CRICKONOMICS

CRICKONOMICS

The Anatomy of Modern Cricket

Stefan Szymanski & Tim Wigmore

BLOOMSBURY SPORT
LONDON · OXFORD · NEW YORK · NEW DELHI · SYDNEY

BLOOMSBURY SPORT
Bloomsbury Publishing Plc
50 Bedford Square, London, WC1B 3DP, UK
29 Earlsfort Terrace, Dublin 2, Ireland

BLOOMSBURY, BLOOMSBURY SPORT and the Diana logo are trademarks of Bloomsbury
Publishing Plc

First published in Great Britain 2022
This paperback edition published 2023

A catalogue record for this book is available from the British Library

ISBN: PB: 978-1-4729-9273-4; TPB: 978-1-4729-9274-1; ePub: 978-1-4729-9272-7;
ePDF: 978-1-4729-9277-2

2 4 6 8 10 9 7 5 3 1

Typeset in Adobe Garamond Pro by Deanta Global Publishing Services, Chennai, India
Printed and bound in Great Britain by CPI Group (UK) Ltd., Croydon, CR0 4YY

To find out more about our authors and books visit www.bloomsbury.com and sign up for
our newsletters

CONTENTS

INTRODUCTION

The greatest myth about cricket is that the sport is conservative, impervious to change. The story of cricket has been one of constant evolution – even though some of the loudest voices have asserted that each of these changes would spell its demise.

We think about the history of the game as four eras of evolution. First came the early development of the sport in the 18th century, when it acquired rules and records and established itself – if only temporarily – as England's pre-eminent team sport. Second was the middle-class respectability that cricket won in the Victorian era, when it spread to the British colonies. Third came the development of the professional game in the early 20th century, when international games – Test matches – gained primacy in the sport. Fourth was the embrace of television, and the growth of limited-overs cricket, from the 1970s onwards.

We conceive of *Crickonomics* as the story of cricket's fifth era: the sport in the new millennium. It is a tale of the rise of India, the growth of women's cricket, and the mysteries of the Duckworth-Lewis Method. It is the story of the full professionalisation of the sport, the impact of Twenty20, and the game spreading to new frontiers. It is about traditional divides in cricket – between private and state schools, in England and Australia alike, in how batters and bowlers are valued, and of biased selectors. It is the tale of what the fans actually want. And it is about the widening gaps between the sport's wealthiest and poorest countries, models for bridging these gaps, and the future of cricket.

We have engaged in these questions in a spirit of curiosity. Although Stefan and Tim, the two authors, are both half-Polish and grew up in England, we come at these questions from different perspectives. Stefan is a sports economist, who delights in using data to answer questions. Tim is a sports journalist, who is used to asking players and administrators alike lots of annoying questions. Over many transatlantic Zoom chats and late-night emails, we have produced a book that neither of us could have written alone. The questions in this book are ones that, in cricket's previous ages, we would simply not have had the tools to answer.

Which Ashes rivals are more reliant on children from private schools? Why have India improved so dramatically? Can countries without much cash follow New Zealand's lead? What really makes fans go to a day at the cricket? How are Afghan refugees changing the game? And why does the traditional caricature of the provenance of England Test cricketers – batters from private schools in the South, bowlers from state schools in the North – remain oddly accurate?

We hope you enjoy finding out the answers – and debating the questions that remain open – as much as we did.

PART ONE

CENTRES OF POWER: NEW AND OLD

1

BATTERS AND BOWLERS, NATURE AND NURTURE

Once upon a time, there were 'Gentlemen' and 'Players'. Gentlemen were members of the leisured class, unencumbered by the tiresome business of having to make a living; players were members of the working class, which usually meant little leisure and lots of labour. In 1806, 42 years before Karl Marx and Friedrich Engels published *The Communist Manifesto*, English cricket inaugurated an annual skirmish in the class war: the Gentlemen v Players match. The game would be played most years until 1962, sometimes as often as four times a year. In 274 games over 156 years, the Players notched up 125 victories and the Gentlemen 68, with 80 draws and one tie. If that sounds lopsided, consider that the Players frequently loaned men to the Gentlemen just to make a game of it.

Today, the notion that a bunch of amateurs could compete with professionals seems absurd. But, although the professionals were paid to play, the amateurs had some real advantages. In the 19th century, cricket played a significant role in the curriculum of the English public schools, from whose ranks most of the Gentlemen were selected. Schooling for the working class was more rudimentary and involved little sport. The Gentlemen were well-versed in the game by the age of 18; their opponents were normally already working for a living – generally as labourers – and they would have limited opportunities to practise.

In his history of the game, published in 1950, Sir Pelham Warner (a Gentleman, of course) observed that the Players' domination had a lot to do with bowling. In the late 19th century, they would sometimes field seven or eight bowlers, while the Gentlemen struggled to produce any decent ones at all. One quarter of the Players' victories were by an innings.

While England's public schools could produce enough talent to sustain batting in the first-class game, they conspicuously failed to nurture anything close to the equivalent in bowling. Fred Spofforth, the great Australian fast bowler who settled in England, took note of the asymmetry, sharing his opinions in the 1904 edition of *Wisden Cricketers' Almanack*. 'Meeting the editor of this interesting Almanack at Lord's during the cricket season he asked how it was the professionals were so much better bowlers than the Gentlemen, adding that the latter very rarely produced a first-class bowler,' Spofforth began. He notes that 'all the advantages' enjoyed by amateurs – 'they are better looked after, clothed and fed' and played on better pitches growing up – should have helped the Gentlemen to be better at the physically arduous task of bowling.

Yet they were not. Spofforth suggests several factors that helped the professionals succeed as bowlers. Manual labour would have built muscle and endurance, 'he really works hard and often and starts early, for this is the great secret, because it gives elasticity to the muscles without which it is almost impossible to excel'.

Next, he says, a professional would often practise on bad pitches where 'probably the faster he bowls the greater the success'. Young amateurs, by contrast, failed particularly badly when they tried to bowl spin – this, he lamented, 'is just like trying to teach a child to run before it can walk'. Lacking strength, amateur bowlers could not maintain their standards over long spells – 'had they bowled harder and longer when quite young and stretched their arms to the full extent they would never find the work too laborious'. Most fundamentally, 'the real reason why the sons of gentleman don't succeed as bowlers is that they don't do the necessary work when young'.

Perhaps that is part of the reason why students at elite schools simply preferred batting. 'The young collegian playing on really first-class pitches finds the batting too good and therefore prefers to pay more attention to the latter as he gets more fun out of it and it is not so irksome, so he lets, while young, the opportunity of being a bowler slip at the very time he should work his hardest,' Spofforth wrote.

Spofforth's writing might leave you with the impression that he was a Player, with a low opinion of Gentlemen. But he was a Gentleman himself;

privately educated in Australia, he worked first in a bank and then made his fortune in the tea trading business. One of the finest bowlers of his time – known as 'Demon', he took 94 Test wickets at an average of 18.4 – Spofforth never played as a professional. In the 1890s, after he settled in England, he turned out three times for the Gentlemen against the Players, featuring in two draws and one defeat. Perhaps Spofforth did not think that young gentlemen in general lacked application, but rather that *English* young gentlemen did.

*　*　*

From the dawn of cricket, batting has always held more cachet than bowling. In the 18th century, the rural aristocracy of England specifically brought in their farm labourers to bowl (and field) so that they could concentrate on the skill they considered more elegant and refined. This is how professionalism in cricket emerged: the labourers had to be paid. Naturally, the elite schools of England, preparing the leaders of the Empire, tended to focus on the elitist skill of batting rather than the working-class toil of bowling.

The sun finally set on the Empire around the same time as the Gentlemen v Players game ended, and the English schools changed their business model accordingly. The days when the wealthy could simply put their son's name down for Eton are long gone. Instead, Eton and other fee-paying schools (now known as independent schools), practise a more refined elitism, seeking to attract and admit the smartest pupils, focusing increasingly on academic achievement and potential in their highly selective admissions process.

Yet independent schools still place considerable emphasis on sports, particularly cricket. Millfield School, perhaps the pre-eminent cricket school in the UK, invested £2.6 million in the cricket and golf centres it opened in 2020. Millfield has produced a lot of elite athletes, including professional cricketers. We compiled a list of schools attended by 291 male England players born after 1946, with a focus on the schools they attended between the ages of 11 and 16. If a child switched schools, we credited the school where he spent the most time – an imperfect solution, but one that struck us as the fairest. Millfield topped the list in our data, alongside Tonbridge, but each only produced four England players, a surprisingly low number for the most successful schools. Two others – Blundell's and Felsted, both independent schools – produced three each.

There is not one great centre for the production of men's England cricketers – they come from all over the place in geographical terms. But not in institutional terms: if there is a centre, it's the institution of the independent school itself. In the postwar period, between 6% and 9% of students have attended fee-paying schools, yet their share of England players in this period is around 24%. Even this number understates their influence once we deduct the almost 15% of England players who were educated abroad – many at private school. First, when considering only students educated in the UK, the share from independent schools is 28%. Second, we have classified players who moved to private schools at age 15 or later as state-educated, since they spent more of their secondary education at state schools. Joe Root, for example, was a pupil at the state-funded King Ecgbert School until he won a scholarship to the fee-paying Worksop College at 15; we classify him as state-educated, but his development was shaped by private school too.

The UK public education system underwent a fundamental shift in the 1970s, abandoning the selective system which allocated children at 11, based on a written examination, either to elite grammar schools or to 'secondary moderns' that offered a less academic education. This system was replaced by the non-selective 'comprehensive' school system. Some old grammar schools converted to independent schools, and a small number of local authorities chose to preserve the state-funded selective system, but most grammar schools became comprehensives.

This shift was associated with a decline of elite sports in state schools that is reflected in our data. Of England players born between 1945 and 1965, only 22% came from independent schools. Ever since, independent schools have accounted for 32% of all players. This seems not so much a matter of class as of money. Back in the days of Gentlemen v Players, a cricketing Professor Higgins could probably have identified a player's team by his accent alone, the traditional class-marker of English society. Today, it is not your accent but your family's income that will land you on either side of the great divide. According to one study, the income of parents who sent their children to private schools was a staggering 89% higher on average than that of parents who sent their children to state schools.

Despite all the upheaval in the educational system, some traditions persist. Independent schools still produce more batters than bowlers. This is illustrated in Table 1.1, which shows the share of batters and bowlers from each school type broken into three postwar periods (the third period, 1986–1999, is incomplete as new players make their debut). In each period, independent schools produced a greater share of batters than bowlers. Almost 40% of batters born since 1986 went to independent schools, double the percentage born from 1946–1965.

Table 1.1: The share of men's Test match bowlers and batters, dependent on school type attended, for players born in each two-decade period

	Test match bowlers			Test match batters		
	1946–1965	1966–1985	1986–1999	1946–1965	1966–1985	1986–1999
comprehensive	21.7%	64.9%	46.9%	23.4%	55.1%	39.5%
grammar	24.6%	3.9%	9.4%	25.5%	5.1%	7.0%
independent	17.4%	13.0%	31.3%	19.1%	20.4%	39.5%
overseas	15.9%	16.9%	12.5%	12.8%	17.3%	14.0%
secondary modern	20.3%	0.0%	0.0%	19.1%	0.0%	0.0%
unknown	0.0%	1.3%	0.0%	0.0%	2.0%	0.0%

The transition of the educational system led to the decrease in selective grammar schools, whose share of batters and bowlers fell from around 25% to less than 5%. It has since recovered to around 10%, thanks partly to an increase in the proportion of children educated at the surviving state grammar schools, which have been expanding since the 1980s.

The overall decline in the state sector can be seen by tallying the totals for grammar, secondary modern and comprehensive schools. The overall state school share of players born from 1946–1965 added up to 67% of bowlers and 68% of batters; it was 69% and 60% respectively from 1966–1985. Then, it fell to only 56% and 47% for players born from 1986–1999.

The share of Test runs and wickets taken depending on the type of school attended appears to tell a slightly different story. As far as bowling is concerned, the independent school share fell significantly from the first period to the second, and then rose dramatically in the third period. In terms of runs scored, the independent school share rose dramatically from the first to the second period, and then fell back in the third period, as Table 1.2 shows.

Table 1.2: Share of men's Test match wickets taken and runs scored by school type and birth decades

	Test match wickets			Test match runs		
	1946–1965	1966–1985	1986–1999	1946–1965	1966–1985	1986–1999
comprehensive	10.6%	79.3%	50.1%	9.8%	36.2%	51.5%
grammar	19.9%	3.9%	9.8%	19.3%	4.8%	2.9%
independent	18.0%	5.9%	39.9%	18.9%	41.7%	33.3%
overseas	13.7%	10.8%	0.2%	16.3%	17.3%	12.3%
secondary modern	37.9%	0.0%	0.0%	35.6%	0.0%	0.0%
unknown	0.0%	1.4%	0.0%	0.0%	0.4%	0.0%

This table is liable to be distorted by exceptional individuals. Stuart Broad – the son of Chris, another England Test player – was born in 1986 and educated at Oakham School. He accounts for over one-third of all Test wickets taken by the third birth cohort; without him, the share of wickets taken by independently educated cricketers would be only 6%, much as it was for the 1966–1985 cohort, rather than 40%. By contrast, the most prolific independently educated Test batter in the cohort is Jonny Bairstow, who has produced only 11% of the cohort's total.

Turning to ODIs, Table 1.3 shows that the influence of Broad's bowling is not as prominent in this format. Here, state-school bowlers have tended to hold their own, but the growing dominance of independent schools in runs scored seems clear.

Table 1.3: Share of ODI wickets taken and runs scored by school type and birth decades

	ODI wickets			ODI runs		
	1946–1965	1966–1985	1986–1999	1946–1965	1966–1985	1986–1999
comprehensive	12.5%	77.0%	63.9%	14.4%	42.0%	40.2%
grammar	18.2%	1.7%	8.7%	18.5%	0.7%	7.6%
independent	19.7%	4.2%	23.3%	17.6%	33.3%	32.7%
overseas	11.5%	15.7%	4.2%	18.8%	23.7%	19.4%
secondary modern	38.1%	0.0%	0.0%	30.7%	0.0%	0.0%
unknown	0.0%	1.4%	0.0%	0.0%	0.3%	0.0%

* * *

Secondary school, somewhere between the ages of 11 and 15, is where batters typically hone their talent. The main requirement for talented young batters at this age is regular practice, and that is exactly what private schools are able to provide. They have the resources that enable young players to play regularly.

'It's a great place to play,' Zak Crawley, the England Test batter, said of Tonbridge, the independent school he attended. 'The facilities there are brilliant for people who want to be pro sportsmen. I could come down whenever I wanted to the nets and practise with some other boys there. And it was great to play on such a beautiful ground. It gave me a lot of motivation that I wanted to do this for a living, because I was just enjoying my cricket so much.'

Nathan Leamon, England's data analyst, who previously worked as a teacher at a number of private schools, believes that attending an elite school particularly helps budding batters. 'With batting, access to good facilities, professional coaching, and good pitches is a huge advantage,' he says.

For teenage cricketers, 'I think you do need more practice on the batting front than the bowling,' observes Stuart Welch, the director of cricket at Cranleigh School. 'The volume and intensity of practice for batters pre-16 years old appears to be a strong indicator of adult success,' says David Court, the player identification lead for the England and Wales Cricket Board. 'This isn't only deliberate practice as defined in the literature but should include a high volume of play. In my experience there is more opportunity for this practice and play in schools with good facilities and programmes, combined with a group of peers who are interested in the sport.'

As in the 19th century, most pitches at independent schools favour batting. The reverse is often true for the pitches at state schools: a curse for batting but a boon for bowling. This is as much a psychological explanation as anything else: young players tend to develop those skills that bring the greatest rewards. At independent schools 'most coaches are ex-batters' and 'pitches are batter-friendly,' observes Chris Morgan, the director of sport at Tonbridge.

Batters from independent schools may also get more chances to impress those who matter in county academies. School coaches' links to county sides mean that batters from private schools are more likely to be seen by the right people frequently enough – a potentially crucial edge. 'Batters in general need more chances because they fail more often,' says Leamon. 'Whenever there is a bias towards players from more privileged backgrounds, it is likely to affect batters more than bowlers.'

* * *

Bowling is a different proposition: the genetic lottery plays a much bigger role. 'You can't put in what God left out,' says Morgan from Tonbridge.

Batters of all sorts of physiques can become elite. Small batters can thrive in Test cricket – Don Bradman, statistically the greatest batter of all time, was 5ft 7in; Sachin Tendulkar is 5ft 5in. Tall players can also flourish: Tony Greig was 6ft 6in, and Kevin Pietersen 6ft 4in. Zak Crawley and Ollie Pope embody the contrasting body types that can reach the top: Crawley is 6ft 5in, Pope only 5ft 9in. Even rotund batters can excel, as Inzamam-ul-Haq could attest: he weighed over 100 kilos, but made 25 Test centuries.

But for bowlers, size matters. Jimmy Anderson is only considered to be of middling height for a pace bowler – yet he is 6ft 2in, placing him among the 6% tallest males for his age in the UK. While there are exceptions, such as Dale Steyn, Kemar Roach and Lasith Malinga, fast bowlers tend to be of above-average height. The vaunted modern Australian pace trio is typical: Pat Cummins is 6ft 4in; Josh Hazlewood and Mitchell Starc are 6ft 5in. The celebrated West Indies pace attack of the 1980s and 1990s were often even taller: Courtney Walsh was 6ft 5in, Curtly Ambrose 6ft 7in, and Joel Garner 6ft 8in; heady heights that helped them produce a potent cocktail of pace and bounce.

A growth spurt can be a catalyst to focus on bowling. As one Australian Test bowler told a group of academics studying the development of fast bowlers, 'I had talent both bat and ball, but I didn't really sort of start to bowl fast until I got to about 16 or 17. I really sort of shot up, grew about four or five inches, very quickly filled out a bit, and all of a sudden bowled a yard or two quicker than I did the year before.'

Conversely, some pace bowlers who show early promise fizzle out: they might have been tall for their age group but their height advantage fades as they grow older. The best fast bowlers in their early teens often drop off because they rely too heavily on their natural endowments. 'A lot of times their skill set remains at that level, whereas others, apart from catching up physically in size have also learnt a few other skills along the way,' said one fast-bowling coach in the Australian study.

Endurance matters as well. 'Bowling has a far higher threshold in terms of physical requirements than batting,' Leamon observes. 'The proportion of the population that has the physical requirements to bowl fast and the robustness to do so day in day out without getting injured is fairly tiny.'

Trying to become a Test seam bowler is certainly a more risky venture than becoming a batter, such are the biomechanical stresses caused by bowling fast. One study of adult bowling injuries found that not bowling enough could be just as likely to lead to injury as bowling too much. Cricket Australia currently recommend that youth pace bowlers should avoid more than two consecutive bowling days and more than four days in any one week, with a week without any bowling in every 10–12. Similar problems arise for pitchers in high-school baseball in the United States. In recent decades, there has been a crisis of injuries as youth pitchers have been called on to play more games. Major League Baseball teams draft players from high school at 18 or from college at 22. There is evidence that college pitchers go on to have better careers, with a majority of candidates for the Cy Young Award (given annually to the best Major League Baseball pitcher) coming from college rather than high-school draftees. The implication is that the college graduates have not been overworked too young.

While there has been less research on spinners – partly because there are fewer of them – they are generally thought to develop even later than seamers. 'Batting and fast bowling lend themselves to earlier talent identification than spin,' says Carl Crowe, a leading spin-bowling coach. 'Spinners often don't mature for years because you need more time to learn your art. Spinners don't peak till their late 20s.'

It is common for elite spinners to start out as fast bowlers, rendering early talent identification even harder. Muttiah Muralitharan, the most prolific Test wicket-taker of all time, bowled medium-pace until switching to off-spin aged 14; Anil Kumble, Derek Underwood, and Sunil Narine also converted to spin in their teens. 'As all youngsters do, I wanted to be a fast bowler,' Underwood told

The Cricket Monthly. 'When it came to the transition between youth cricket and adult cricket I was no longer quick anymore, and one had to adapt to a different set of circumstances.'

* * *

The evidence suggests that a privileged education confers a greater advantage on batters than on bowlers. The abundant practice and coaching that private schools make possible for children between the ages of 11 and 16 are more likely to benefit a batter than a bowler. 'It's easier to make a batter. I would say fast bowling is an athletic pursuit, batting a coached skill,' said Morgan. 'The key traits that make you a good batter tend to be learned rather than inherent,' Leamon observed. It is harder to identify fast-bowling talent at an early age than batting talent, because height and physique are crucial for bowlers and children physically mature at different rates.

'It's certainly easier to identify a batter at a younger age than it is a seamer,' Welch explains. 'You don't know how quick they're likely to be – the mechanics might be very good, but they might have reached their peak in terms of their development. So you might have a tall seamer aged 13 or 14 that might not grow that much, which then hinders his development.' The study of 11 leading Australian international fast bowlers found that eight of them did not specialise as fast bowlers until late in development – around the age of 17, too late for school to have much of an impact.

The intensity of competition among independent schools also plays a role. Elite schools will prioritise batting simply because identifying school-age talent is a surer bet. 'Cricket scholarships are most often given to batters,' says Jonathan Arscott, formerly the cricket master at Tonbridge. Among private schools, especially since the 1990s, 'it's now a competitive market for cricket talent, and mostly for batting talent.'

If wealthy private schools have the resources to lavish on batters, other schools may simply not need much money to nurture bowlers. The cost of developing bowling talent may simply be lower in general terms. 'Bowling is essentially a closed skill, and one which can be practised very effectively with a minimum of equipment, facilities and coaching,' says Leamon.

The old leisure versus labour distinction that characterised the distinction between Gentlemen and Players may still play some role too. 'Bowling seam is hard work, batting is fun,' says Arscott. 'Public school pupils generally have options. Batting for a living v The City is a close call. Bowling seam for a living v The City – well you have got to love bowling seam and love being knackered after every game, and you have got to have more significant application and determination with respect to fitness.'

* * *

We have seen how a private education increases your chances to play representative cricket for one of England's senior teams. The path to that level will differ for each player, beginning with their school days – but it will inevitably pass through county cricket.

County youth development programmes start around the age of eight or nine, and they run teams from each cohort, from under-10s to under-18s. Players are recommended by schools or local clubs, and many counties run trials to identify talent. By the time players reach the age of 17 or 18, then, the counties have a good idea of the talent in their area.

The next critical step is the England Under-19s. At 18, the best single predictor of eventually playing for England is playing for the under-19s: it is the royal road to the England national team. England have been playing under-19 Test matches since 1974. Out of 192 England senior Test players who have appeared since then, 52% have played first for the under-19s. David Court, who chairs the selectors of the under-19s, told us that the figure has been 63% since 2000.

Court seemed surprised when we suggested that this is a remarkable strike rate. 'What's it like in football?' he asked, so we looked. Under-19 is not the right comparison, since by that time, most footballers are already professionals and may have appeared for the senior team. A better comparison is under-17 – just before most footballers turn professional. Under-17 international football is a serious business, the World Cup is considered a marker of future potential, and England play regularly – 142 games between 2010 and 2020. We counted the number of active professional footballers in June 2021 who have played for the England senior team (102) – only 43% had played for the under-17s.

The ECB has proven itself remarkably good at identifying talent at under-19 level. And it's not just about the number of players. A list of former under-19 players reads like a roll call of modern English Test stars: Michael Vaughan, Alastair Cook, Marcus Trescothick, Ian Bell, Andrew Flintoff, Ben Stokes, Joe Root, Graeme Swann, Jimmy Anderson, and Stuart Broad. While 52% of England senior Test players went through the under-19s, they produced 61% of Test runs and a remarkable 69% of Test wickets. If it's hard to spot a bowler at 15, it seems pretty easy at 18.

We quizzed Court about how the process works. The ECB try to develop a smooth transitional process for elite players from junior sides to the senior squad. Court coordinates a team of 12 scouts spread out around the country. Based on recommendations from county youth academies, they target around 60 players a year. Below under-19, they focus on regional competitions, aiming to keep the talent pool as large as possible.

Trying to respond to regional disparities is part of the strategy, 'We've just started a pilot programme with ECB, Yorkshire, Lancashire and Leicestershire, where we've put some money in to employ a community talent champion. For want of a better word, they are community scouts going out into non-affiliated cricket, not played in the normal structured way, and try to identify talent and bring them into the pathway – to try to address our imbalance in the player population. Our aim is to have people from the community identify people in the community and bring them in – hopefully this will increase the diversity in our playing system.'

Technology is used too. Ben Jones completed a PhD at the University of Bangor in 2019, which was sponsored by the ECB. Jones' PhD was based on detailed interviews with top players, trying to figure out what separated the mere elite – county players – from the super elite – Test players. He used a data analysis method known as machine learning to pick out those individual characteristics that most accurately predict the difference. The process whittles down more than 650 factors to a shortlist of 14 to 18.

The ECB have used these findings to inform how they identify youth talent. They asked Hannah Jowitt, who works on pathway management for the ECB, to study machine learning, with a view to expanding its application to their databases.

Some of the indicators identified so far are unsurprising: the amount of time you've spent playing cricket, or the age you started playing. Others are less obvious. For batters, more variety in training routines turned out to be beneficial. Random-varied practice requires the learner to switch without warning among the skills being practised, rather than focusing for an extended period of time on a particular shot. Another factor that stands out for Court is how fast you move from junior to senior cricket. 'The speed of transition is a key indicator, how many opportunities players have had, how quickly do they produce significant early performances.'

While playing for the under-19s is an excellent predictor of future success, the ECB say they don't want this to create an unfair bias in the selection process later on. Court says that England are wary of the sunk cost fallacy – the dangers of sticking to a past decision just because you have already invested in it. 'There are still plenty of players who haven't played under-19 who will one day play for England.' Non-selection at under-19 can act as a spur to improve performance; Court cites Zak Crawley, who was overlooked for the under-19s, as one example.

Court says that those who attend private schools 'get a privilege bias – it's something we talk about, not so much in terms of school but in terms of practice. To try and combat this, the ECB don't direct scouts to watch school games, instead asking them to look at county games at under-18 and 2nd XI level.'

The aim is to avoid unconscious bias in favour of those from private schools. Once you know the track record of wealthy schools, you might be predisposed to assess their pupils more generously. Instead of looking at a school's name, then, they will look at hours of practice. If players are roughly at the same level but some of them had four times the playing opportunities, the other ones may well have the higher potential.

These strategies help us understand the success of the under-19s in identifying bowling talent. When it comes to bowling, Court says that they focus more on raw talent than on current performance, 'Bowling fast is important, not necessarily control. We know from history that the best fast bowlers have been fast but not necessarily able to control it at an early stage. Control comes from the volume of coaching, being able to bowl fast is a better predictor of future success.'

For the past two centuries, it has been impossible to disentangle schooling from the development of English cricket talent. The division of labour has persisted – private schools develop batting talent, while bowlers emerge only towards the end of the educational career, and are more likely to pass through the state sector. These historic biases are a waste of talent and promote a socially divisive image of cricket. They also mean that Spofforth's observations continue to resonate.

2

THE STRANGE CONSERVATISM OF KERRY PACKER, AND WHY COVID-19 WILL ACCELERATE THE RISE OF CLUB CRICKET

'C'mon Aussie, C'mon,' was the slogan of a revolution: the theme tune of Kerry Packer's World Series Cricket (WSC). It was ingenious – cheeky and playing to fans' patriotism while telling them that the best Australian cricketers could now be found in WSC. The breakaway cricket competition that Packer launched in 1977 hijacked many of the world's best cricketers for the next two years. Today, WSC is remembered as an extraordinarily tumultuous time in the world game – and one that, from commercialisation and the popularisation of limited-overs cricket to day-night matches and helmets, changed the sport irrevocably.

But there was a strange conservatism to the anthem – and, really, to all World Series Cricket. The anthem was based on the traditional notion of the game: that nation v nation competition represented the pinnacle. If Packer lacked the legitimacy that official Test status would bring, assembling the best players in the world into teams representing nations – WSC Australia, WSC West Indies and the WSC World XI, who tussled in 'Supertests' – was the next best thing.

Packer does not appear to have really considered trying to get people to care about Melbourne v Sydney, or challenge the fundamental organisational structure of the sport. In persuading cricket fans to gravitate towards his rebel version of the international game, Packer did not challenge the orthodoxy that international cricket was the highest version of the sport. His breakaway league was predicated upon the idea that fans wanted to watch international cricket – so that is what he gave them. A true challenge to the primacy of international cricket would have to wait another three decades.

* * *

There are 95 full members and 20 associate members of the Global Association of International Sports Federations (GAISF). This covers most significant sports played in the world, but there are probably at least 100 more sports governing bodies outside this elite group, including the World Elephant Polo Association, the International Axe Throwing Federation and the International Modern Arnis Federation (a martial art developed in the Philippines). Even within the GAISF there are some minor sports, such as fistball (popular in Germany, not to be confused with handball), kick volleyball (popular in Indonesia and Malaysia) and tug of war.

There are many organised sports, but few can claim to have a significant global following. Restricting ourselves to team sports, Google Knol – Google's defunct version of Wikipedia – listed the top 10 team sports (in order) as football, cricket, basketball, baseball, rugby union, field hockey, volleyball, ice hockey, American football and rugby league. What stands out from this list is that, even at the pinnacle of world sports, relatively few generate any serious revenue. Of course, football makes by far the most money globally. The four sports prominent in the US – basketball, baseball, American football and ice hockey are all big money spinners, but mostly only in North America.

A measure of revenue generation is the salary that a professional can command. A top field-hockey player could hope to make up to $100,000 a year and a top pro-volleyball player a similar amount. There are no public statistics on the number of professionals in these two sports, but the numbers are small. Rugby league has a very narrow appeal – popular only in parts of England, France, Australia, South Africa and New Zealand and barely known elsewhere. Rugby union has a wider market, but can still only be considered a regional rather than global sport. Outside of the big five (soccer and the four mostly American sports) earning a salary of more than $1 million would represent superstar status. In the big five, a salary of $1 million is no big deal.

Cricket's position in this hierarchy has always been strange. Given the sport's popularity in India – with about 18% of the world's population – it can fairly claim to be one of the most popular sports on the globe. In some ways, you might compare it with rugby union – with a roughly similar status in England, Australia, New Zealand and South Africa. Union lacks cricket's following in South Asia and the Caribbean, but it has a strong following in the Pacific Islands, France and Ireland, some following in Argentina and Japan, and has shown signs of early growth in countries as disparate as the US, Georgia, Brazil and Lebanon. Rugby sevens made its debut at the 2016 Olympics, a sure way to raise a sport's international profile.

Cricket is also similar to rugby in that, from their earliest days, spectator interest has revolved around international competition. England first played Australia at cricket in 1877; a team representing Canada had defeated a team representing the US in 1844, in the first known international fixture in any sport. The first rugby international was between Scotland and England in 1871. This is not a coincidence. The men organising rugby and cricket shared the same vision, based on amateurism and an aversion to what they thought of as the avarice of commercialism, which was embodied in the new American sport of baseball and the emerging sport of Association football. Cricket differed from rugby in that it allowed professionals to play alongside amateurs. Rugby union refused to countenance such an arrangement, leading to the split between union and league in 1895. In union the amateurs remained firmly in control.

The contrast with the big five sports is striking. There are as many nations potentially interested in baseball as there are in cricket and rugby – alongside the United States, Cuba and the Dominican Republic, Mexico, Venezuela, Canada, Japan, South Korea, Taiwan can all field credible international teams. While baseball is heavily skewed towards the domestic club game, the sport's world championship – the World Baseball Classic – now features 20 teams.

Football's World Cup is a different matter. The most popular sporting event on the planet, it is hard to avoid the competition anywhere in the world. But still, it is only played once every four years, compared to the 100 or so professional club leagues that operate around the world, year in, year out. The accountants

Deloitte reckon that only 15% of all revenue in European football goes through the hands of FIFA, UEFA and the national associations – and this includes the money from the Champions League. International representative competition itself is probably worth less than 10% of total revenue. By contrast Jon Long, the former head of strategy for the International Cricket Council, estimated that in 2000 only around 10% of the sport's total wealth came from club matches.

Ever since the Ashes were created in 1882, international cricket has been lauded as the acme of the sport. With periodic exceptions, domestic cricket has faced a perpetual struggle for relevance and attention, its very existence reliant on being subsidised by international matches. While in other major sports, the best players from around the world compete against each other for clubs, international cricket has essentially had a monopoly on best v best action. County cricket has been enriched by global greats – Somerset fielded Viv Richards and Joel Garner alongside Ian Botham – but this was a complement to international cricket, not a challenge to it.

Club matches have served as loss leaders for cricket boards – nurseries for the international team and ways of developing talent, as opposed to revenue-generating sources in their own right. As Stefan, along with Ian Preston and Stephen F. Ross, noted in a paper in 2000, which advocated the development of a club-based structure, cricket had an 'absence of a strong club competition which is a characteristic of all the successful team sports.'

* * *

Before making his fortune selling cigarettes in India, Lalit Modi studied in America. There, he observed a sporting structure that was the antithesis to cricket's: international competition was a sideshow to Major League Baseball and the National Basketball Association. American football did not have any need for international competition at all; the National Football League was long established as the most lucrative sports league in the world. Modi wondered whether India could emulate the NFL's franchise system, building a league, structured on city lines, with the best cricketers in the world. That way, India's cricket fans would not need to wait until hosting a World Cup to see all the best players in the world together; they could see them every year.

Modi's gambit failed. In 1996, the Board of Control for Cricket in India rejected his idea for a one-day league lasting four to six weeks played between different cities.

Eleven years later, Modi tried again. India was now considerably richer; the cricket board's global clout had grown commensurately. Cricket had a new format – T20 – ideally suited to an inter-city league. And, perhaps most importantly, someone had already got there first. The Indian Cricket League – featuring six city-based teams, representing Delhi, Chandigarh, Chennai, Hyderabad, Kolkata and Mumbai – launched in November 2007. Like World Series Cricket, this was a rebel competition, not sanctioned by the board. Unlike Packer's structure, this one was not based on nation v nation competition, but sought to get fans to commit to city v city matches.

Even before a ball had been bowled in the IPL, it had already earned the Board of Control for Cricket (BCCI) in India almost £1 billion: £500 million in a 10-year broadcasting contract, and a further £367 million in franchise fees paid by team owners.

At a stroke, the fundamental economic model of cricket was transformed. No longer would the BCCI be overwhelmingly dependent upon international games for its revenue. India would not merely be the most lucrative international side in the world, but they would now be able to earn huge sums from their domestic matches. Ultimately, India could become like the US in baseball or basketball: the home of a league so lucrative, and so international in its player pool, that it would no longer need the cash it once generated from bilateral international fixtures.

Before the IPL, only around 2% of the Indian board's total broadcasting rights came from domestic cricket. From 2018, when a $510 million-a-year contract for IPL broadcasting rights began, the BCCI now earned 71% of broadcasting rights from the IPL, with the rest from India's home matches. So for every rupee they earn from home internationals each year, the BCCI now earn 2.5 from the IPL. While internationals remain worth slightly more on a per game basis, the overall discrepancy is only likely to grow: it is far easier to grow a league than increase the number of internationals. Though the ICC's global events are vibrant, the BCCI's share of income from these – $50 million a year from 2016 to 2023 – is puny compared to what it generates from the IPL. For the first time, Indian cricket is not reliant upon the Indian national team for its riches.

* * *

Most of the great West Indies Test team of the 1970s and 1980s returned, year after year, to county cricket. They did so both because it offered a chance for them to develop their games – at the time, there was scant international cricket played in other countries during the English summer – and because it paid better than playing international cricket. Yet a player's attractiveness to domestic teams abroad was still driven largely by international displays; players needed international cricket as the gateway to more lucrative domestic leagues. With international matches seldom clashing with county cricket, players did not have to choose between club and country.

By the late 1990s and 2000s, national boards were able to pay players more, making international cricket the most lucrative source of work for nearly all players. Due to the state of the country's politics, economy and cricket board, Zimbabwe were an exception, contributing to a spate of players retiring and taking up domestic contracts abroad, predominantly in county cricket, in the early 2000s. In almost all other cases, international cricket offered both the greatest potential source of sporting prestige and of cash: sporting and economic incentives favoured players committing to international cricket.

During the first IPL season, in 2008, five New Zealand players arrived late for their Test tour of England. By staying later in the IPL and missing warm-up matches in England ahead of the Test series, New Zealand's players could earn more money. These basic economic incentives would recalibrate the status of Test cricket around the world in the years ahead.

Now, it was possible for players to earn far more playing in T20 leagues than in international games. By 2016, the Federation of International Cricketers' Associations (FICA), the global players' union, found that leading players could earn more playing in the IPL, and two other lucrative T20 leagues, than in international cricket for all countries bar India, Australia and England.

Where once players had been dependent upon the international game to make their name, and win prestigious contracts abroad, now T20 leagues were their own pathway: players could progress up and down leagues. By 2018–2019, FICA found, 541 players had overseas contracts in short-format leagues, with 124 representing at least two overseas domestic sides. Players didn't even need international cricket to fill gaps in their schedule: between November 2018 and March 2020, June 2019 – when the ODI World Cup was played – was the only month without a major short-format league in the world game.

The circuit was so relentless that standards in some international games were hollowed out. Why watch West Indies in bilateral T20 fixtures when their stars were more likely to be playing in a T20 league? When West Indies toured Australia in 2015–2016, and were thrashed in the Test series, seven of their leading players – including Chris Gayle, Kieron Pollard, Dwayne Bravo and Andre Russell – were absent from the national team. They were still in Australia, only they were playing in the Big Bash. The shifts were self-perpetuating. As international cricket became less attractive for fans, so broadcasting rights for matches became less lucrative relative to domestic leagues, in turn increasing the economic incentives for players to prefer club over country.

In T20, club cricket can rival the standard of the international game. The quality of cricket in the IPL – with four overseas players per team, and the deepest stocks of domestic talent anywhere in the world – is already greater than the average T20 international between Full Members, analysis by the cricket data company CricViz has shown. T20 leagues in South Africa, the West Indies, Pakistan were also found to be of a higher standard than the average T20 match between Full Members.

The market for coaches has followed a similar trajectory to that of players. Stephen Fleming – who has reached eight IPL finals as a coach – has never coached in international cricket. Ricky Ponting, Mahela Jayawardene and Shane Bond have dabbled in international cricket without committing to a head-coach role. The franchise world offers a challenge as stimulating and the basic economic equation all employees crave: more money for less work. 'It was an offer I had to take,' Bond explained of leaving his job as New Zealand bowling coach to take up the same post at Mumbai Indians in 2015. 'When you're away

200–250 days a year, it's certainly demanding. This way I get to spend a lot more time based at home.'

Mike Hesson is understood to earn considerably more as Royal Challengers Bangalore's director of cricket operations than he did leading New Zealand to No.2 in the Test rankings and the 2015 World Cup final. Even for those who don't get an IPL job, a portfolio of other T20 jobs – say, at least two from the Pakistan Super League, Bangladesh Premier League, Big Bash and Caribbean Premier League – can add up to a package worth more than any international jobs outside Australia, England and India.

As they impinged on the calendar ever more, T20 leagues also undermined international cricket by limiting the time that could be given over to the international game. Many countries sought to avoid clashes with both their own T20 leagues and the IPL. In the case of West Indies, for instance, this meant playing no international games during either the two months given over to the IPL or the month of the Caribbean Premier League – a total of three months a year.

In the IPL's early years, many countries continued to schedule home internationals during the competition – part naivety and part greed. But should boards now have the temerity to try to compete with the IPL, it is they who will look second-rate in comparison: players, fan interest and broadcasting dollars will all gravitate to the IPL. In April 2021, five leading South African players – including their entire first-choice pace-bowling attack – left midway through their ODI series against Pakistan to join the IPL.

At the end of 2017, the ICC effectively granted a global window to the IPL, with the new Future Tours Programme avoiding clashes between leading international fixtures and the IPL. It was belated recognition of a simple truth. Before the IPL, international cricket was a 12-month-a-year sport; now, it is a 10-month-a-year one.

* * *

When the Covid-19 pandemic curtailed professional sport for several months, a funny thing happened: many international boards saved money. Unless Australia, England or India are involved, almost all bilateral international games lose money. And so for all the vast disruption caused by Covid-19, having to cancel matches was actually a relief to many boards. That some boards are economically better off playing fewer matches highlights how unsustainable the entire structure of international cricket has become.

Long before Covid, one of the most salient trends in the world game was the dwindling value of broadcasting rights for matches involving the sport's middle classes. Essentially, as broadcasting rights for the IPL, and even the copycat state T20 leagues, have soared, Indian broadcasters have had less cash to spend on matches in other countries – even India games overseas. A similar effect has been felt in England: as broadcasting costs for England's home summer have soared, so broadcasters have become more selective in which other cricket they bid for, and more disciplined in what they are prepared to spend. The upshot of these shifts in the broadcasting market has been to make more international cricket less viable.

At the end of 2019, Ireland cancelled a one-off Test match against Bangladesh, which had been scheduled for May 2020. Cricket Ireland's chief executive, Warren Deutrom, said that staging the match would cost around €1 million, and there was 'little expectation of creating revenue streams to cover the costs'.

Financial pressures are making Test cricket, and even shorter formats of international cricket, harder to sustain in many more-established countries. Worldwide, most Test matches lose around $500,000 net. Even New Zealand, the inaugural World Test champions, now stage only four home Tests a year. Despite the elevation of Afghanistan and Ireland to Test cricket in 2017, the number of Test matches worldwide has gradually been going down: from 204 – an average of 51 a year – between 2001 and 2004, to 181 from 2016 to 2019, an average of 45 a year.

As cricket slowly resumed after the first wave of the pandemic, domestic cricket proved more resilient than the international game. Other than in England – the second biggest market in the world game – no international cricket at all involving Full Members took place between June and 30 October, 2020. In the same period, the marquee T20 leagues, the Caribbean Premier League and IPL went ahead, while T20 tournaments were also played in countries including Afghanistan, Bangladesh, England, Ireland and Sri Lanka.

The cost of charter flights, quarantine restrictions, and different travel rules between different countries seemed to make it easier to stage T20 leagues than international series. If players from a particular country were unable, or unwilling, to travel to a T20 league, the league could always find replacement players; if they could not travel to an away tour, the hosting side would be left without another nation to play.

The basic economics of T20 leagues were also far better suited to the age of Covid than most international series. In the space of a month, a home board could optimistically fit in 12 limited-overs fixtures – two three-match series in T20Is and ODIs alike. Yet in the space of only 24 days in August and September 2020, the Caribbean Premier League fitted in 33 games – their entire tournament.

While the direct impact of Covid-19 will lessen in the years ahead, one of its legacies will be to accelerate the growing importance of club cricket within the game's ecosystem. At the height of the pandemic, Tom Harrison, chief executive of the England and Wales Cricket Board, declared that the new Hundred competition would now be 'even more important'.

Long before Covid, the ECB was worried about its dependence upon bilateral international cricket for revenue, this was part of the rationale for the launch of The Hundred. Instead of a home summer whose value would depend upon the attractiveness of the touring sides – essentially leaving the ECB with a shortfall in the two years out of every four when neither Australia nor India were playing a Test series – the ECB hoped that The Hundred would generate the same amounts of cash every year, creating less volatile revenue streams. In 2018, the ECB's annual strategic report included the 'status of Test cricket' as a major threat to its future financial stability for the first time.

As club cricket becomes more prominent and lucrative, bilateral fixtures between international cricket's middle classes face being rationalised further: these games simply don't pay the bills. All boards are 'going to have to really, really scrutinise where the loss-making cricket is,' said Wasim Khan, the former chief executive of the Pakistan Cricket Board. 'It might be that you look at lessening the number of Test matches within a series … Shorter tours may well become the norm moving forward as every country looks at how they can cost-cut.'

The economic crisis caused by Covid-19 will lead to reductions in advertising and broadcasting budgets, making matches more expensive to stage. 'If the broadcast revenues fall significantly, then more and more series outside of England and India matches, in particular, are going to become unviable,' said Johnny Grave, the chief executive of Cricket West Indies. He highlighted tours such as New Zealand flying to the Caribbean for, say, three T20Is and three one-day internationals as the sort of series that already lost the home board money but would now be impossible to justify.

As Covid-19 ravaged the world game, it emphasised club cricket's growing clout. The T20 World Cup, scheduled to begin in October 2020, was postponed. At the same time, the 2020 edition of the IPL, rescheduled from April, was staged. For all the difficulties – quarantine periods, moving the tournament to the UAE and the absence of crowds – the IPL set new broadcasting records, attracting a 24% increase on the 2019 season.

The success accelerated the IPL's plans to expand the tournament to 10 teams, from 2022. The change will necessitate playing more matches, further intensifying the stress on the international calendar.

* * *

Many years of human existence have been given over to comparing the careers of Sachin Tendulkar and Virat Kohli. But to understand the contours of cricket's shift, perhaps most revealing is to examine who they played for.

Tendulkar is the first – and, surely, only – man to play 200 Test matches during a remarkable 24-year international career. A small measure of his longevity is that Tendulkar played international cricket against players born in six consecutive decades from the 1940s to the 1990s. Along the way, Tendulkar only had time to fit in 43 first-class games for Mumbai, his state. After making his Test debut, Tendulkar played just 35 more first-class games for Mumbai in 24 years – barely one-tenth of Mumbai's number of fixtures in this time. Tendulkar, essentially, was an India player who occasionally turned out for his home state. No matter that Mumbai were India's dominant side; like all domestic teams, they knew that they would have to cede players to international cricket.

The dominance of country over club was even more pronounced in one-day internationals. Alongside his 463 ODIs for India, Tendulkar only fitted in 17 List-A games for Mumbai. Whether you wanted to see Tendulkar bat against the red ball or the white one, you needed to see him playing for India.

Like Tendulkar, Kohli can seldom be glimpsed batting against a red ball in Indian domestic cricket. His last Ranji Trophy match for Delhi was back in 2012. But in the most popular format of the sport, the relationship is inverted. By the start of 2022, Kohli had played 207 IPL games to go with his 95 T20 internationals. So where Tendulkar played five Tests for every Ranji Trophy game, Kohli has played more than two IPL games for every India T20 match. If you want to see Kohli play T20, the easiest way to do so is to turn on the IPL.

In the years ahead it seems certain that the world's best cricketers, from India and elsewhere, will spend more of their time playing in club matches – above all the IPL. The broad trajectory of cricket's journey is unmistakable; the question is how much space is left for the international game.

'Market forces will ultimately determine what's gonna happen,' a former senior figure in the ICC said in 2020. 'Bilateral cricket outside of the big three members – maybe four or five at a pinch – has been dying for the last half-dozen years, if not more.'

With every passing year cricket's structure is coming to look a little more like that of football or basketball. While global international tournaments will retain a huge following, fans' day-to-day focus will increasingly be on club games and – beyond marquee series involving Australia, England and India – bilateral fixtures will have to accept a diminished role. From a balance between international and domestic sport that was the antithesis of football and basketball, cricket has already moved about halfway to bridging this gap; as the IPL expands, its balance will become even closer to those sports.

It is a shift that, for all his radicalism, even Packer did not envisage. If he had, World Series Cricket would have needed a new anthem.

3

AN URBAN SPORT IN A RURAL COUNTRY: THE CHALLENGE OF INDIAN CRICKET

Many sports have a rural myth. The countryside carries cultural connotations of purity and simplicity, and it is frequently meant to represent the nation itself, in contradistinction to cosmopolitan cities. For Indian cricket, that myth is captured in the movie *Lagaan*, set in the fictional village of Champaner. Faced with an oppressive tax imposed by the colonial British, the farmers of the village agree to play a game of cricket. If they win they are exempted from the tax, if they lose they have to pay three times the amount.

Happily, the hero Bhuvan hits a six to clinch a one-wicket victory: this is Bollywood, after all. The imperialists not only lose on the field; they also agree to leave the area altogether. Part of the film's appeal (it has spawned a large literature on this question) is its identification with rural India. The vast majority of Indians lived in villages in 1893, when the film is set, and they still do today. According to most recent census data, around 800 million Indians live in villages of less than 1500 people. Fewer than 200 million Indians live in towns or cities with populations greater than 100,000.

Champaner is a fictional village. Village cricket is a real phenomenon in England, but in India it is about as real as Champaner. Certainly, there is almost nothing written about it. The great historians of Indian cricket Ramachandra Guha, Boria Majumdar and Mihir Bose speak at great length about cricket in cities, but have little to say about cricket in a rural setting. Jonathan Rice writes in the *Wisden On India* anthology, 'In India it has probably always been an urban sport, with pick-up matches being played on the maidans of Delhi, Kolkata and Mumbai rather than in the villages far away from the noise and skyscrapers of the great subcontinental cities … The Indian national team is made up of men from the cities. There are very few boys from the local equivalent of Bowral or Pudsey or Unity Village, Guyana – M.S. Dhoni being the exception that proves the rule.' Even the use of Dhoni as a counter-example is revealing: Ranchi, his home town, has a population of one million.

The first known reference to cricket in India is at Khambhat in 1721, in what is now the state of Gujarat. The first recorded first-class match was between Chennai and Kolkata in 1864. But from the late 19th century until Independence, the acknowledged centre of cricket in India was Mumbai. The cornerstone of the city's dominance was the competition that eventually came to be known as the Pentangular. It was first played in 1877, between the Europeans and the Parsis, Zoroastrians of Iranian descent who dominated trade in the city. It became the Triangular when the Hindus were included in 1906, the Quadrangular in 1912 with the addition of the Muslims, and it acquired its final name when 'The Rest', comprising Buddhists, Jews and Indian Christians, were given a team in 1937. Mahatma Gandhi, famously, was no lover of cricket, partly because of the association with British imperialism. But he also worried about the communal antagonisms promoted by competitions like the geometrically-named tournament.

Mumbai's reputation still drew cricketers from far and wide, just as the city attracted migrants from the rural villages in search of economic opportunities. While the earliest Indian cricketers came from the social elites, talented players from poorer backgrounds quickly made their mark; Majumdar even describes the period of the Indian game from 1880 to 1947 as 'cricket as egalitarianism'. Most celebrated among these were the Palwankar brothers, the greatest of whom was Baloo. Born in Dharwad, a small city more than 300 miles south of Mumbai, into the Chamar caste, who were generally shunned by higher caste Hindus, he moved to Mumbai in 1896. He played in the first game between the Hindus and Europeans in 1906, establishing his fame by bowling the team to victory. In doing so, he overcame, as far as possible within these systems, the prejudices of British rule and Hindu caste.

Still, most players were drawn from the richer classes. Great names of this era include C.K. Nayadu, the son of a high-caste landlord from Andhra Pradesh;

Vijay Merchant, from a family of wealthy Gujarati industrialists; and D.B. Deodhar, a Professor of Sanskrit from Pune. What unites them all is that they were drawn to Mumbai to play cricket. Independence in 1947 brought about the end of the Pentangular, and ceded pre-eminence to the Ranji Trophy. First played in 1934, it became the dominant form of domestic cricket in India and remained so until the creation of the IPL in 2008.

India comprises 28 states and eight union territories. All the states and four of the territories have their own Ranji Trophy teams. But Mumbai also has its own team, separate from the state of Maharashtra in which it is located; Vadodara, also known as Baroda, has its own team as well, as do the regions of Saurashtra and Vidarbha. Finally, Railways and Services represent the transport system and the army.

This regionalisation of competition should have enabled talent from all over the country to blossom on sporting merit. But in the early years of the Indian nation state, educational records appear to have counted for more. Majumdar writes that 'non-cricketing, chiefly academic, qualifications played a leading role in determining a cricketer's recruitment, remuneration, level of appointment and job promotions. The policies adopted by corporate houses made it mandatory for player recruits to have a college degree. This prioritisation of non-cricketing qualifications was instrumental in alienating the relatively underprivileged from the game.' Domestically, the team that represented the city Mumbai continued to dominate. In the first sixty years after Independence, Mumbai won 28 Ranji Trophies.

The domestic organisation of the game did not seem to help India in international competition. While hockey was competitive into the 1970s – the Indian men's team won the gold medal at the Moscow Olympics in 1980 – cricket has emerged as the unquestionably dominant sport. Yet the national team's results were consistently disappointing. India played their first Test match in 1932; in none of the first seven decades did India win more Tests than they lost. By 2000, India had won just 61 of their 330 Tests while losing 109 – almost two defeats for every victory. Since their own elevation to Test status in 1952, their great rivals Pakistan had won 74 Tests while losing 62: an overall win-loss ratio of 1.19, more than double India's puny success rate.

The reasons for India's underperformance were multilayered. Infrastructure and facilities were often poor. The team lacked fast bowlers – so batters had scant preparation for what they would encounter at international level. Fitness and fielding were often shoddy. The upshot was a team whose spinners could make them formidable at home but could not compete on unfavourable wickets overseas. Until 2000, India had won only 13 of their 155 away Tests; their win-loss ratio of 0.19 abroad compared badly to Pakistan's 0.65.

You might expect that India's population of almost 1.4 billion people would all but assure its cricket dominance. But if 80% of those people live in remote villages, many of whom are subsistence farmers with little access to sport or sporting competition, regional disparities mean that the population advantage is less impressive. Gandhi wanted India to reject materialism and celebrate its rural traditions. But since Independence, most Indian politicians have believed that India's future lies in modernisation, and that, among other things, means urbanisation.

Throughout the world, people who live in cities tend to have higher incomes, better services, are less likely to be unemployed and more likely to be well educated. And they live longer – in India, rural life expectancy is currently 68 years; in the city, life expectancy is 72.6. The benefits of urbanisation on living standards have been studied extensively by economists. Ultimately, the reasons are quite simple, falling under the ungainly title of 'agglomeration externalities' – a well-educated population, for instance, does not only benefit the individual citizens but society as a whole. This is why the government will step in to subsidise the transaction, as is the case with elementary education.

Agglomeration externalities are a by-product of people living close to each other. For instance, the scent of fresh bread wafting over from a bakery will make the coffee shop next door more attractive as well. A tiny village, to stay with the baked goods theme, will not be able to sustain a French pastry shop, so nobody gets chocolate croissants. In a big city, you can get any sweet your heart desires. Once you have a significant number of people living close together, the possibilities for expanding such agglomeration externalities are endless.

Sport provides an obvious example of that logic. To play professional sport, you need someone to play against, and you need an audience – cities offer a plentiful supply of both. Sport is urban because a large number of players can travel short distances to play each other, while cities have a large supply of potential spectators. Almost every major sports team is located in a city of some size. Urban environments also provide the competitive environment to develop talent and the opportunity to learn from rivals. Indian cricket started in the cities because that was where the British played their games. But once in Indian hands, the cities thrived because Indian players, like the Palwankars, migrated to the urban centres.

Indian policy makers have long struggled to balance the desire to create a more equal society, respecting Gandhi's legacy, with the desire to see the economy grow through urbanisation. That happens when people migrate from rural areas to cities, largely because of the differences in wages – in other words, urbanisation is born of inequality and depends on it. Influential Indian economists such as Arvind Panagariya have argued that Indian policy should give up its Gandhian roots along with its desire for greater equality and instead actively foster the urbanisation that will bring prosperity to the country.

Whether that is sound advice or not, India remains one of the least urbanised countries in the world. If we look at the main cricketing nations, New Zealand is the most urbanised at 87%, then Australia at 86%, the UK 84%, South Africa 67%, Bangladesh 38%, Pakistan 37% and then India 35%. Only Sri Lanka, at 19%, is more rural. About 55% of the world's population now lives in cities; India remains one of the largest outliers.

India did not set out on the path to increasing urbanisation until the 1970s. In 1971, only 18% of the population was urban, not so very different from the rate of 14% recorded in the 1941 census, the last before Independence. In the past 50 years, the urbanisation rate has almost doubled. Despite the abject poverty in urban slums, greater urbanisation is correlated with greater wealth (GDP). More GDP is correlated with more sporting success, such as Olympic medals won. Where the arrows of causality point within this framework is a matter for debate, but it is tempting to think that India's low levels of urbanisation held back its cricketing development.

What is not subject to debate is Indian cricket's remarkable improvement in the 21st century. Between 1994 and 2004 India won as many Tests as it lost.

Between 2004 and June 2021 India won 85 Tests and lost 47, within striking distance of bringing their all-time record to parity.

Prior to 1994, the organisation of cricket in India was essentially amateur. Professionalisation, by definition, implies money changing hands; only amateurs play for free. Indian cricket did not simply change because of a desire to do better, but rather because it finally acquired some financial muscle.

When India won the World Cup in 1983, only a small fraction of the Indian population could witness it; in 1980, only 1% of Indian households had a TV. Cricket was both a catalyst for, and beneficiary of, the TV boom. In the 1980s, TV spread in the cities; by 1990, 15% of households had a set. In the 1990s, access broadened to reach a good part of rural India – by 2000, Doordarshan, the national TV network, could reach 70% of households. Two types of programmes, which lent themselves ideally to families and even communities watching together, were particularly well positioned to benefit from the surge: soap operas and live sport.

Until 1993, the Board of Control for Cricket in India (BCCI) obtained no revenue from their ownership of Indian cricket broadcast rights. Incredibly, Doordarshan actually charged the BCCI to carry their games on TV. When the BCCI tried to sell its rights to a foreign broadcaster, Doordarshan persuaded the government to block access. The BCCI took legal action and obtained a landmark ruling from the Indian Supreme Court in 1995, securing their freedom to sell broadcast rights in the open market.

The contract the BCCI signed in 1993 was for US $600,000. The next broadcasting rights, in 2000, fetched $55 million. In 2006, the rights were sold for $549 million. The first IPL rights, in 2008, fetched $920 million over 10 years. The BCCI cancelled the contract after one season; Sony retained the rights – but are now paying $1.6 billion over the following nine years.

Suddenly, Indian cricket was awash in cash. The BCCI created a National Cricket Academy, based in the traditional strongholds of Mumbai, Chennai, Delhi and Kolkata, to start a professional training programme for elite cricketers. Foreign coaches were drafted to spread the latest ideas, paying particular attention to boosting India's fitness and fielding, traditional weak points. Indian cricket entered a new era.

Economists differentiate between the 'intensive margin', which would here mean increased spending on developing the skills of players coming from the traditional cricketing centres, and the 'extensive margin', such as searching for new talent outside of the traditional centres. Can we find evidence that India's rise is associated with expansion on the extensive margin? And if so, whereabouts on that margin? Has India gone out to find players in the vast untapped rural communities of the country, or has it searched in newly urbanising regions?

Before looking at the data, it is worth exploring why it matters. Take the example of M.S. Dhoni, the poster-child for extending the reach of Indian cricket. 'M.S. Dhoni opened the doors for Indian players from small towns and obscure backwater states,' the Indian MP and diplomat Shashi Tharoor wrote when Dhoni announced his international retirement in 2020. 'By rising from humble origins in the backward state of Jharkhand, including working as a railway ticket-collector in order to afford to pursue the sport, he ushered in a democratisation of India's big-city elite cricketing culture.'

Tharoor's tribute encapsulates one of the abiding images of Dhoni. He was not merely a brilliant cricketer, who led India to the T20 and ODI World Cups, but also the emblem for a broader shift in Indian cricket. Dhoni hailed from Ranchi, a city in the east of the country that had scant pedigree producing leading cricketers. Before Dhoni, it produced only one Indian cricketer – Rajesh Chauhan, an unexceptional off-spinner who played in the 1990s.

For many, Dhoni's emergence meant that a new age in Indian cricket had dawned: stars could now come from anywhere. But Ranchi is not quite 'anywhere'. It is a city of over one million; yes, there are over two dozen Indian cities larger than Ranchi, but it is not a small town by any standards and is the state capital of Jharkhand. What had happened to Ranchi is a population explosion. In 1971 its population was 266,545 according to the census. When the results of the 2021 census are published, they are likely to show that the population has more than quadrupled in 50 years.

In 2011, K.R. Guruprasad published a book called *India's Small Town Cricket Heroes*, which identified 11 'small town' players who had emerged in the new era of Indian cricket. Of these, three hailed from cities with populations larger than one million (Dhoni, Praveen Kumar and Virender Sehwag), three more from cities ranging from 400,000 to 900,000 (Harbhajan Singh, Ravindra Jadeja and R. Vinay Kumar) and three more from towns of more than 100,000 (Iqbal Abdullah, Suresh Raina, and S. Sreesanth). Of course, if you are from Mumbai, every town is a small town, but 100,000 represents a substantial urban agglomeration. For example, a town of that size could be expected to have at least three high schools, promoting healthy inter-school rivalry in sports competitions.

'Rural', too, is an elastic word. Sreesanth's father worked for a life insurance company, his mother is a chartered accountant, and the family moved around. He was born in the town of Kothamangalam (population, 114, 574), and until around the age of eight, he lived in the tiny village of Kakur. Then, his family moved to Ernakulam, the centre of metropolitan Kochi, with a population of more than two million. Of the 11 'small-town heroes', only one hails from a genuine village – Ashok Dinda from Naichampar in Bengal – and only one comes from a truly small town, Munaf Patel from Ikhar in Gujarat.

A more recent example of emergent rural cricket is the left-arm quick bowler Thangarasu Natarajan. He grew up in Chinnappampatti, a village 20 miles outside the city of Salem in Tamil Nadu. Salem has a population of nearly one million, but Chinnappampatti really is a village.

His father was a day labourer in the weaving industry; his mother sold snacks at a roadside shop. Natarajan learned to play cricket with a tennis ball, developing his yorker, 'Bowling yorkers is something that came naturally to me while playing tennis-ball cricket,' he recalled. 'I used to bowl them slightly wide with the tennis ball because the batters would take a swipe at the straighter deliveries.' Natarajan did not bowl with a hard ball until the age of 20.

Chennai is not only the state capital of Tamil Nadu, but one of the country's traditional cricket centres – and that is where Natarajan moved to play league cricket. At the start of 2015, he made his first-class debut for Tamil Nadu, taking three wickets. This success came at a cost: Natarajan was called for throwing, and had to remodel his bowling action. He wasn't selected for Tamil Nadu in any other matches, in any format, over the next two years. By the age of 25, Natarajan seemed in danger of drifting out of the game.

He got another chance when the Tamil Nadu Premier League launched in 2016. There, he excelled; his yorker was so reliable that he bowled it six consecutive times to defend 12 runs in a Super Over. With all matches televised, and IPL scouts attending games, Natarajan was coveted at the next IPL auction. He made his professional T20 debut for Tamil Nadu in January 2017. By the end of the following month, Natarajan had been signed by Kings XI Punjab for INR 3 crore ($400,000), the highest fee for any uncapped Indian player.

Despite an underwhelming debut IPL season, another fine Tamil Nadu Premier League campaign secured a contract with Sunrisers Hyderabad in 2018. The following season, Natarajan showed how his skills could transfer to the IPL, making him indispensable with his death bowling. He was promptly taken to Australia, making his debut in all three formats during India's tour.

* * *

The creation of the IPL in 2008 has brought a new level of rigour and professionalism to the process of identifying young talent. IPL talent-ID schemes have operated alongside traditional state structures, rather than replacing them – effectively increasing the chances for young talent to be noticed.

'In the past in Indian cricket, when young players were looking for opportunities, the only place they got them was from their own state associations,' Rahul Dravid told *The Cricketer* magazine in 2020. 'The great thing about the IPL is you can come from Karnataka and play for Mumbai. You have eight franchises looking out for all the best players. It's like having an extra eight pairs of eyes looking out for talent all over the country.'

While the IPL has increased the incentives for aspiring cricketers and introduced another layer of talent identification, these effects have been amplified by broader changes. The IPL has inspired a raft of copycat state leagues. Essentially, these are miniature versions of the IPL – with franchise teams and player drafts. The most prominent such leagues are in Tamil Nadu and Karnataka.

As Natarajan's tale attests, state T20 tournaments have increased the number of potential pathways to professional cricket in India, especially for later developers. Where once only an elite coterie of Indian cricketers – those in the national squad and the few best domestic players – made enough money from cricket, salaries for domestic players have mushroomed in this century. Even players who don't get coveted IPL contracts can now earn a good wage through the Ranji Trophy and state T20 leagues. This has made cricket a more stable career and easier to commit to for those without family wealth to lean upon.

Another recent phenomenon, offering an alternative route into the professional game, is the growth of private academies. The most significant of these is the MRF Pace Foundation.

It took until 1980 for the first Indian pace bowler, Kapil Dev, to reach 100 Test wickets – by then, they had played Test cricket for 48 years. In 1987, Ravi Mammen, the managing director of the Madras Rubber Factory, was fed up with Indian batters being bullied by quick bowlers. He vowed to help India develop their own stock of pace bowlers and started the MRF foundation. It promptly enlisted Dennis Lillee, one of the greatest fast bowlers of all time, as director.

When Lillee arrived at the foundation for the first time, in September 1987, he told T.A. Sekhar, MRF's chief coach, 'I want a running coach, I want a dietitian, I want a swimming pool and I want practice wickets which will be very similar to Australia. I want to do video analysis of the bowlers.' Lillee, and the foundation, got them all. Each intake trains at the foundation for around three months a year.

By the end of 2021, 17 Indian Test bowlers were MRF graduates. Many had come from non-traditional cricket centres, being scouted or spotted at talent trials of the sort common among private academies. Zaheer Khan, MRF's most famous alumni with 610 international wickets, came from the small town of Shrirampur in Maharashtra, considered a cricketing backwater. Zaheer was not selected for Mumbai's team in the Ranji Trophy, but Sekhar used his contacts to secure a trial at Baroda, who then signed him up. Sreesanth and Munaf Patel both also attended MRF before making their first-class debuts; Irfan Pathan, R.P. Singh and Ashish Nehra were other graduates, with MRF making a concerted effort to identify left-arm quicks.

In January 2021, India sealed an astounding series victory with a depleted team while inflicting Australia's first defeat at Brisbane in 33 years. At the heart of that victory was a hastily assembled pace attack that may be a harbinger of India's cricketing future. Taking the new ball with Natarajan, making his Test debut, was Mohammed Siraj, the son of an auto rickshaw driver in Hyderabad who started playing the game at the age of 12. The first-change seamer was Shardul Thakur, who grew up in Palgarh – a small town of 70,000 almost 100 kilometres from Mumbai – and used to lug his cricket kit on the train to Mumbai before breaking into their Ranji Trophy team. The fourth seamer, Navdeep Saini, hails from Karnal, a town of 350,000 people in Haryana, which had never previously produced a Test cricketer; his father was a driver for the Haryana government and Saini earned money playing in local tennis-ball tournaments, where he was seen by a Delhi bowler who helped him move to the capital.

When Dhoni was born, in 1981, there was really only one pathway to the professional Indian game: the traditional route, through the state systems. Now, there are four potential pathways: the state system, the IPL, state T20 leagues, and private academies. The search for cricketing talent in India, wherever it is from, has never been so extensive.

* * *

To look at the relationship between urbanisation and cricket and at the changing distribution of cricketers over time, we identified the birthplace and birthday of every recorded first-class player in Indian cricket history and matched their records with the census closest to the date of their birth.

Table 3.1 on the following page illustrates the share of the six biggest producers of first-class cricketers by state and by city, based on players born between 1901 and 2000. The upper panel shows a steady and significant decline in the share of players from states that dominated the game for most of the 20th century (bearing in mind that the career of a player born in 1950 could reach into the 1980s). From more than 80% of players born between 1901 and 1930 (and therefore active in the period before independence), the six largest states have seen their share drop to less than one-third of players born in the period 1991 to 2000. The six states have consistently represented about 36% of the total population in the censuses since 1901. Their contribution of first-class cricketers has now roughly fallen into line with their population share.

The share of the big six cities has also declined, as can be seen from the lower panel of Table 3.1, but less dramatically. From a share of around 30% for players born in the first half of the 20th century, their contribution fell to just over 20% of players born in the 1980s. As of June 2021, the share had fallen to only 14% of players born in the 1990s, although this cohort is still active, and so these numbers might change over time.

To put this in context, these cities accounted for a little over 1% of India's population in the early decades of the 20th century but for more than 30% of first-class players – which means that the odds of playing were about 35 times larger if you were from the big cities. The share of the big six cities' in total population has increased with urbanisation and now accounts for nearly 6% of the national total, even while their share of first-class players has fallen. As a result, the odds in favour of the big cities over the rest now stand at about 3:1. The advantage players get from growing up in a big city remains significant, but is far less pronounced.

Table 3.1: Share of six largest producers of first-class cricketers by state and city

State	1901–1930	1931–1950	1951–1960	1961–1970	1971–1980	1981–1990	1991–2000
Maharashtra	98	130	71	115	172	235	76
Gujarat	45	79	40	62	95	159	88
Bengal	43	51	34	29	51	75	40
Punjab	19	31	27	33	55	59	26
Karnataka	19	43	19	32	46	85	20
Tamil Nadu	17	26	15	24	45	81	21
India	298	576	383	641	1040	1579	835
Top six share	80.9%	62.5%	53.8%	46.0%	44.6%	44.0%	32.5%

City	1901–1930	1931–1950	1951–1960	1961–1970	1971–1980	1981–1990	1991–2000
Mumbai	39	52	22	43	64	90	21
Delhi	1	18	22	35	60	64	49
Kolkata	37	41	32	26	33	35	14
Chennai	11	21	9	13	31	55	9
Hyderabad	1	14	7	9	30	49	22
Bangalore	9	26	8	10	26	40	9
India	298	576	383	641	1040	1579	835
Top six share	32.9%	29.9%	26.1%	21.2%	23.5%	21.1%	14.9%

The character of the Indian team has changed accordingly. While the share of national team players from particular states or cities are highly volatile – a small number of them will change the percentages dramatically – the biggest six states can lay claim to a dwindling number of India's runs and wickets. They contributed 76% of Indian players born between 1951 and 1961. Their share has fallen in every subsequent decade, reaching the lowest point in Indian cricket history in the decade of players born between 1991 and 2001 with 51%. A higher proportion of Indian international players than ever before come from beyond the traditional Indian cricket centres.

Table 3.2: Share of Indian Test cricketers from the big six states, by decade of birth

	1901	1911	1921	1931	1941	1951	1961	1971	1981	1991	2001
Bengal	0	1	1	1	1	2	3	1	12	0	0
Gujarat	1	1	5	4	3	5	3	8	6	18	0
Karnataka	0	0	0	2	4	3	3	8	6	6	1
Maharashtra	5	8	9	18	10	11	8	15	14	15	2
Punjab	2	7	1	1	1	4	7	5	13	10	2
Tamil Nadu	1	1	1	3	2	4	5	3	10	6	1
Big six	9	18	17	29	21	29	29	40	61	55	6
Grand Total	12	19	23	30	31	38	43	63	101	108	11
Big six share	75%	95%	74%	97%	68%	76%	67%	63%	60%	51%	55%

The data, then, confirms the impression that the traditional cricketing strongholds have declined, with some evidence of an acceleration of this trend in recent years. Where, then, is the new talent coming from? If we consider players born before 1950, most originated from Maharashtra and Gujarat on the western coast. But when we consider players born after 1980, while these traditional strongholds continue to produce a good number of players, other regions now also contribute significantly. Urban environments may still dominate, but urban environments spread across the whole country.

No one state stands out as a new hotspot of Indian talent. Uttar Pradesh and Andhra Pradesh were both significant producers of first-class players in the early 20th century, and they have grown a bit faster than others. States such as Himachal Pradesh and Jharkhand, Dhoni's home state, have seen large increases from a low base, but the absolute numbers are not large. Beyond the traditional cricketing centres, we see a broadening spread of players from all regions of India.

Much the same can be said about individual cities. Vadodara and Kanpur have always been cricket strongholds, and they have seen their contribution grow relatively fast over the century; cities such as Mysore or Jodhpur never produced many cricketers and still don't. It's the same picture: the game gradually seeps into all corners of the country, and the established concentrations are changing only slowly.

And what of the small towns and rural India? We divided cities into population bands and then identified the proportion of the total population found in those bands, together with the share of first-class cricketers born in the decade of the census year. The results are illustrated in Table 3.3.

As we noted, most Indians live in rural areas. The data combines rural areas with towns and cities of less than 100,000 people. Matching each individual player (of whom there are more than 5000) with each urban location in the Indian census (of which there are 337) is not trivial, and errors are possible. For example, players often identify their birthplace as the suburb of a city, which may accidentally get included in the rural category. If anything, the percentage of first-class players allocated to the category of 'rural and towns less than 100,000' may be an overstatement.

Table 3.3 suggests that the overwhelming majority of first-class players come from larger urban areas. Around one-third come from cities of over one million, which account for less than 10% of the total population. Perhaps more interesting are the medium-sized cities in the next two categories. Cities in the half million to one million range and the 100,000 to half-million range each account for only 3% or so of the Indian population, but they produce 10–20% of first-class players. These shares seem to have fallen somewhat in recent decades, but they are still large. The share of smaller towns and rural India is far below their share of population, although there are real signs of an increase in recent years.

Table 3.3: Population and first-class cricketer shares by urban area size

Urban area population group	Population share	Share of first-class players	Population share	Share of first-class players	Population share	Share of first-class players	Population share	Share of first-class players
	1961	1961	1971	1971	1981	1981	1991	1991
Over 1,000,000	4.2%	27.7%	5.2%	28.5%	6.3%	36.1%	8.4%	33.2%
500,000–1,000,000	0.9%	10.7%	1.4%	12.1%	2.9%	16.2%	2.6%	11.4%
100,000–500,000	3.8%	37.5%	4.0%	33.4%	3.5%	22.0%	3.6%	20.4%
Rural and towns less than 100,000	91.0%	24.1%	89.4%	26.0%	87.2%	25.7%	85.4%	34.9%

Indian cricket's new wealth has led to a new, rather nice, problem: where to spend the money. As of 2022, the BCCI's annual revenue amounts to around US $700 million, about 50 cents for every person in the country – clearly, the BCCI needs to be selective. The 2021 census, once published, is expected to demonstrate another large jump in the urbanisation rate. The dilemma for the BCCI is this. They can either direct the money towards the newly urbanising talent, who are being drawn into the long-established cricket networks of the cities, or they can focus on tapping into the vast rural pool of potential talent.

The experience of the past two decades – and of India's Test series victory in Australia in 2021 – suggests that if more players from beyond the middle-classes in big cities are given opportunities to make good on their talents, they will help India to win more.

4

AN ASHES EDUCATION – WHY CRICKET'S OLDEST RIVALRY IS THE BATTLE OF PRIVATE SCHOOLS

On a Saturday in May 2016, Zak Crawley and Ollie Pope faced each other in a school game between Tonbridge against Cranleigh. The two captained their sides in the 50-over match, one of the most anticipated fixtures for both schools every year.

Cranleigh won the toss and decided to bat first at their home ground, renowned as among the best batting surfaces in schools cricket. Pope, who batted at No.3 alongside his wicketkeeping duties, was soon at the crease.

Those at the game recall Pope settling into his innings with orthodox strokes, and then unfurling his full repertoire. After he had hit a flurry of boundaries straight over mid-on and mid-off against a seamer, Crawley moved the two fielders back to the boundary, which necessitated bringing third man and fine leg into the inner ring. Pope promptly scooped the next two balls over the wicketkeeper, taking advantage of the newly created gaps behind the wicket.

Pope's controlled 120 from 119 balls underpinned Cranleigh's 311 for 4 from their 50 overs. If they were going to get close, Tonbridge needed their own captain and normal No.3, Crawley, to produce a defining innings of his own. Before his team's innings, Crawley went to Ian Baldock, the Tonbridge coach, and said, 'I want to open.' Even though Tonbridge fell to a 20-run defeat, Crawley scored 140 – 'an astonishing innings from a young schoolboy', according to Tonbridge's cricket master.

The game was a glimpse of England's future. Crawley and Pope, who were born a month apart in 1998, were only 18, and they had yet to make their county debuts. Within three and a half years, they would be playing Test cricket.

Through their skill and hard work, Crawley and Pope became Test cricketers. They also benefited from the training and development regimes that only exclusive schools such as Tonbridge (boarding fees £42,105 per year) and Cranleigh (£39,330) can afford.

* * *

The Ashes is one of the oldest sporting contests in the world and emblematic of the complex and fraught relationship between England and Australia. The Ashes are deeply woven into the history of the two countries, bringing out the best and the worst in each.

Records of cricket in Australia go back to the 1820s; an English team first toured in 1862. Their aims were both commercial and political. The tours could be very lucrative, in part due to the wealth created by the gold rush of the 1850s. But to the English gentry, the central purpose of cricket competition was to bind England to its colonies.

The link is illustrated by Lord Harris, an old Etonian and later a Conservative politician. When he became Governor of Bombay in 1890, he would disparage India's potential to excel at the game while playing an active role in encouraging cricket development in the country. He chaired the first meeting of the Imperial Cricket Council, which eventually evolved into the present-day governing body, the International Cricket Council.

In 1878/79, Harris led a tour to Australia that included a match in Sydney against New South Wales. The game kept bookmakers busy; the locals were strongly favoured to win. Each side brought their own umpires. As the game proved unexpectedly tight, the crowd, convinced the English umpire was biased, became agitated. The New South Wales team asked Harris to withdraw his umpire on grounds of incompetence. He refused. In response, the crowd stormed the pitch. Harris later complained that he 'in defending Coulthard [the umpire] from being attacked, was struck by some larrikin with a stick'.

Two of the main elements of an enduring narrative were established: the English are snobbish cheats, the Australians aggressive louts. The final piece fell into place over the next few years: the Australians were clearly better at the game that the English had invented, and hence it was declared, after a bitter defeat on

English soil in 1882, that English cricket was dead and 'the body will be cremated and the ashes taken to Australia'. Charles Alcock, who was instrumental in creating the fixture, wrote the obituary, 'Sacred to the memory of England's supremacy in the cricket-field which expired on the 29th day of August, at the Oval'. Barring the occasional brief reversal, there has been little reason to revise this assessment since.

The most fraught and debated series in Ashes history is the Bodyline tour of 1932/33. The outline of the story is familiar to most cricket fans. The greatest batter of all time is in his pomp: Bradman the Australian. The English, knowing they cannot win by conventional means, adopt 'leg-theory' – which essentially meant bowling fast at the head and body of the Australians. The ploy works, and England regain the Ashes.

However ingenious a strategy it might have been on the ground, Bodyline precipitated a political crisis – Australian hostility was such that many wanted to end cricketing ties altogether. At the AGM of the prestigious St George Cricket Club in Sydney, one member asked if the Australian team would still be sent on tour to England. A member of the New South Wales Cricket Association executive replied, 'It has to go. We cannot afford, from an Empire point of view, to allow the Tests to be abandoned. They mean more than cricket. They mean friendships between England, Australia, South Africa, New Zealand and the West Indies.' As the Australian cricket historian Chris Harte observed, 'That was the crunch. The concern was about the Empire.'

Douglas Jardine (captain, Winchester and Oxford) and Plum Warner (tour manager, Rugby and Oxford) were, from an Australian point of view, the villains. Harold Larwood and Bill Voce, the English bowlers who put Bodyline into practice, were largely absolved of responsibility by the Australian public – they were just carrying out orders, and Larwood would settle happily in Australia. The ones who gave the orders were another matter: posh Establishment figures, snobbish Englishmen who could not win in a fair fight. Warner would later be accused of editing the official records to conceal his involvement in the scheme. Some Australians are still riled by the mere mention of Jardine's name.

Such conflicts are never just about cricket. The scorn for privileged Englishmen from fancy schools sneering at Australians runs deep, fed by other histories such as the Gallipoli landings in 1915, when First World War English generals sent thousands of Australians and New Zealanders to futile slaughter. Irish ancestry makes other Australians tend to distrust imperialist Englishmen – an estimated 30% of Australians are of Irish descent, and many of their ancestors were sent to Australia as convicts, often sentenced for rebellion against British rule in Ireland.

* * *

It's not unreasonable to associate cricket with English elitism: the posh English schools of the 19th century played a significant role in the expansion of the game and British imperialism. Elite school cricket was and – as the tales of Crawley and Pope attest – still is a major part of the Establishment. The longest continually contested game in any sport is the annual Eton v Harrow cricket match, which began in 1805 and still has a slot at Lord's every year. There is a record of Westminster playing Charterhouse in 1794, and Winchester has played Eton and Harrow since 1825. These games have always been more than sport. The historian J.A. Mangan has documented the relationship between games such as cricket, the Victorian public school, and its role in imperialism. 'Cricket was the pre-eminent instrument of moral training,' he wrote.

Naturally, when Australians look at English teams, they notice the significant representation of the privately educated, from Harris and Jardine to Peter May (Charterhouse) and Ted Dexter (Radley) or Colin Cowdrey (Tonbridge) and Mike Brearley (City of London School) to Andrew Strauss (Radley) and Alastair Cook (Bedford School). We identified the schools that 228 out of 255 (89%) England Ashes players attended in the post-war period; 33% went to independent, fee-paying schools in the UK. These percentages understate the significance of independent schools, since we excluded pupils who transferred to independent schools after starting at a state high school. The over-representation of private schools is striking – on average in the post-war era they have accounted for only about 7–8% of secondary school-age children. For children educated in the UK, the probability of playing in an Ashes Test for England was about six times larger if you went to private school.

At times, more than half of England players were private school alumni – in 1950, twice in 1956, and once in 1961. The British school system was different back then. The state system had three types of school – grammar, secondary modern, and technical. Children sat an exam called the 'eleven-plus' (named after the age at which you took it), and the roughly 10% who passed went to grammar schools. Most of the rest went to secondary modern schools.

Going to grammar school brought significant advantages in terms of funding and status. Unlike secondary moderns, grammar schools were expected to prepare students for a university education. Grammar schools also had better sports facilities; England players who did not come from private schools were frequently grammar-school alumni. It was not uncommon in the early postwar years for eight or nine of England's team to have been educated at either private or grammar schools, typically with a fairly even split between the two.

This all changed in the 1960s with the end of selective schooling in the state sector. By the 1980s, the era of Ian Botham and David Gower, most members of the team who had been educated in Britain were from state schools, generally comprehensive. A number of players educated overseas began to appear as well. The team for Botham's Ashes in 1981 contained only two privately educated players – Mike Brearley and Gower. By the 1990s, England regularly put out teams that included more players educated abroad than educated at private school.

The England team of 2005, who so memorably regained the Ashes, were largely a product of the comprehensive system, with a little help from overseas. The only privately educated players in that England side were Andrew Strauss and Ian Bell. Then, beginning with the addition of Alastair Cook, Matt Prior and Stuart Broad, private schools became more important. Throughout the 2010s there were either four or five private school graduates in every Ashes team; the last time there were fewer than four was in 2007.

It's not hard to draw parallels with politics. From 1945 to 1961, the five British Prime Ministers all went to private school, and three of them were Etonians. The following five either went to grammar school (Harold Wilson, Edward Heath and Margaret Thatcher) or left school early (Jim Callaghan and John Major). Since Tony Blair came to power in 1997, three of the five prime ministers went to private school, including two Etonians; only Gordon Brown and Theresa May (predominantly) attended nonselective state schools.

* * *

In 2013, an article on the Australian Broadcasting Corporation (ABC) website highlighted the 'extraordinary' advantage enjoyed by English cricketers who went to elite schools. Journalist Steve Cannane's piece contrasts the dominance of privately educated players in the England side with 'the cricket curse facing private schoolboys' in Australia and asks 'what private schools are doing wrong?'

The ABC article spoke of a common perception in Australian cricket: if there is discrimination against children educated at a certain type of school, it is against those from private schools who, it is claimed, are widely derided as too soft.

Ed Cowan, who played 18 Tests for Australia from 2011 to 2013 as a top-order batter, is an old boy from Cranbrook School in Sydney (fees of A$38,862 [£21,300] for senior day pupils in 2021). A prolific player in junior cricket, Cowan said that the Australian stereotype of players from elite schools lacking toughness counted against him. 'Perception is often reality when it comes to selection,' Cowan wrote. 'Throughout my career, even as a junior, I have battled against a perception that a kid who went to a good school and had a degree must be soft as butter … My upbringing and education in any other walk of life would make me an insider … In Australian cricket, it leaves me an outsider.'

'In cricketing terms Ed Cowan comes from a disadvantaged background,' writes Cannane. 'Despite having access to the best facilities and good coaches, cricketers from elite private schools across Sydney are up against it when it comes to making it into the Test arena.'

When Cowan made his Test debut in 2011, *The Australian*'s headline read: 'Ed Cowan smashes through the private-school barrier'. The article said, 'There have been any number of conspicuous exceptions to the rule – Lindsay Hassett, Ian and Greg Chappell and David Boon springing quickly to mind – but broadly speaking the bluebloods of Australian cricket have tended to graduate from the blue-collar ranks.'

Just how many exceptions to the rule have there been? We assembled the schooling data for Australian Ashes cricketers since 1945. We were surprised by the results.

Australia has expensive private schools that charge handsome fees, just like England. Many of them have been around a long time: The King's School, Sydney (1831), Launceston Church Grammar School, Tasmania (1846) and Hale School, Perth (1858). The majority of schools are state funded and non-selective. But there is a third category – Catholic schools. Apart from the religious element, these schools may look similar to the elite high-fee schools, but many charge relatively modest fees and are administered by the Catholic Education Office. Even so, they are certainly a form of private education.

Perhaps surprisingly, about 35% of Australian children attend private schools, more than half of which are Catholic schools. One reason for this is the substantial government funding of schools outside the state system, which has expanded significantly since the 1970s. Accordingly, the share of privately educated students has risen significantly in the past 50 years – from around 25% to the current 35%. The percentage of privately educated children has been consistently higher than in England, where it has fluctuated fairly narrowly around the 7.5% level.

A striking number of recent Australian players did attend private schools. The list includes Pat Cummins, long ranked as the No.1 Test bowler in the world (St Paul's Grammar School in Sydney, which charges A$17,784 a year); James Pattinson (Haileybury City, Melbourne, A$33,560 a year); Cameron Bancroft (Aquinas College, Perth – the same school as Australia's coach Justin Langer, A$17,991 for day pupils and A$24,282 for boarders); the Marsh brothers, Mitchell and Shaun (Wesley College, Western Australia, A$25,541); and new star Cameron Green (Scotch College, Western Australia, A$28,600 for day pupils and A$54,600 for boarders).

To this list can be added Joe Burns, Chris Lynn and Mitchell Swepson (who all attended St Joseph's Nudgee College in Brisbane within four years of each other, A$16,300 for day pupils and A$38,470 for boarders); Marcus Stoinis (Hale School, A$26,910 for day pupils and A$51,660 for boarders); Matt Renshaw (Brisbane Grammar School, A$28,230) and Ashton Agar (De La Salle College in Victoria, A$12,689). A few players attended religious schools with more affordable fees – Jhye Richardson went to Emmanuel Catholic College in Western Australia, which charges A$7,073 a year; Travis Head went to Trinity College in South Australia, A$6,930. But among players from private schools, more expensive and exclusive schools dominate.

Since 1945, 31.4% of Australian Ashes players have attended private schools, barely different from England's 32.9%. Indeed, there are actually more Tests where the Australian private-school graduates were in a majority – 13 times, compared to England's four. In 77 post-war Ashes games (40%), the Australian team had more privately educated players than the English; in another 11%, the proportions were the same.

The Australian Test team is scarcely more blue collar than the English one. In both countries private schools are major nurseries of Ashes cricketers. An Ashes series limited to privately educated children would not look as different to the real Ashes as Australians might like to think.

* * *

Not only have Australian Ashes teams included roughly as many privately educated Ashes players as England; they also appear to be following a similar trend. Figure 4.1 below shows that, from 1945 onwards, the share of privately educated players in the Ashes teams declined. The fraction stabilised in the 1970s, and then from the 1990s onwards started to rise again.

The trend is particularly noticeable in the past decade or so. From 2010 to the end of the 2019 Ashes, 45% of England's Ashes players educated in the country were privately educated, compared to 44% of Australian Ashes players. So much for the Australian 'private-school barrier': Australian private schools are now comfortably producing a disproportionate share of international players.

Figure 4.1: Share of privately educated players in Ashes teams (five game moving average), 1946–2018

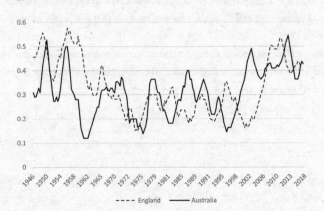

What explains the recent trend? In a 2012 study of English schools, Francis Green, Stephen Machin, Richard Murphy and Yu Zhu found that the wage gap between private school and state school graduates had increased since the 1960s. It seems that the advantage of better facilities and greater resources has increased across the board.

When comparing England and Australia, not everything is the same. In both countries, the share of runs produced by privately educated batters is roughly the same as their share in the proportion of players – about one-third each. But when it comes to wickets taken, the countries are different. In Australia the percentage of wickets taken is in line with the runs. Yet privately educated English players took only about 17% of England's wickets – one-sixth of wickets compared to one-third of runs. English private schools specialise in batting; the Australian equivalents do not. We have already explored the English private school preference for batting – the Australian approach seems worthy of further research.

There are clearly other important differences, both economic and cultural, which affect the production of cricket talent. For example, the Australian school system gives cricketers a significant advantage over their English rivals: more time to practise. English schools play cricket in the summer term, but the programme of matches is often disrupted by exams. But while England operates a three-term model, Australia operates a four-term model. Two of these – terms one and four – are given over to cricket, at the start and the end of the year. Even when children have exams, at the end of term four, that still leaves all of term one for cricket.

The Ashes are many things: a clash between Australia and the mother country; cricket's most storied rivalry; the place where cricketing legends are forged. They are also a battle of the private schools.

5

THE RISE OF NEW ZEALAND: BY LUCK OR DESIGN?

As Kane Williamson lifted the inaugural World Test Championship on a bright midsummer's evening in Hampshire in June 2021, it put the seal on the greatest era in New Zealand men's cricket. New Zealand had already reached consecutive ODI World Cup finals; now, they had won a global event by defeating India, the behemoths of the modern game.

Few triumphs can claim to have been so popular with neutral fans. Partly, this reflected the sense that victory for New Zealand in a global event was overdue, after losing the 2019 World Cup final through the arcane – and rapidly scrapped – boundary countback rule. It also reflected admiration for the spirit with which New Zealand played under Williamson and his predecessor, Brendon McCullum. But the popularity of New Zealand's win also reflected the feeling that, in cricket's age of the Big Three – Australia, England and India – they showed how interlopers could also thrive. 'It was a victory for the small guys,' Mike Atherton wrote. In *The Australian*, Gideon Haigh said that, 'Were it not for New Zealand's skill, spirit and ingenuity, the game would feel even more than it does like a slightly seedy racket for the benefit of India, Australia and England, so busy hogging the big bilateral fixtures and ICC events ... Watch the Black Caps go cheerfully and also mercilessly about their work, and you're consoled that, once cricketers take the field, cricket is 11 versus 11, rather than GDP versus GDP, as significant as the latter is in a resource-dependent world.'

The contrast between the cricketing resources of New Zealand and the vanquished Indian team was incredible. The final pitted a team representing a nation of five million against one representing 1.4 billion, and a board with annual revenue of £28 million against one with £380 million. New Zealand have the smallest population of the 12 Test-playing countries and, before the Covid-19 pandemic, had lower annual revenues than Surrey County Cricket Club. And yet there was little sense of New Zealand's victory being a huge surprise: the side were already ranked No.1 in Test and one-day international cricket. By the end of the year, New Zealand would reach another World Cup final, in the T20 World Cup. It meant that, within three years, they had reached the finals of the World Cups or World Test Championships in all three formats of the international game.

* * *

In cricket terms New Zealand is the equivalent of a photographic negative of the West Indies. Both have a similar sized population – 5 million (NZ) and 6 million (WI) – and were comfortably the two smallest Test nations until the admission of Ireland. Both comprise a collection of small islands. New Zealand is a single nation, the West Indies cricket team subsumes 10 countries and four dependent territories.

Both teams made their Test debut within two years of each other, in 1928 and 1930. But while West Indies quickly made an impact, New Zealand took 26 years to win a Test. From the 1960s to the 1990s, the West Indies produced some of the greatest players and teams in the history of the game and embarked on a 15-year undefeated run in Test series.

By 2000, the West Indies and New Zealand had vastly different records. The West Indies had won 134 Tests, lost 93, tied one and drawn 126 – a win-loss ratio of 1.44, which was the second best in Test cricket, below only Australia. New Zealand had won just 44 of their 276 Tests while losing 111, giving them a win-loss ratio of 0.39 – the second worst of any Test side, ahead of only Zimbabwe. Even in ODI cricket, traditionally New Zealand's strength, the differences were vast. West Indies had a win-loss ratio of 1.66 – once again, the second best of any nation, but this time behind South Africa. New Zealand's win-loss ratio was 0.76, placing them seventh in the world. And while West Indies had won the first two World Cups, and reached the final in the third, New Zealand still hadn't got to a World Cup final.

New Zealand's history did not suggest that they would be able to thrive in the 21st-century game. When people thought of New Zealand's cricket team – and they rarely did – it was mostly for mustachioed medium-pace bowlers, a breed known as dibbly-dobblers who bowled wicket-to-wicket seam at barely 70mph. Admiring their kits was often the most exciting part of watching New Zealand play.

But since 2000, the fortunes of New Zealand and West Indies – at least in Test and ODI cricket – have gone into reverse. In Tests, New Zealand have won 63 and lost 64; West Indies have won 43 and lost 108. In ODIs, New Zealand have won 217 and lost 194, a win-loss ratio of 1.11. The West Indies have won 169 and lost 243, a win-loss ratio of 0.69.

New Zealand's record since 2013 has been extraordinary. From their clash with West Indies at the start of their home summer in 2013–2014 to November 2021, New Zealand won 35 Tests and lost 17 – a win-loss ratio of 2.06, narrowly ahead of India as the best in the world in this period. In the same period, West Indies have won 17 Tests but lost 37, a win-loss ratio of 0.46. The difference is equally stark in ODIs: New Zealand have won 78 and lost 43, giving a win-loss ratio of 1.81 – narrowly below India as the best in the world. West Indies' record, once again, is almost the inverse of New Zealand's – they have won 43 ODIs while losing 72 to give a win-loss ratio of 0.60.

So New Zealand's success on the global stage has been in keeping with their general excellence. From a side considered among the lower echelons of Full Member nations, New Zealand have repositioned themselves as the most formidable side beyond the big three. Here is how they did it.

* * *

At the start of 1999, New Zealand were ranked eighth in ODIs and Tests alike – in both cases, only narrowly above Zimbabwe as the lowest-ranked of the Test nations at the time. In cricket terms, this was unsurprising: apart from during the 1980s, when their team included Martin Crowe and Richard Hadlee, New Zealand had seldom been much better. But in a broader context, New Zealand's cricket underperformance was puzzling given the proud sporting traditions of the nation.

Per capita, the 46 Olympic gold medals New Zealand had won by the end of the 2016 Games placed it sixth worldwide in the all-time list, two places ahead of Jamaica. The country's success in contesting the America's Cup in yachting has been extraordinary. And then there's rugby.

Perhaps no team in any sport can match the sustained dominance of the All Blacks over more than a century. The team has an all-time win percentage of 77%. They hold the longest unbeaten streak in international rugby – 23 games – and the longest winning home streak – 47 games. Out of 577 games since they started playing in 1903, they have never endured a period of weakness – their worst losing streak is six games, in 1949–1950; they lost five in a row in 1998, four in 1929–1930 and three in 1970–1971, 1973 and 1994. All other defeats have come in pairs or singles. The team's alleged weak point is the Rugby World Cup, which they have won only three out of nine times.

Against this background, the modest success of the cricket team was perceived as something of a national embarrassment.

* * *

The tale of cricket in New Zealand is really the tale of New Zealand Cricket (NZC), the sport's governing body and its modernisation. The story begins in 1995. It was not an auspicious year for the sport in New Zealand. It is best remembered for three players – Dion Nash, Stephen Fleming and Matthew Hart – confessing to smoking marijuana on their tour of South Africa. Fleming later said that 'more than half the squad were involved'.

In a sense the pot incident was in keeping with the lack of professionalism in New Zealand at the time. This was an era when the country's domestic cricketers were semi-professional; even many national team players juggled other jobs alongside their international commitments. John Wright, who played for New Zealand from 1978 to 1993, recalled that getting a contract with an English county was like 'winning the lottery'. It was the only way to be a full-time cricketer. On one Test tour to England, Wright's telephone bill home dwarfed his entire tour fee.

As the pot scandal unfolded, the board of NZC decided to seek out new highs. He set up a committee to review the administration of the game, chaired by John Hood, who would later become vice-chancellor of Oxford University. The report recommended a drastic step. Until then, the board comprised 13 members, all drawn from the six provincial associations that administered the highest level of the domestic game, and all unpaid part-timers. The Hood Report recommended replacing them with a seven-person board of professional administrators with relevant experience for the activities that they were running. In effectively replacing cricket enthusiasts with business people, it required the current board to vote themselves off the board. Remarkably enough, they did.

The outgoing board's most dramatic gesture was to appoint Christopher Doig, one of the world's leading operatic tenors, to become chief executive. Doig had longstanding connections to cricket, but the decision provoked a lot of snide jokes about how at least the national anthem would now be sung properly. Yet the raft of reforms pushed through by Doig and his successors now draws widespread admiration – in cricket and beyond. 'NZC has been heralded as leading the non-profit sporting world in governance practices,' wrote Trish Bradbury and Ian O'Boyle, two academics who have written extensively on sports governance issues, in 2015. Even the All Blacks have learnt from their initiatives.

New Zealand may provide clues as to how other mid-sized nations can compensate for their financial disadvantages with Australia, England and India. Here are eight factors that we believe have given New Zealand the best chance to thrive in the age of the big three:

1. Professional governance

The traditional model of governance of sports organisations is the representative model, in which groups within a sport federate together and nominate membership of governing committees to represent their interests. In the New Zealand context this meant that club representatives were elected to provincial committees and provincial representatives were voted onto the national board, often with quotas to ensure that each province was represented in proportion to its size.

The intention of this is to fairly represent each individual interest group within the sport. The downside is that it often leads to factionalism and poor decision-making. For example, everyone might agree that a national centre of excellence is a good idea, but local politics might lead to disagreement over the location, leading to horse-trading among provinces and a final decision that is preferred by the majority, but is not necessarily in everybody's best interests. The Hood Report recommended the creation of an independent board structure with 'the appropriate mix of business management, media and marketing, strategic, cricket-playing and cricket administrative experience' who were not 'representatives of particular provinces or other sectional interests'.

It's no coincidence that NZC adopted this approach in the 1990s. For more than a decade prior to this, New Zealand had been going through an economic reform process known as 'Rogernomics', named after Roger Douglas, the finance minister between 1984 and 1988. Although Douglas was part of the Labour government, his policies closely resembled Reagonomics in the US and Thatcherism in the UK. The driving ideology of Rogernomics was efficiency and incentives – ending bureaucracy and regulation, while allowing markets to operate freely. The legacy of Rogernomics is still hotly debated in New Zealand today. Many believe that the economy had become sclerotic and needed to be freed up; many others argue that the costs, in terms of unemployment, increased inequality and worsening poverty among the most deprived groups in society, were unpalatable.

While NZC embraced these reforms, other countries have not modernised their governance in the same way. The Cricket West Indies board have rejected a series of reports calling for independent governance to replace the existing model – of two representatives per territory, which resembled New Zealand's board before 1995. West Indies' model was called 'antiquated', 'obsolete' and 'anachronistic' in an independent report commissioned by the Prime Ministerial Committee on the Governance of West Indies Cricket in 2015. Partly these difficulties have reflected the political diversity of the West Indies, which is unique in international cricket.

Factionalism has also characterised the administration of Sri Lankan cricket. 'The board is still elected by 140-plus members, many of whom hail from clubs and associations that are either defunct or add nothing to the health of cricket on the island,' the journalist Andrew Fidel Fernando wrote for ESPNcricinfo in 2021. 'Many of the electors are in the game for personal gain. It is small-scale politicking for which board members are essentially elected.'

2. Raising funding and interest in the sport

World-leading governance can only take a sports team so far – they also need cash to develop. During his five-year tenure from 1995, Doig oversaw a near tripling of NZC's revenue from NZ$7 million to NZ$22 million. This was an era of increasing TV revenues in all countries, but NZC's performance was exceptional. Over the same period the revenue of the England and Wales Cricket Board only increased by 50%. Since 2001 NZC's revenues have almost trebled again, reaching more than NZ$60 million in 2020.

Much of this extra revenue came from increases in sponsorship income, which in turn stemmed from an improved profile of the game within New Zealand. This did not come, at least initially, through an improved performance of the national team. But NZC found other ways to engage with its cricket public.

Doig encouraged a focus on entertainment. As one journalist snootily observed in 1995, 'New Zealand Cricket chief executive Christopher Doig's plans to make one-day cricket more of a spectacle were certainly demonstrated yesterday. Live music added an extra dimension, although the drumming accompanying fours and sixes seemed out of place.'

Perhaps the most tantalising innovation of this period was Cricket Max, a short-form version of the game invented by Martin Crowe. The game allocated each team two innings of ten overs each. To encourage straight hitting a trapezoidal area was marked out behind the bowler, in which no fielder could be placed, and any runs scored in this area counted double – so a straight six was worth 12 runs.

With NZC's encouragement, the first official Cricket Max game was played at Cornwall Park, Auckland, in February 1996 and attracted an impressive crowd of more than 5000. Following this pilot, NZC created two competitions at provincial level for the following season. The experiment was a success and crowds were good. But the real purpose had been to create a TV-friendly version of cricket for Sky. The early games attracted TV audiences comparable to the extremely popular Super 12 Rugby. At a time of scant broadcasting interest in other domestic cricket, Sky reputedly paid NZ$ 500,000 a year for it.

As the game became established in New Zealand, NZC tried to persuade other cricket nations to adopt it. England played a series at the end of 1997 and a West Indian side toured in 1999–2000. India played a Max game to mark the start of their 2002 tour; Sachin Tendulkar scored 72 off 27 balls. But NZC struggled to generate any interest at the ICC. One problem was the simple number of adaptations – for many it was just too different from cricket. Matthew Engel said that it begged 'the question of why the New Zealanders do not simply play baseball'. In many ways, Cricket Max was the precursor to Twenty20.

Just as New Zealand changed at professional level, so they also innovated at the grassroots. Concerned by declining participation figures, administrators appointed Alex Astle as the first national development manager in 1998. The New Zealand administration 'shifted its attention for the first time from solely high-performance cricket to also include community or grassroots cricket,' Astle said.

Compared to England, New Zealand was a generation earlier in embracing hybrid formats to keep the sport vibrant at grassroots. Clubs were encouraged to play shorter forms – or even matches with fewer players. In Wellington, 'dual-pitch' cricket was introduced for children. This entails two matches being played at the same time on pitches next to each other – so when a batter has finished their innings on one pitch they would go and field on the other pitch. Making cricket more adaptable and accessible has helped New Zealand grow their participants and fanbase.

3. A streamlined domestic system

For much of the 20th century, professional cricketers were mostly found in England, the one country that could sustain a professional domestic competition. By the 1990s the growth of TV and sponsorship revenues meant that an increasing number of top cricketers could make a living out of the game. But the path to full professionalisation of players was often fraught, with labour-management disputes commonplace.

At the turn of the century, there were still no professional contracts at all for the hundred or so domestic players in New Zealand; the only professional contracts, introduced in 1995, were for leading national players. The lack of professionalism in the domestic game meant that standards were low, and many players left the sport early because they weren't paid enough.

The formation of the New Zealand Cricket Players Association in 2001 and the negotiation of a fixed player pool to be distributed from NZC revenues marked the beginning of the fully professional domestic cricket era in the country.

This was also the catalyst to improve coaching. Coaches at the six domestic teams became professional, working year-round rather than just in the summer. Under the old system 'the characters you could pick were pretty much people who were in jobs that could afford to take two or three months off, so clearly you weren't always getting the best people,' says Mike Hesson, who worked in various coaching roles for Otago from 1996, and was national coach from 2012 to 2018.

The professionalisation of the domestic game in New Zealand has been made easier by the structure of domestic cricket. For all three formats of the game, New Zealand have the same six provincial associations playing against each other, a system that ensures a concentration of talent.

Other mid-sized Test nations have fragmented competitive structures. In Pakistan, the Quaid-e-Azam Trophy, the first-class domestic competition, has frequently included more than 20 teams – a mix of regional and departmental teams – and in 2014–2015 featured 26 sides. In Sri Lanka, to the exasperation of former greats such as Mahela Jayawardene and Kumar Sangakkara, the quality of the domestic game has been eroded by more and more teams acquiring first-class status. There are now 26 first-class teams in Sri Lanka, diluting the talent pool, creating a chasm between the domestic and international game and meaning that payments to players are spread too thinly. With the need to pay match-fees for all first-class players, only around 30 male cricketers in the country – compared to New Zealand's 116 – could be described as genuine full-time professionals, according to Andrew Fidel Fernando, a leading Sri Lankan cricket journalist.

When Tom Moody was appointed Sri Lanka's director of cricket in 2021, he said that the domestic system stifles Sri Lankan cricket. 'It's not a system that supports excellence,' Moody lamented. 'When there's a 26-team club competition, it's a very big ask for any player, regardless of how many club runs he's got, to step on to the international arena. It's an enormous gulf.'

Yet in recent years, there is evidence of rivals learning from New Zealand. From 2019–2020, the Quaid-e-Azam Trophy was reduced from 16 teams to six, concentrating the talent pool and allowing for greater focus on maintaining the grounds that stage such games.

4. Improving infrastructure

The state of grounds in New Zealand was emblematic of the lack of professionalism. Regional teams would criss-cross the country playing games at small grounds in small towns: in 2002–2003, New Zealand domestic matches were played at 24 different grounds. While this brought the domestic game to all parts of the country, it came at a cost. 'Many of the venues just didn't have practice or playing facilities that were going to help develop players,' Hesson recalls.

In 2005, the New Zealand Cricket Players Association pressed NZC to introduce a 'warrant of fitness' – essentially, criteria for playing and practice facilities which any ground hosting domestic cricket had to meet. The warrant of fitness helped to improve the quality of pitches in New Zealand, which have changed from traditional green seamers to being more conducive for batting: the overall batting average in New Zealand first-class cricket rose from 28, in the period from 1999 to 2008, to 32 from 2008 to 2021. The shift, former fast bowler Simon Doull has said, means that batters have more experience of building long innings on the sorts of good batting wickets that are common in Test cricket. Since 2010, averages in New Zealand domestic cricket have been higher than anywhere else in the world, and the closest of anywhere in the world to the average in Test cricket.

Table 5.1: First-class averages in domestic cricket, 2010 – June 2021

Country	Average
New Zealand	31.4
Afghanistan	29.84
Australia	29.46
Bangladesh	29.44
India	29.22
England	29.04
Sri Lanka	27.7
South Africa	27.23
Ireland	26.46
Zimbabwe	26.14
Pakistan	25.34
West Indies	23.52

Source: CricViz

After England were thrashed in India in 2021, skipper Joe Root called for county pitches to be made better for batters to help prepare players for Test cricket. 'You want guys to come into this environment of Test cricket and have that knowledge of what it's like to go out in the second innings and know the opposition have 450 on the board,' he said. 'They need to find ways of making games last four days, giving spinners the opportunity to bowl and learning to bowl at different stages of the game.'

The transformation in pitches in New Zealand was a microcosm of the wider improvements in facilities in the country. 'Perhaps Christopher Doig's greatest legacy to NZC will be the development of the NZ Cricket Academy and High Performance Centre with facilities widely accepted as being the best of their kind in the world,' said John Anderson, who chaired NZC between 1995 and 2008. These developments were continued by his successor, Martin Snedden.

The High Performance Centre at Lincoln University, which opened in 2018, is considered one of the best of its kind. Its new marquee cover and climate control system allows the temperature to be manipulated, and so enables players to play outside in match conditions for 12 months a year, rather than resorting to indoor nets during the winter.

Pakistan is a notable instance of a country that has been slower to recognise the importance of upgrading facilities. In 2018, Misbah-ul-Haq, the former captain, shared video footage of the changing room for Sui Northern Gas Pipelines Limited, his side, during the first round of the Quaid-e-Azam trophy, Pakistan's national first-class competition. As ESPNcricinfo reported, 'The footage showed squalid toilets with worn tiling, paint peeling off damp walls that had mould growing on them. In the two rooms directly in front of the toilets, several kitbags were sprawled; they might last have had a maintenance call before Misbah made his debut, such was the state of dereliction. There was no air-conditioning, one solitary ceiling fan hummed half-heartedly in what would have been a sweltering room for 22 people to sit in.'

When he shared the footage, Misbah emphasised that the conditions at Lahore City Cricket Association Ground were unfit to nurture international cricketers. He later said, 'The first-class cricketers are the only ones we have that will go on to represent Pakistan at international level. So we need to provide them with the requisite facilities and make domestic cricket competitive, otherwise you can never improve the standard of cricket in your country.'

5. An enlightened attitude towards franchise T20 leagues

When the IPL launched in 2008 it recalibrated the relationship between domestic and international cricket. Players – especially those from outside the big three – could now earn more playing in foreign T20 leagues than the international game. In the very first season of the IPL, in 2008, New Zealand allowed a coterie of players to fly in just two days before the Lord's Test: better that, they reasoned, than antagonise the players by mandating that they return earlier and risk losing them altogether to the free market. New Zealand frequently allowed players to miss low-key internationals to play in T20 leagues. The board also rationalised their international fixture list, to avoid direct clashes with the IPL whenever they could.

Some of New Zealand's rivals attempted to deny this reality – or deluded themselves that appeals to patriotism would trump economic realities. Until their humiliation in the 2015 World Cup, England were scornful of the IPL, which was at the root of Kevin Pietersen's schism with the side. In the first decade of the IPL, West Indies routinely scheduled home internationals that clashed with lucrative T20 leagues – even the IPL – forcing players to choose between the international game and earning life-changing sums away from it.

Cricket West Indies' inflexible selection policy compounded the problem. It was long mandated that players had to play in the domestic 50-over tournament to be eligible for the national one-day international team – even though the domestic tournament clashed with major T20 leagues. In 2015, Phil Simmons was suspended as West Indies head coach for objecting to the continued exclusion of Dwayne Bravo and Kieron Pollard from the ODI team. Both were proven, experienced international players who were available and wanted to play – but, because they had contracts in the Big Bash, which clashed with the domestic 50-over tournament, they weren't deemed eligible for selection. Apart from the T20 World Cup, which does not clash with any major leagues, the West Indies were routinely depleted throughout the 2010s.

A.B. de Villiers' retirement from South Africa, a year before the 2019 World Cup, was driven by his desire to play in lucrative T20 tournaments around major internationals. The board refused to allow De Villiers to 'pick and choose,' as he termed it, leading him to retire from international cricket altogether. New Zealand's enlightened pragmatism has ensured that, barring injuries, they have been at full strength for the games that matter most. Had NZC tried to limit the participation of players in leagues, 'you would end up with players retiring earlier, potentially prioritising IPL over international cricket,' Hesson says.

6. Not bleeding money on their own T20 league

The years after the formation of the IPL were T20 cricket's gold-rush period, as investors and boards ceaselessly sought to create lucrative leagues of their own. The formula was simple: the same players recycled from other leagues around the world. Many would represent teams who were given the same names – often ending in Kings or Stars – in indistinguishable kits. Chris Gayle, the Bradman of

T20, has played T20s for 28 different teams, including for franchises in leagues staged by Afghanistan, Bangladesh, South Africa and Zimbabwe.

Leagues hoped that, by recruiting stars like Gayle, they would generate lucrative commercial deals, sponsors and broadcasters. But they displayed a lack of understanding of cricket's commercial landscape – above all, a naive belief that they could attract a sizable Indian audience, despite Indian cricketers being barred from playing in foreign T20 leagues. The Sri Lanka Premier League played only a solitary season, in 2012, before collapsing because it was not deemed commercially viable. Cricket South Africa lost £11 million on the Global T20 League, which was cancelled before its launch in 2017. Three weeks before it was due to launch in 2019, the first season of the Euro T20 Slam – featuring sides from Ireland, Scotland and the Netherlands – was cancelled. Some franchise leagues have become renowned as hotbeds of match-fixing, with owners even known to make money by betting against their teams, and pressurising their own players to deliberately underperform.

Of the 12 ICC Full Members, New Zealand is the only one that has not tried to create a glitzy T20 tournament built around new teams, rather than those that mimicked traditional sides in domestic first-class cricket. Instead, they were content to build an undemonstrative and unflashy league based on local players and local media interest. It was a conservative decision – but a pragmatic one, rooted in an understanding of their local market. NZC's wisdom ensured that the board did not haemorrhage cash on their domestic T20 league, and could instead build a sustainable competition tailored to New Zealand's needs.

7. A culture that puts the national team first

Culture is perhaps New Zealand's greatest advantage – and the hardest to replicate. A combination of history – the relative lack of regional divides – and the small geography and ease of travel within the country have created a culture in which the six districts are tasked with furthering the interests of the national team first, and winning themselves second, mirroring the system in New Zealand Rugby.

Provincial sides balance their own strategies – after all, it is in New Zealand's interests for domestic sides to experiment – with serving the national team. As head coach of New Zealand from 2012 to 2018, Hesson occasionally directly influenced domestic selection for what he perceived as the good of the national team. Soon after taking over, Hesson called up the Northern Districts head coach to ask if B.J. Watling – who normally opened for the side and played as a specialist batter – could keep wicket and bat in the middle order; Watling would become arguably New Zealand's best Test wicketkeeper. Hesson also asked Canterbury if they could shuffle Tom Latham down to the middle order in the one-day side, where he would also keep wicket – mirroring the role that he would play for New Zealand in the 2019 World Cup.

The collaboration between NZC and domestic sides also manifests itself in other ways. At times major associations have encouraged young players to move to different teams for a year or two to increase their chances of getting game-time. Players who live in one major association but play in another can also get full access to training facilities during the off-season. A portion of each domestic head coach's salary is directly paid by NZC; developing international players is part of each coach's Key Performance Indicators, formalising the link between domestic teams and the international side.

In rival countries, relations between the domestic side and national team are not always as smooth. Counties, against the wishes of the England team, have long given contracts to overseas players immediately before they embark on tours of England. Several Australian Test cricketers acclimatised in county cricket before the 2019 Ashes. Marnus Labuschagne identified his stint with Glamorgan as pivotal to his brilliant series. 'It really did help me a lot playing in these conditions, learning the small intricate things that you need to change from game to game, innings to innings playing on greener wickets,' he said.

The close relationship between domestic sides and the national team has also enabled New Zealand to prioritise the A team. New Zealand's A-team programme was once behind its rivals; now, it is at least the equal of any nation bar India. As recently as 2011, New Zealand played no A-team matches at all in an entire year; nor did they play any in 2002 or 2003. In 2018, Cricket New Zealand reduced their domestic first-class programme from 10 rounds to eight in 2018 to fund increasing investment in their A-team programme – a decision possible because of a collective understanding of the need to prioritise the national team. New

Zealand have used their A team to accelerate the development of players of interest to the national team: for instance, Rachin Ravindra, an all-rounder who bowls spin – a comparative rarity in the country – made his New Zealand A debut before playing his first domestic game after excelling for New Zealand Under-19s.

In June 2021, New Zealand made six changes to their side for the second Test against England, resting leading players so they could prepare for the World Test Championship final. Even without many leading players, they cruised to an eight-wicket victory. Both New Zealand's top wicket-taker, Matt Henry, and top run-scorer, Will Young, in the victory were then omitted for the final. England batter Graham Gooch famously likened facing New Zealand's bowling attack during the years of Richard Hadlee to facing 'the World XI at one end, Ilford seconds at the other'. Now, New Zealand have developed a system with depth.

8. No selection by committee

Traditionally, selection in cricket was done by committee. This entails a chairman of selectors, or a group of selectors, selecting the squad or team; officially, the captain and coach often haven't got a say. There is a long history of selection being influenced by nepotism or personal favouritism – and the captain ending up with a team he didn't want.

'My God, look what they've sent me!' England captain Archie MacLaren exclaimed in 1902, when seeing his side for an Ashes Test. In 1953, England sought an all-rounder to give the side more balance. Chairman of selectors Freddy Brown stumbled upon a solution: himself. Aged 42, Brown played his final Test match. In 1988, the chairman of selectors, Peter May, selected his godson Chris Cowdrey – who averaged 19 in Test cricket, and had not played a Test for three years, during which he had averaged 30 in the County Championship for Kent – to captain England against West Indies. Cowdrey made a duck and five, England lost by 10 wickets, and he never played for England again.

Even in modern times, tensions around picking the team have persisted. In 2008, England selected Darren Pattinson, a 28-year-old fast bowler whose family had emigrated from Australia when he was six and had only played six County

Championship matches, to make his Test debut against South Africa. 'It does look a confused selection,' England captain Michael Vaughan said after the game. 'I felt sorry for him, because he'd obviously not been in the set-up and didn't know anyone.' Vaughan had wanted Simon Jones to be picked. In the West Indies, South Africa, Afghanistan, Zimbabwe and beyond in recent years, there have been allegations of some form of bias – regional, racial, or nepotism – affecting team selection, or simply different preferences between the selectors and captain and coach causing confusion over the best team. Using a selection committee is a standard way to guard against perceived bias, such as towards players from a certain region – but this can blur accountability and create less continuity in selection.

Selection by committee has lingered in cricket long after it was regarded as an anachronism in other sports. In English football, Alf Ramsey made assuming full condition over selection a condition of accepting the manager's job in 1962; he would win the World Cup four years later.

While some variant of the committee model has lingered in other nations, New Zealand have simplified their selection method, following the football model. In 2012 they reformed their selection process, making the head coach the head selector. This meant that the coach could always pick exactly the squad and team that he wanted, and ensured more stability of selection. New Zealand's small player pool, and their relative lack of international fixtures – creating scope for the head coach to watch domestic cricket – means that the system is ideally suited for the country.

'The bigger the selection structure, the more problems you're likely to have,' Hesson said. With the head coach chief selector, 'when you got picked in the team you actually knew that the person who picked you rated you, and therefore that gave you some confidence.'

* * *

It's hard to say if there was ever such a thing as a New Zealand masterplan. The Hood Report is recognised as a landmark document framing an agenda for reform, but many of the good things that have happened to cricket in New Zealand emerged from individual initiatives. No amount of sound administration can guarantee the emergence of players like Brendon McCullum, Kane Williamson, Ross Taylor, Trent Boult and Tim Southee. But NZC have overseen the evolution of men's cricket from an amateur sport with low status to a professionalised organisation that has risen to international pre-eminence. New Zealand's players are benefiting from a structure set-up to prolong their careers and maximise the nation's cricketing talent. Unlike Rogernomics, which produced both winners and losers, NZC's modernisation seems to have produced nothing but winners.

Compared to other mid-resourced Test nations, New Zealand has some considerable natural advantages. Perhaps most significantly, it is one of the wealthiest nations in the world on a per capita basis. After NZC embraced professionalism, the sport has attracted a number of cricketing immigrants, largely from southern Africa – including Grant Elliott, whose six secured New Zealand's place in the 2015 World Cup final, and Devon Conway, Colin de Grandhomme and Neil Wagner, who all played in the team that won the World Test Championship. This quartet all emigrated to New Zealand in their 20s.

Sometimes, rugby is framed as a disadvantage for NZC. And while it is true that most of the best athletes have historically gravitated towards rugby, the presence of such a world-leading sports team is better understood as an advantage for cricket. When captain McCullum and coach Hesson plotted New Zealand's revival in January 2013 after the side were bowled out for 45 at Cape Town in McCullum's first Test as skipper, they discussed the All Blacks. 'We had the greatest example right in front of us in the All Blacks. Yeah it's a different sport – but it's the same attitudes required,' McCullum said in 2018. 'So we looked at what worked for them and how they portrayed themselves in the public and why the public are endeared to the All Blacks as well.'

As cricket has entered the professional age, rugby has provided a template for NZC's administrators to follow. The professionalisation of rugby, in 1995, came in the same year as NZC had begun to embrace professionalism. NZC have sought to learn from New Zealand Rugby's collaborative relationship with domestic teams, and a culture in which the needs of domestic sides are subordinate to the needs of the national team. Administrators have frequently moved between the two sports – David White, NZC's chief executive since 2011, previously worked for Wellington Hurricanes and Auckland Blues. New Zealand's size makes it easy for the cricket team to pinch the ideas from one of the best sports teams in the world. 'There's a natural cross-pollination because it's a small population and people bump into each other,' said John Bracewell, who was New Zealand head coach from 2003 to 2008.

In recent years other countries have tried to copy aspects of the New Zealand approach. Ireland, who became a Full Member in 2017, have ostentatiously tried to become the 'European New Zealand'. When Ireland reformed their governance in 2009, it was modelled upon New Zealand's. More recently, New Zealand have been 'one of the foremost models we used in benchmarking Ireland's strategic plan,' the Cricket Ireland chief executive Warren Deutrom explained. Information supplied by NZC 'has been incredibly helpful to us as a guide,' Deutrom said. New Zealand's approach to hosting Tests – finding boutique venues for lower-profile matches – has informed Ireland's thinking on hosting internationals. Cricket Ireland have recruited several officials from New Zealand, and have studied how they developed their provincial competitions. A heightened emphasis on A-team cricket is also borrowed from New Zealand's playbook.

Such flattering attempts to learn from New Zealand cannot obscure that their status, like those of all bar the Big Three, remains hazardous. The player pool will always be finite, rendering them vulnerable to a few inopportune injuries. Managing the competing demands of T20 leagues and international cricket will become even more arduous in the years ahead, as the biggest leagues expand. And it is possible that, as other boards with similar budgets mimic New Zealand's strategies, their competitive advantage will be eroded.

There is no simple template for success in international sport, nor any guarantees of sustained success. But, in an age of financial polarisation in cricket, New Zealand have found a model that allows them to defy these inequities.

PART TWO

PIONEERS

6

WOMEN'S CRICKET – A HISTORY OF INNOVATION

'It was not very wonderful [i.e. surprising] that Catherine, who had by
nature nothing heroic about her, should prefer cricket, baseball, riding on
horseback, and running about the country at the age of fourteen, to books'

Jane Austen, *Northanger Abbey*

Was one of the most consequential innovations in cricket pioneered by a woman? Quite possibly. Jane Austen's *Northanger Abbey*, written in 1803, is usually quoted to show that baseball was played in England long before the Knickerbocker Club of New York wrote the first official rules in 1845 – but it also suggests that there was nothing strange about girls playing cricket at the beginning of the 19th century. That would certainly have been true in rural Hampshire, where Austen grew up. It was 30 miles from Austen's childhood home that the first recorded women's cricket match was played in 1745, featuring the women of Bramley and Hambledon, two villages in Surrey.

John Willes was the first man to bowl with a round arm – or 'straight arm', as it was known at the time – in first-class cricket in the 1820s. But it may not have been his idea. The story goes that his sister, Christiana, was so bothered by having to bowl underarm while wearing skirts that she took to bowling round arm when she played with her brother in a barn in Tonford, near Canterbury. Willes is then said to have imported the style to the first-class game. While overarm bowling is now customary, Willes' technique has some resemblance to that of modern slingy bowlers such as Lasith Malinga or Fidel Edwards, who both bowl with a very round arm.

Overarm bowling's origin story is disputed. There is a theory that the style was common in the 18th century but had died out in the 1790s because the all-powerful Hambledon club in Hampshire outlawed it. What we do know is that Willes' method contravened the Laws at the time he used it. He was no-balled playing for Kent against MCC at Lord's in July 1822. He reacted by throwing down the ball in disgust, mounting his horse and riding off, never to return to cricket. Despite this, overarm bowling became more popular in the 1820s; in 1828, the Laws were modified to permit bowling with a round arm. On Willes' tombstone, it is inscribed, 'He was the first to introduce round-arm bowling in cricket.'

Of course, the story of Christiana Willes may be nothing but a charming invention, though Willes would hardly have been the first man to get credit for a woman's idea. The tale appears to have originated with an article in *Cricket* magazine published in 1907 and written by Edward Hodges, who was considered something of an expert on early 18th-century cricket. He also happened to be Christiana's son. Hodges' recollection was part of an interview published in the same edition of the magazine that recorded his death, making it close to a dying declaration.

What we do know is that aristocratic women played cricket in the 18th century; the Countess of Derby was a noted exponent. On seeing her play, the Duke of Dorset observed, 'What is human life, but a game of cricket? And if so, why should not the ladies play it as well as we?' The British Museum owns a very fine 1778 painting by John Collet, *Miss Wicket and Miss Trigger*. It shows two elegant ladies, one wielding a gun, the other a cricket bat. But the game was not restricted to aristocrats. Women's village games were often played, pitting the married against the unmarried – a practice common among men, too. As with men's games, women's matches were typically occasions for gambling, often for substantial amounts. Neither was drinking uncommon; the matches appear to have been very festive occasions. Yet by the 1830s, Victorian men had driven women out of the game, which they now declared only a gentlemanly one.

* * *

By the 1890s, women started to reclaim their cricketing heritage, with advocates now stressing the game's potential contribution to health and wellbeing. Some reactionaries continued to argue that ladies were too frail to withstand vigorous exercise, but women such as Bessie Rayner Parkes led an intellectual revolt. A pioneer feminist, she founded the *English Woman's Journal* in 1858, whose pages proclaimed, side by side, a woman's right to higher education and the benefits of healthy exercise. The creation of women's colleges at Cambridge (Girton, 1869) and Oxford (Lady Margaret Hall, 1878) enabled some young women to organise themselves to play sports in the same ways that men's colleges did. But while men focused on cricket, rowing and the newly emerging football, women took to field hockey.

In the 1870s, this was a relatively new sport – the first club was formed in 1849, and the Hockey Association would not come into being until 1886. Women were already playing the game informally at college, and the first women's club was formed in 1887. Nine women's clubs banded together to form the Ladies' Hockey Association in 1895. They immediately applied to join the Hockey Association and were rejected. Kathleen McCrone, in her history of English women's physical education and the struggle for emancipation, relates that they received 'a curt and disdainful refusal, on the grounds that its interest was solely in men's clubs'. Undeterred, they renamed themselves the All England Women's Hockey Association and rapidly established hockey as the leading team sport for girls and women in England. They inaugurated international competition in 1896, and the women's game quickly spread across Europe and much of the world.

There are some scattered references to women playing cricket between the 1860s and 1880s, but not until the 1890s did regular competition emerge. Two male entrepreneurs organised two all-professional women's teams in 1890, perhaps the first professional women's sports competition in history, but the experiment was shortlived. Things went better when women organised themselves – the White Heather Club, which was formed in 1887, revived women's club cricket, which was popular enough by 1895 for the popular journal *Cricket* to condescend, 'The New Woman is taking up cricket, evidently with the same energy which has characterized her in other and more important spheres of life.' In the following 30 years women's cricket made little progress, largely due to the lack of institutional support. As Rafaelle Nicholson puts it in her history of women's cricket in Britain, 'numerous accounts from this period point to the informal playing of cricket during girlhood, curtailed by opposition as they became young women.'

The formation of the Women's Cricket Association (WCA) in 1926 created a central body to organise women's cricket in England for the first time. The pent-up demand was such that within a year, the WCA had 347 individual members and 46 affiliated organisations. A crucial principle of the WCA was separate development – they would avoid playing mixed matches, and try to forge a distinct identity as a women's game. The WCA needed the goodwill of men's clubs to allow them to play on club grounds. But the experience of male hockey's exclusivity (many women's cricketers were also hockey players) and the Football Association's decision to ban women's football in 1921 showed the pitfalls of being reliant on the men's game.

In 1934, the Australian Women's Cricket Council invited the WCA to send a team to compete for the Ashes. The squad were captained by Betty Archdale, who was the daughter of Helen Archdale, a suffragette who had been imprisoned for breaking windows on Whitehall.

Unlike the men, the women had to pay for their own passage – £80 per head (the equivalent of about £6,000 in 2021). At least they had their modest expenses covered in Australia. The cost of travel meant that only better-off players could go. By this time, women's league cricket was emerging in the northern mill towns and producing some high-calibre players, but they were unable to afford the time off or the cost of the passage. More importantly, the squad could only include single women; married women were 'not allowed' to leave their families. The women were told not to smoke, drink or gamble or – most importantly of all – 'be accompanied by a man'.

England won the series and returned with a healthy profit of £1,229,13s – the equivalent of about £90,000 in 2021. Australia's Test tour of England in 1937 marked a new first: Marjorie Pollard became the first women to be a radio sports commentator, announcing the first women's Test match covered by the BBC.

After the Second World War, women's cricket continued its slow growth, but often in spite – rather than because – of the attitudes of leading figures in the men's game. A comment by Len Hutton, England's captain from 1952 to 1955, is typical. According to Brian Johnston, the famous commentator, the two were fielding in a charity match in 1963, and Johnston asked what Hutton thought of women's cricket: 'absurd, just like a man trying to knit'.

* * *

W.G. Grace is generally credited with establishing the modern game of cricket between the 1870s and the First World War. He dominated the sport on the pitch and, as he well knew, attracted large crowds. 'They've come to watch me bat,' he once told an umpire as he picked up a broken bail and placed it back on to the stumps after being bowled. Grace also played a significant role in the game's administration and the establishment of the county system.

Rachael Heyhoe Flint can reasonably be considered his equivalent in women's cricket. She played for England from 1960 (when *Wisden* first began to cover women's cricket annually) until 1982, averaging 45.5 in Tests and 58.5 in ODIs. As England captain between 1966 and 1978, she never lost a match. She was an indefatigable promoter of the women's game – often writing match reports on her own games – and was elevated to the House of Lords in 2010. Her death in 2017 was mourned throughout the sport.

Heyhoe Flint forged strategic alliances with male cricketers to advance the women's game, which included securing recognition by the MCC and Lord's. The custodians of Lord's refused to stage a women's match until 1976. Lord's had never even considered admitting a woman as a member, but with the passing of the Sex Discrimination Act by the UK government in 1975, Heyhoe Flint threatened MCC with legal action unless they relented. It would take her until 1998 to win that battle.

Perhaps her greatest triumph was the creation of the cricket World Cup. Tony Cozier, the eminent West Indies commentator, called the first men's World Cup 'perhaps the boldest and most ambitious innovation the game has known since the legalisation of overarm bowling'. But the women got there first.

'Women are not always second-best in the game of cricket. It was the women after all, who staged the first ever cricket World Cup – an idea born out of a few after-dinner brandies on a night in 1971,' Heyhoe Flint recalled in her autobiography. She was staying at businessman Jack Hayward's Sussex home during a weekend playing cricket at Eastbourne. Though she modestly gave him all the credit, the two hatched the plan for the first Women's World Cup together.

Over brandy, they discussed how to invigorate women's cricket, which remained in its familiar position: deprived of attention, publicity or funding, entirely amateur and with only three nations – Australia, England and New Zealand – even playing semi-regular international fixtures. She had boundless ambitions for the women's game and Hayward had the cash. He had already supported England women tours to Jamaica; now, he agreed to spend £40,000 to help cover the cost of staging the World Cup in England, which would be run by the International Women's Cricket Council.

The seven teams that assembled in England for the inaugural World Cup in 1973 illustrate the state of women's cricket at the time. Together with Australia, England and New Zealand, there were two teams from the Caribbean: Jamaica and Trinidad & Tobago, rather than a West Indies team; the Caribbean Women's Cricket Federation had yet to be formed. There was a Young England side, comprising players unwanted by the full squad, and an International XI of players either unwanted by the nations competing or from countries that weren't represented at all. Originally, the international team was meant to include the best South African talent, but the players withdrew after protests about including them during apartheid. There was no Asian representation. Even with Hayward's support, touring countries had to pay for their own flights and equipment. It even fell to the players themselves to promote the tournament: Heyhoe Flint wrote match reports on England's games for *The Daily Telegraph*.

Inauspiciously, the first game of the tournament, at Kew Green, was rained off without a ball being bowled. With only lukewarm support from English administrators, matches were played at a hotchpotch of venues – Bournemouth, St Albans, Tring, Sittingbourne, Dartford, Bletchley and Kirby Muxloe. The final took place at a venue more fitting international cricket: Edgbaston, the designated host because Lord's refused a request to hold the final.

After rain scuppered the opening fixture, the sun came out: only one other match was abandoned. The tournament was well received, benefiting from being staged in areas that did not host men's international cricket. And the World Cup had the luck that all competitions crave: a successful home team. The last game pitted the Ashes rivals against each other, and England triumphed over Australia by 92 runs in front of a crowd of 1,500 spectators. Heyhoe Flint scored 64 and was presented with the trophy by Princess Anne.

Like all the players in the competition, Enid Bakewell, who scored a match-winning 118 in the final, was an amateur. 'I had to work part-time to get time off to play cricket,' said Bakewell, who was a swimming instructor. 'During the tournament I wasn't being paid, so I'd go without hairdos and makeup when I was playing. We didn't really have any training sessions. We'd just get together on the day.'

While women's cricket struggled to survive the indifference of men's administrators, the tournament galvanised public interest. 'I can recall that the inaugural tournament created huge public awareness of the very existence of women's cricket,' Heyhoe Flint told ESPNcricinfo in 2008. 'That was a great bonus because even though the first recorded writings about women's cricket were in 1745, the general public in the UK were still very ignorant about us.'

The success of the World Cup was the catalyst for the men's game to act on plans to form a copycat competition. Three days before the final at Edgbaston, the International Cricket Conference – the forerunner to the International Cricket Council – voted to approve England's proposal for a 60-over World Cup. Two years later, the first men's World Cup was played in England. This time, naturally, Lord's eagerly hosted the final.

* * *

Heyhoe Flint once said that she spent her life challenging male supremacy. Even in death she continues to do so. In 2021, Clare Connor became MCC's first female president; one of her first acts was to propose erecting a statue at Lord's to Heyhoe Flint. Only a very few MCC members have grumbled about 'gesture politics'.

But not all opposition has come from misogynists. The WCA, both before and after the Heyhoe Flint era, was exceedingly white. The cricket scholar and journalist Rafaelle Nicholson, the author of *Ladies and Lords; A History of Women's Cricket in Britain*, has documented the treatment of women's cricketers.

Several times, for instance, Indians have felt strongly that the English were cheating, claims that led to a confrontation during a tour by India in 1986. A WCA official was quoted as responding that 'the Indians are a race who will always find something to complain about'.

Heyhoe Flint was an ardent supporter of cricket tours to South Africa during apartheid. In 1970, when the scheduled cricket tour by South Africa met with political opposition, she was involved in fundraising to cover policing and other costs so that the tour might go ahead. She actively participated in the unsuccessful campaign to persuade MCC to resume cricketing ties with South Africa in 1983. She resigned from the WCA in 1986 in protest at several English women cricketers being banned after participating in a rebel tour of South Africa.

In her autobiography, written in 1978, she set out her views on South Africa and apartheid. She loved the country and confessed that she 'toyed with the idea of going back to South Africa to live'. Her qualification seems grudging, 'South Africa, apartheid apart, is such a wonderful country for a visitor.' But her position was that the apartheid regime was none of her business. 'I found it strange and sad, but retained the view that it was their country, and hardly the place of any English people to criticise,' she decided, concluding, 'Who are we, in any case, to tell the South Africans how to run their country?' She rounds this off with a fine piece of whataboutery, 'And if we are honest, can't we find other examples of oppression, perhaps just as odious, in the recent histories of countries such as Chile and Russia?' There is no evidence she ever disavowed these opinions.

It's safe to say that such views are considered racist today and were thought racist then too. When Heyhoe Flint says 'their' country, she can only mean white South Africans, since these were the only people in a position 'to run their country'. She was not merely collaborating with a despicable regime in the interest of preserving international sport – she was actually contemplating emigrating there.

The discussions about honouring Heyhoe Flint with a statue coincided with the Black Lives Matter protests erupting in 2020. In Bristol, the statue of the 18th-century merchant Edward Colston, who enriched himself in the slave trade, was torn down and thrown into the harbour. In 2021, the Cass Business School in London decided to rename itself the Bayes Business School after acknowledging the slave trade connection of another 18th-century English merchant, John Cass.

As in the United States, Britain's history is deeply tied not just to enslavement and its profits but to racism in many forms. How many of Heyhoe Flint's contemporary English cricketers in the 1970s and 80s disagreed with her? A 1989 poll in *The Cricketer* found that 94% of current and past men's professionals believed that players should be allowed to play or coach in South Africa – at a time when Nelson Mandela was still in jail and the ANC was still an illegal organisation in South Africa. The 1970 campaign in which Heyhoe Flint participated was endorsed by almost the entire male cricketing establishment. Ultimately, Heyhoe Flint lived to see apartheid end in 1991 and the WCA merge with the ECB in 1998.

In August 2021, Lord's announced that they would be building a Heyhoe Flint Gate, not a statue, to be opened in 2022. A cynic might conclude that if Heyhoe Flint's attitudes towards race ever became a big enough embarrassment, then it would be less conspicuous to rename a gate than remove a statue. To be clear, it would be a sham to scapegoat Heyhoe Flint alone and so, by implication, let the numerous male cricketers who implicitly or explicitly supported the apartheid regime off the hook. There is a long history of racism in English men's cricket, implicating virtually the entire male establishment. But by the same token, can you really honour a figure of such historical significance as Heyhoe Flint and simply ignore the racism? It's a genuine conundrum.

* * *

Just as women's cricket was the first to recognise the international potential of a global one-day tournament, so it was also the first to realise the potential of its cousin, T20 cricket.

T20 was launched in England in 2003, initially as a vehicle to allow men's counties to earn cash and so reduce their dependence on the ECB. The phenomenal success of the summer – over a quarter of a million fans attended – instantly spawned imitators the world over, as other nations attempted to mimic the ECB in finding a way to generate cash from domestic matches, which had previously been entirely reliant upon subsidies from the international game.

Some suggested that T20 was best left to domestic cricket, ignoring the format's potential to promote interest in the international game as well. While the men's game initially dithered over whether to make T20 an international format, the women's game was altogether more decisive. On 5 August, 2004, a crowd of around 500 watched England play New Zealand in the inaugural T20 international at Hove; New Zealand triumphed by nine runs. Within 14 months of the first county T20 game, the Women's Cricket Association was nimble enough to recognise the possibilities of T20.

Yet those taking part in the match had no sense that they were pioneers. 'I don't remember us having a sense at all that it was this kind of quite radical new thing that we were doing in international cricket and that it hadn't been done in men's cricket,' recalled Connor, who captained England. 'No one really pointed it out to us and I don't think we had that kind of collective moment of hold on, we're breaking new ground here. Let's have some fun.'

Six months later, New Zealand hosted Australia in the first men's T20 international. The success of the inaugural men's World Twenty20 in 2007 – and the 2009 edition, which also included a parallel women's competition for the first time – confirmed the popularity of T20 at international level. But while the men's game spent the next decade agonising over how much of the stage should be given over to the most popular format of the game, administrators in the women's game had no such doubts.

A comparison between the volume of matches played in the three formats, considering only the 12 Full Member countries, illustrates the contrast. In the men's game in the 2010s, Full Members were involved in 433 Tests, 1204 ODIs and 613 T20Is. In the women's game, Full Members were involved in just eight Tests, 456 ODIs and 522 T20Is. So T20Is accounted for just 27.2% of men's fixtures, but 52.9% of women's fixtures. Even discounting Test matches, which are almost obsolete in the women's game outside of the Ashes, the stark contrast remains. While Full Member men's sides played almost two ODIs for every T20I in the men's game, their women's teams played more T20Is than ODIs.

'We identified early that that was going to be the growth format for cricket, and particularly women's cricket, it was going to take the game into new territories, it was going to drive greater reach and audience,' said Connor, who has been the ECB's head (now manager) of women's cricket since 2007 and also chaired the ICC women's cricket committee. 'It was easier for the women's game to push the international T20 format higher up in terms of number of games and volume because of not having congested schedules with Test cricket. There's much more space.'

* * *

If the women's game could be said to have led the way in its embrace of T20 in the early 2000s, it was also more proactive in reacting to another of the sport's biggest challenges of the era: the need to give international matches greater context and meaning.

Apart from the World Cups, the structure of international cricket remained broadly unchanged between the end of the 19th century and the start of the 21st. Bilateral matches were arranged on an ad-hoc basis, with the number of fixtures in each series determined by a combination of historic rivalries and economic attractiveness rather than by sporting merit. Beyond the world rankings – which some players and fans found confusing – there was no overarching context to the games. Women's cricket was the first to try to create a more compelling structure.

The men's game had long been aware of the problem. Beginning in 2004, there were a series of attempts to introduce a league structure for Tests and ODIs. Yet, somehow, it never quite happened: countries wanted more freedom to control their own schedule. Bangladesh and Zimbabwe successfully lobbied against one plan that would have entailed less Test cricket. While the men's game was bickering over what the future looked like, the women's game was embracing it. This change took two forms.

The first, beginning in 2013, was the introduction of a points system for the Ashes series. With the Ashes only comprising a solitary Test match, but England and Australia playing multi-match series in ODIs and T20Is, the women's game sought an answer to the question of how the destiny of the urn should be decided. In 2010/11, England won five games to Australia's three across the T20I and ODI series – and yet lost the Ashes by virtue of losing the one-off Test.

'For a series with all the cricketing history and tradition and treasure – it's not enough, a one-off Test match. It was a case of, OK, well, how can we do something modern and relevant?' Connor recalled. And so she hit upon the idea to make all matches between England and Australia count towards the Ashes. Over a multi-match series, the winner of each game would receive points; the Ashes were awarded to whoever accrued more points over the series. The multi-format Ashes series was first introduced in 2013 and has quickly become accepted as the way to determine the holders of the women's urn.

The second, and more significant, structural reform in the international game came in January 2014 when the ICC board approved the launch of the Women's ODI Championship. The competition had a simple format: the eight teams would play each opponent in a three-match ODI series, with the results counting towards the league table. After each team had played 21 matches, the top four would secure automatic qualification for the ODI World Cup. This was a more equitable system, giving emerging teams more regular fixtures and allowing countries to plan years in advance.

'We were striving to make women's cricket more relevant, more admired, more attractive, more easy to follow, than perhaps the men's game,' said Connor, who was instrumental in setting up the competition. 'I do remember meetings sitting around with senior men at ICC, and them saying, "Let's take this opportunity in the women's game, because we can." It can be more agile, and we can get things going and do some things that make real sense. Sometimes you can't do that in men's sport.'

The first iteration of the Women's ODI Championship began in August 2014, only seven months after the concept had been agreed – exactly the sort of decisiveness that has often proved impossible to bring to the men's game. Connor said that the relative lack of attention paid to the women's game has encouraged a more dynamic approach. 'It is a bit sad to say – it hasn't carried the same importance. The decision has probably been taken more lightly and therefore more quickly because it's women's cricket – the associated baggage, the associated politics, the associated broadcaster and commercial constraints or relationships are different.'

After two successful editions, the men finally copied the format the women had pioneered. The Cricket World Cup Super League, which launched in 2020, essentially imported the structure of the Women's ODI Championship, using a structured competition to create a league table and determine World Cup qualification. After launching in 2019 the men's World Test Championship used a similar, but more convoluted, points system.

At the same time as women's cricket was driving international cricket towards a more structured model, they also led the sport's reappearance in multisport events, such as the Commonwealth Games in 2022. 'Hopefully, it's paving the way for a much stronger conversation around Olympic participation,' Connor said. Once again, if you wanted to know what was about to happen in the men's game, the surest way was to monitor developments in the women's.

This was merely the latest instance of the quiet radicalism of women's cricket. While their history of innovation has partly been driven by necessity and partly by a less cumbersome decision-making process, Connor also points to the personalities of those at the apex of the women's game: women such as Heyhoe Flint; Australia's Belinda Clark, who was chief executive of Women's Cricket Australia while also being Australian captain; and – we can add – Connor herself. They made careers out of challenging authority.

'The women's game is comprised of people who are used to breaking boundaries or convention,' Connor said. 'I think of myself in that regard, playing in all boys teams for eight years – that was very unusual. You think about the people and the personalities and what drives them? They are people who have kind of been doing something out of the norm by even just playing cricket back in an era where it was virtually an all-male space.'

And so when The Hundred, a completely new competition, launched with a women's match in 2021, it was entirely in keeping with cricket's traditions. Throughout its history, women's cricket has been neglected and underfunded. Yet in spite – or, perhaps, because – of these struggles, it has also been the cradle of innovation.

7

HOW JAYASURIYA AND GILCHRIST TRANSFORMED TEST BATTING – BUT T20 DIDN'T

It was the end of the English summer of 1998, and Sri Lanka found themselves in their usual position: limited to a one-off Test match at the fag end of the season. Even though they had lost their last Test against Sri Lanka in 1993, England were the last country to agree to play them in a multi-match Test series. 'I think they thought that giving us even one Test was a waste of their time,' Sri Lanka opener Sanath Jayasuriya later told *The Cricket Monthly*.

After winning the toss on a fine day at The Oval, Sri Lanka captain Arjuna Ranatunga made a curious decision: to bowl first. As expected, given the fine batting conditions and Sri Lanka's workmanlike pace attack, England cruised to 445 in their first innings, lasting 158.3 overs in the process and batting beyond tea on the second day. Centuries from Graeme Hick and John Crawley had put England in an impregnable position – at least according to the orthodoxy of the time.

'To be honest, we thought the game was over,' England fast bowler Darren Gough recalled. 'If you get 445 in the first innings and bat more than 150 overs, you don't expect to lose.' The only question seemed to be whether Sri Lanka could repel England's bowlers for long enough to hold out for a draw.

On the second evening, Sri Lanka were left with 19 overs to bat. Ordinarily, given England's position, the limit of their ambition would have been to reach stumps with minimal damage. Instead, Jayasuriya got off the mark with an extra cover drive for four off Gough and then laid waste to England's quick bowlers. Sri Lanka reached 79–1 off 19 overs at the end of the second day, with Jayasuriya reaching his half-century in just 58 balls. As the BBC reported at the time,

'Sri Lanka's openers made a mockery of England's claims that the pitch was too slow to score at a fast rate.'

England were familiar with the damage that Jayasuriya could inflict. In the quarter-final of the 1996 World Cup at Faisalabad, his 82 from 44 balls had razed England's bowling attack. Some in the English press had denigrated Jayasuriya as a one-day slogger; the insults, he later said, 'gave me strength'.

On the third day at the Oval, an early wicket brought Aravinda de Silva, the other batting hero of Sri Lanka's 1996 World Cup triumph, to the crease. Jayasuriya and de Silva brought up their 50 partnership within seven overs. On an astounding day, Sri Lanka added 367 runs, taking them one clear of England's total. While it had taken England 158.3 overs to reach 445, Sri Lanka closed the third day on 446 for three off 110 overs – 47.3 fewer than England's first innings.

'It wasn't senseless hitting,' Jayasuriya said. 'We respected the better spells, and we were cautious around the breaks, very keen to hang on to our wicket. And it wasn't all easy. The bounce was a bit hard to gauge on that pitch, so I put the pull shot away. But the pull was Aravinda's strength, so he kept on doing that. There was a long boundary on one side, so I thought it would be tough to clear. At those times I just scored a single and handed it over to Aravinda.' By targeting Ian Salisbury, England's only frontline spinner, the pair ensured that England had to deploy their seamers in longer spells, reducing their effectiveness.

Had Sri Lanka batted at the same pace as England's 2.8 runs an over, it would have taken them until midway through day four to pass their total, leaving them inadequate time to get a meaningful lead, bowl England out again and then chase down a fourth-innings target. But Jayasuriya and de Silva's aggression helped Sri Lanka reach 591, despite their innings lasting fewer overs than England's. Both sides picked up wickets at an almost identical rate; the difference was that Sri Lanka scored a whole run per over more quickly.

After England's first innings, only two results seemed plausible – an England win or a draw. Sri Lanka's ingenuity not only put victory in reach, but their hefty lead rendered an England win impossible.

Rightly, the Test is remembered for Muttiah Muralitharan's performance of a lifetime. In the second innings, he took nine for 65; only a run-out deprived him of a perfect ten. He ended the match with figures of 16 for 220, the fifth best in the history of Test cricket.

Yet it was the alacrity of Sri Lanka's batting that enabled Muralitharan to win the Test. Had they batted at a similar speed to the norm in Test cricket at the time, there would simply not have been enough time for Muralitharan to bowl them to victory. For all Muralitharan's brilliance, Sri Lanka still required 287.5 overs to take 20 England wickets – well over three days of the Test. Only five times in history had a team bowled so many overs and won a Test; these were all in 1955 or earlier, an age when over rates were far higher, allowing more overs to be bowled over the duration of a match. On just three previous occasions in history had a team scored as many as England in their first innings and yet still lost.

The Oval 1998 was not only a triumph for Muralitharan, Jayasuriya and de Silva, it was also a victory for a buccaneering style of Test cricket, aptly sealed when Jayasuriya scythed two sixes to complete a chase of 37. Sri Lanka would never be limited to a solitary Test against England again.

* * *

Ever since being elevated to Test status in 1981, Sri Lanka had given glimpses of such an approach. Perhaps the best illustration was Duleep Mendis. As a Test batter, Mendis was interesting not so much for his results – he averaged an unremarkable 31.64 – but for how he got them.

Sri Lanka's first Test in India took place in Chennai in 1982, seven months after their inaugural Test match, which they had played at home to England. In the Chepauk Stadium, Mendis hit stunning twin centuries: 105 off 123 balls in the first innings – almost double the average scoring-rate in Test cricket at the time – and another 105 in the second. While the exact number of balls that Mendis faced in that innings has been lost to history, it was recorded as four minutes short of four hours – again, strikingly quick for the era.

When Sri Lanka played their first Test in England, at Lord's, Mendis adopted the same approach. He struck 111 from 143 balls in the first innings, three times pulling Ian Botham for six, and reached 94 from just 97 balls when he fell attempting to bring up his century by hitting a rare Botham off-break for six.

Just like in Chennai, Mendis helped Sri Lanka to a draw, defying predictions that they would be swatted aside.

Separated from India by the 50-mile wide Palk Strait, and conveniently located on trade routes between the east and the west, Sri Lanka's history is marked by invasions and the struggle to unite as a single kingdom. The majority Sinhalese population (75%) has been on the island longest, and they converted to Buddhism more than 2000 years ago. In the Middle Ages Tamil invaders from India (Tamil Nadu is the Indian state across the Strait) settled on the island; they are known as the Sri Lankan Tamils (around 11% of the population). Arab traders, whose descendants are known as Sri Lankan Moors, make up around another 10% of the population. The Chinese considered conquest in the 15th century, not long before the Portuguese arrived at the beginning of the 16th century, followed by the Dutch in the 17th century and finally the British – ending the last semblance of Sri Lankan independence in 1815. The remaining 4% or so of the population are known as Indian Tamils, brought from India to work on plantations during the 19th century.

The 19th-century colonialists set out to deliver to the Sri Lankan elites the two dimensions of their culture that they valued most highly: their school system and cricket. A number of the country's most prestigious schools were founded in the heyday of both English public schools and gentlemanly cricket: Royal College in 1835, S. Thomas' College in 1851, St Sebastian's and Wesley College in 1854. As the names suggest, Victorian Christianity was fairly central to the curriculum, both Anglican and Roman Catholic. In the 1860s and 1870s, a number of public metaphysical debates were staged in the country between Christian clerics and Buddhist monks, contributing to a Buddhist revival in Sri Lanka. This in turn led to the creation of a number of Buddhist schools – notably Ananda College in 1886, Maliyadeva College in 1888 and Mahinda College in 1892. Divided by religion, these schools were united by cricket.

Almost all elite schools in Sri Lanka have a 'Big Match', a multi-day game that doubles as the highlight of the local social calendar. These games, which attract abundant media coverage and are often played on international grounds, attract crowds of up to 30,000 – a combination of returning old boys and local cricket fanatics who feel compelled to pick a side to follow. One of the most celebrated matches is the game between the 'Royalists' of Royal College Colombo and 'Thomians' of S. Thomas' College. They have faced each other every year since 1879, in a contest older than the Ashes. In 2018 Prime Minister Ranil Wickremesinghe – an Old Royalist, as they are known – took time out to attend the game, even though the country was under a state of emergency at the time.

The education system in Sri Lanka is run mainly by the government, with more than 10,000 schools under its control. But 66 elite schools, almost all founded before independence in 1948, continue to be self-governing, either as fee-paying or with government financial support. Sri Lankan international cricketers are almost entirely drawn from these schools.

Mendis, for example, is a Thomian. Mahela Jayawardene attended Nalanda College. Murali, though a Hindu of Indian Tamil background, attended St Anthony's, a Roman Catholic school in Kandy.

We compiled a list of 150 players who have represented Sri Lanka in Test cricket. All of them attended one of 40 elite schools, only five of which were founded after 1948. Half of their Test players were drawn from just eight schools. A mere 10 schools produced 80% of the Test runs scored; five schools took over 50% of the Test wickets.

This concentration is also geographic. Colombo and its suburbs account for only about 20% of the country's 25 million population, but 60% of Test cricketers. Apart from Muralitharan, very few Tamils appear in the list of players; many Tamils, especially in the north and east of the country, refuse to identify with Sri Lanka. The country has been torn by civil strife since independence, culminating in a civil war between Tamil separatists and the Sinhalese, in which more than 100,000 people were killed between 1983 and 2009. The war limited opportunities to participate in cricket. While there are concentrations of wealthy Tamils in Colombo, the 'hill country' Tamils from the centre of the country typically come from such poor backgrounds that they are unlikely to get the chance to reach an elite school. Schooling in Sri Lanka is only compulsory until the age of 14; after that, some promising children get scholarships to the elite schools, just as they do in England.

The religious denomination of the elite schools that produce cricketers is notable. Just 7% of Sri Lankans are Christians, yet 36% of Test players went to

Christian schools, with 23% of players attending Roman Catholic schools. While 70% of Sri Lankans are Buddhist, only 42% of Test players attended Buddhist schools. Another 19% of players went to secular schools; we only identified a single Sri Lankan Test player who attended a Hindu school, even though Hindus account for 12% of the population.

School Big Matches have historically been two-innings-a-side games played over two days – though some are now three-day affairs. With matches normally played on excellent pitches, the only way to win was for a side to score quickly enough to give themselves enough time to take 20 wickets. Big Matches have helped shape the kind of batters that Sri Lanka have produced.

'From school days my batting was always on the aggressive side,' Mendis recalled. 'Within two days we've got to finish the game. At that small age it was cultivated in you that you've got to go for runs.'

The importance of these matches has been heightened by Sri Lanka's willingness to promote young players very quickly. Anura Tennekoon was still at S. Thomas' College when he made his debut for Ceylon in 1965; he was only 18 and had never played a club game in the country. In 1972, aged 19, Mendis hit 184 for S. Thomas' College in the Big Match. Later that year, he was selected for Sri Lanka against Pakistan in a three-day game.

In Sri Lanka's first Test, Arjuna Ranatunga – who would later captain the team for 11 years – made his debut at the age of 18 years, 78 days. Ranatunga was a pupil of the Buddhist Ananda College in Colombo, and he represented Ananda in 'Big Matches' against Nalanda College, the great Buddhist school rivalry. Ranatunga took guard for the first time in Test cricket with Sri Lanka 34 for four. His counterattacking response, stroking 54 in 96 balls, was an innings straight out of a Big Match. Between them, Ananda and Nalanda have produced 33 of the 150 Sri Lankan Test cricketers in our list, and 31% of Sri Lanka's Test runs; their bowling contribution is less impressive – less than 4%.

* * *

Geography shaped Sri Lanka's early development as a cricket nation. Until their 1965–1966 tour to Australia, England travelled by boat to the antipodes. Handily for Sri Lanka, it was a natural stopping point after the Suez Canal. From

1882, when Ivo Bligh first led England down under to 'recover those Ashes', England's long voyages were broken up by a stopover in Colombo. The same logic applied when Australia made the journey in the opposite direction.

Stops were short, only a day or two, reflecting Sri Lanka's lowly status in world cricket. And so the Australian and English tourists only granted Sri Lanka a match of a single day. Long before the inception of one-day cricket, these matches – known as 'the whistlestops' – were two-innings-a-side affairs. The format made forcing a victory essentially impossible. Instead, a premium was put on entertainment – above all, fast scoring – as Nicholas Brookes, a historian of Sri Lankan cricket, has noted. In 1961, C.I. Gunasekera famously hit Australian left-arm wrist spinner Lindsay Kline for 24 in a single over. It was the sort of ebullient batsmanship that the crowds who packed in to see the whistlestops valued above all. These games contributed to a rich culture of aggressive batsmanship in Sri Lankan cricket.

One-day cricket proved the gateway to Sri Lanka gaining Test status. Sri Lanka defeated Pakistan in two one-day games in 1976 and beat India in the 1979 World Cup, when Mendis scored a freewheeling 64 not out. When Sri Lanka gained Test status, they imported a batting philosophy similar to that in one-day cricket.

'The boys started playing well in the one-day game, automatically the same thinking came into Test cricket,' Mendis recalls. 'We were used to the short game right from the start, until 1981 when we got Test status. Most of the players – they are on the attacking side,' he said. 'I think that was always there.'

In the mid-1990s, Sri Lanka's batters ushered in a revolution. Vowing to take the exploitation of the fielding restrictions in one-day international cricket to a new level, Sri Lanka promoted Jayasuriya and Romesh Kaluwitharana – alumni of St Servatius' College, Matara, and St Sebastian's College, Moratuwa, both Roman Catholic elite schools – to open the innings. In the process they inverted the traditional norms of one-day cricket, which dictated that teams kept wickets in hand for the final overs, and then accelerated. Instead, Sri Lanka's method was to lead from the front: attacking with impunity during the 15 overs of fielding restrictions, they would get ahead of the run rate and allow their middle order to bat without pressure and score quickly.

The innovation paid off. Jayasuriya and Kaluwitharana opened throughout the 1996 World Cup, culminating in Sri Lanka's victory over Australia in the final in Lahore, only 14 years after their elevation from Associate members of the ICC. The two – especially the more consistent Jayasuriya – gave Sri Lanka a series of remarkable starts, which included looting 117 from the first 15 overs against India and 121 from the first 15 against England. Sri Lanka were not just world champions, they had also profoundly changed the game.

Each year, the five *Wisden* Cricketers of the Year are awarded on the basis of a player's influence on the previous English summer. In 1997, Jayasuriya became the first player to win the award without playing in England, reflecting how counties and the English team tried to replicate his pyrotechnics when opening the innings.

Yet Sri Lanka's impact was not restricted to the ODI game. In 1995–1996, a few months before co-hosting the World Cup, Sri Lanka toured Australia. Although they were mauled on the field, it was one of the most tumultuous tours of the decade. The nadir came in the Boxing Day Test at the Melbourne Cricket Ground. In front of a crowd of 55,000, umpire Darrell Hair called Muralitharan seven times for throwing after judging his bowling action to be illegal, setting in motion years of controversy.

Arjuna Ranatunga, Sri Lanka's captain, would later credit the team's more aggressive approach on the pitch to this harrowing experience. As Sri Lanka became more confrontational after Boxing Day 1995, their Test batting also became more enterprising. In the next match, they recalled Jayasuriya for his first Test in 15 months. At the time, Jayasuriya had an underwhelming average of 30.6 from 16 Tests. All but one of these had come batting in the middle order, normally at No.6. But Jayasuriya was recalled in a new position: he would open the batting, replicating his one-day international role.

Batting first, Australia reached 502 for nine declared, putting them on course to complete a 3–0 series whitewash. With around an hour to play on the second evening when Sri Lanka began their innings, Jayasuriya cover drove the great Glenn McGrath for six, and reached 47 from 44 balls by the close to signal their new approach. He fell the next morning, but in the second innings, Jayasuriya's rapid 112 – his maiden Test century – announced the arrival of a Test opener unshackled by the old conventions about dutifully playing himself in.

A year and a week after their Oval heist, Sri Lanka welcomed Australia for a three-match Test series: their first meeting since that stormy series in Australia. In the meantime, Australia had succeeded Sri Lanka as World Cup champions.

In the first Test, conditions favoured bowlers, especially spin; no side passed 234 in any innings as the game hurtled to a finish on the third evening. But while Australia tried to survive through caution, Sri Lanka recognised that calculated risk-taking was the best way to score runs: Sri Lanka scored at 3.53 an over in the Test, almost a whole run an over more than Australia's sedate 2.57.

Repeating their trick of The Oval, only in a lower-scoring game, Sri Lanka won despite facing far fewer overs, 93.2 – barely a day's worth of batting – to Australia's 127.3.

It was a classic display of guerrilla cricket. Just as in Lahore during the World Cup final, Aravinda de Silva was Player of the Match for his innings of 78 and 31 not out.

When they reached a fraught 60 for four in their run chase of 95, Ranatunga smashed Shane Warne for a four and six in consecutive balls to end any jitters. It ensured that Sri Lanka defeated Australia for the first time in a Test match – and that after two rain-ruined final Tests, Ranatunga would ultimately be triumphant in his last series against Australia. It was Ranatunga's final revenge, and the end of an era of high-octane rivalry between the two nations. A few weeks later, Australia would begin their record-setting run of 16 consecutive Test victories.

* * *

In November 1999, Australia prepared for their first summer under the captaincy of Steve Waugh. Before their first home Test of the summer, against Pakistan, John Buchanan, Australia's new head coach, gave a talk to the squad about 'climbing Everest'.

'Stephen Waugh had the mantra of taking the road less travelled – he definitely wanted to play far more aggressively,' Buchanan recalled. 'We were both keen to find ways and means of playing the game differently to anyone else, and so meant we looked at the game from a technical point of view, from a physical point of view, from a mental point of view, and a tactical point of view.'

As part of this approach, Australia resolved to be more assertive with the bat. Even though they were recognised as the best Test side in the world, their batting approach was in keeping with the orthodoxy of the times. In the four and a half years since toppling West Indies in the Caribbean to take over the No.1 ranking, Australia had scored at a slovenly 2.95 an over, placing them fourth among the nine Test nations at the time, behind West Indies, Pakistan and the leaders, Sri Lanka.

Australia's rate of scoring was entirely in keeping with the norm for Test cricket. Not since 1921 had the average scoring rate in a year of Tests exceeded three per six-ball over. Test cricket was a mature game; this simply seemed to be the way that it was played.

Of course, such a modest scoring rate came at a cost: draws. In the previous two years, Australia had drawn four Tests in which they were dominant but had not gone on to win – despite first innings leads of 149, 123, 28 (before setting their opponents a target of 419) and 110. In each case, Australia's problem was a lack of time to bowl opponents out in the fourth innings, with the opposition lasting 61, 122, 86 and 68 overs in the final innings to secure a draw, on occasion abetted by the weather. Over the first innings of these four games, Australia had scored at modest rates: 2.82 an over, 2.55, a funereal 2.23, and 3.07. Scoring too slowly had cost Australia wins. If they were to convert their dominance more efficiently, Australia needed to score more quickly.

The team developed 'the idea of being able to try to be in a position to really advance the game on day one, if we batted first,' Buchanan recalled. 'If we could do that at a relatively good rate then we had a huge amount of momentum in the game, and it would take other teams a significant time – if they were good enough – to prevent us from putting together a win. One of the ways that we were broadly looking at our batting was that we wanted to be able to be quite aggressive in our playing, and really take the game on.'

In the first game of the Australian summer, Australia handed a Test debut to Adam Gilchrist. He had already shown himself to be a thrilling left-handed opener in ODI cricket, playing in a similar way to Jayasuriya as Australia won the 1999 World Cup. Now, he usurped veteran Ian Healy as Test wicketkeeper in a symbol of Australia's newly aggressive approach.

On debut, Gilchrist struck 81 off just 88 balls. He helped Australia amass 575 in their first innings at 4.13 an over. Pakistan had scored 367 in their first innings and managed 281 in their second innings yet still lost. It was exactly the sort of game that the old Australia would have dominated but only drawn.

In Buchanan's second game, Gilchrist gave an even more extraordinary illustration of his approach. In the fourth innings of the game, he entered with Australia a perilous 126 for five, needing what seemed like a fanciful 369 to win.

'You never know,' partner Justin Langer told Gilchrist when he arrived at the crease. Gilchrist smote 149 not out, from just 163 balls, sharing a rollicking stand of 238 with Langer to clinch a stunning victory. 'He could be playing in his own backyard,' captain Waugh gushed.

'The way that Adam Gilchrist really took on the Pakistan attack – that, I think, was the launch pad of that real belief in the side that we could attack from anywhere, we could be in any position within the game and still believe we can win it,' Buchanan said. 'He just embodied that whole approach. So he's coming in the order at six or seven. The game has got a lot of shape by that stage – good or bad or medium, whatever – first or second innings. And he was able – in the main – to put that shape to one side and just play his own natural free-flowing attacking game.'

Australia rejected the traditional trade-off in batting: between average and strike-rate. Instead, they were able both to score more consistently – the average runs per Australian wicket surged from 34.1 in the four years before Gilchrist's debut to 45.9 in the four years after – and more quickly.

Gilchrist was a phenomenon. But while he was at the apex of Australia's radical new approach, players already in the side also became markedly more aggressive.

When Gilchrist was picked, Ricky Ponting had played 28 Tests and had a strike rate of 46. Over his next 28 Tests, that soared to 69. Langer was renowned as a stodgy accumulator: he had a strike rate of just 41 in November 1999. Langer was about to turn 29; it seemed to be just the way that he played. But from then on, he had a strike rate of 58. The transformation in Australian batting was two-fold: they picked more aggressive players, like Gilchrist and Matthew Hayden, who was recalled the following year; and those already in the side played more assertively. From scoring at 2.95 an over in their four years before Gilchrist's debut, Australia scored at 3.80 an over in the next four years. The difference was almost a whole run an over – 76 runs in a day of 90 overs.

From 1997 to 1999, Australia had sometimes struggled to convert their advantages into victories. No longer: Gilchrist's debut was the second Test in a sequence of 16 consecutive victories, which remains an all-time record.

Waugh's Australia were not merely a great team; they also changed their sport. 'His side played in such a way that they basically took the draw out of the equation,' England skipper Nasser Hussain observed in *Wisden Cricketers' Almanack* in 2004. 'They would score their runs at four an over, declare early and leave as much time as possible to bowl the opposition out twice.'

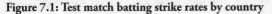

Australia became far and away the dominant side in world cricket at the beginning of the 2000s. They increased their strike rate more dramatically than anyone else; between 2000 and 2003, they scored 20% more quickly than the other Test

Figure 7.1: Test match batting strike rates by country

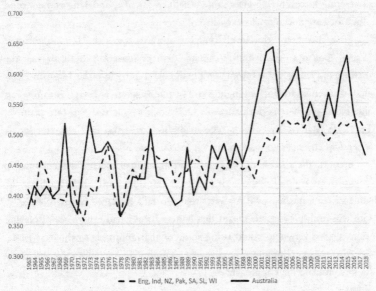

nations, a prolonged gap over the rest of the field that no side has matched since data on strike rates started to be consistently recorded in the 1960s. But other nations were also increasing their scoring at the same time.

The solid line in Figure 7.1 shows the Test run-rate of Australia, which starts to rise in 1999, from 48 per 100 balls, to 54 in 2000, 59 in 2001 and 64 in 2002, where it peaks. The other major Test nations start from a lower base and do not start to rise until 2000, when the strike rate increases from 45 per 100 balls to 48 in 2001, 50 in 2002, and then, after regressing a little, reaches 53 in 2005 – catching up with the Australians who are by this time returning to earth.

There are a lot of fluctuations from year to year in this chart, which runs from 1963 until 2018, but the period 2000–2005 clearly indicates a step change. In every other period, rises and falls are quickly reversed. But in this period, Test-batting strike rates around the world found a new equilibrium, which has not been reversed.

We cannot know for sure what caused this shift. But the data suggests two interacting forces. Stefan gives more weight to the first, and Tim to the second – but they are not mutually exclusive.

First, run rates were already nudging upwards across the Test game before Waugh took over as Australia's captain, perhaps reflecting the impact of the increase in ODI run rates from 1992 gradually seeping into the Test game. Test sides showed a growing willingness to fast-track aggressive batters into the Test side based on their performances in ODI cricket. Gilchrist was one example; England's Marcus Trescothick, who made his Test debut in 2000, and India's Virender Sehwag, who made his debut in 2001, are others.

Second, the success of Australia's batting approach may have encouraged imitators. As Figure 7.2 shows, it took rival Test sides until 2005 to achieve the same increase in their own run rates that Australia managed from 1998–2000. Cricket's multiple formats meant that batters already had experience of playing more aggressively, and could bring some of that approach to the Test game. Selectors could pick more aggressive players to imitate Australia and consciously look to emulate their approach.

Figure 7.2: Test match batting strike rates indexed to 1998 (100)

	Australia	The Rest*
1998	100	100
1999	107	101
2000	119	97
2001	131	106
2002	141	112
2003	143	110
2004	123	116
2005	126	119
2006	130	117
2007	135	117

*The rest includes England, India, New Zealand,
Pakistan, South Africa, Sri Lanka and West Indies*

'He has transformed Test cricket,' Simon Barnes wrote of Steve Waugh in *Wisden* in 2003. 'Over the past four years, his Australians played in a manner that was once unthinkable. A captain is usually assessed on the way he operates his bowlers and sets his field, for it is supposed to be the fielding captain who controls the tempo of a match. Waugh is, of course, spectacularly good at all that. But it is the way he manages his batting line-up that is revolutionary.

'Under Waugh, Australia's batting has become the most intimidating aspect of modern cricket. The Australian batters seek to frighten opponents every bit as much as the fast-bowling quartet of the 1980s West Indians. They all act the same way, and they're all coming to get you,' Barnes wrote, detailing how rivals were imitating them. 'Other nations are following the Australian lead, but they're not as good at it yet.'

Australia 'absolutely' encouraged England to be more aggressive with the bat, recalls Michael Vaughan, who became captain in 2003 and led England to victory in the famous 2005 Ashes series. 'We knew that they were scoring at about 3.6 an over … You can't beat an Australian side unless you're actually scoring for five days, so yeah we went more aggressive.'

The most extreme example of soaring Test strike rates was found in wicketkeepers. Even before Gilchrist's debut – as England selecting Alec Stewart ahead of Jack Russell showed – batting was already becoming a more important factor in determining which wicketkeepers were picked. From a meagre average of 23.6 in Tests in the 1980s, wicketkeepers averaged 27.3 in the 1990s. This then soared again, to 31.8, in the 2000s – and, even with Gilchrist retiring in 2008, reached 33.6 in the 2010s.

But keepers since Gilchrist haven't just been better batters – they've also scored at a dramatically faster rate. From the 1990s to the 2000s, the strike rates of wicketkeepers increased from 44 to 53: they went from scoring at the same rate as the top six to scoring at a strike rate of three more, suggesting that countries were consciously trying to create their own mini-Gilchrists – keepers who couldn't just bat well, but could score quickly. Only in 2001 did England first select Stewart as a wicketkeeper-batter at No.7; England later selected Matt Prior, Jonny Bairstow and Jos Buttler on account of their batting. New Zealand's Brendon McCullum, India's M.S. Dhoni and Rishabh Pant, Pakistan's Sarfaraz Ahmed, and South Africa's Quinton de Kock all kept wicket and batted in a similar style to Gilchrist, even if none could quite emulate him. He scored seven Test centuries at quicker than a run a ball (no previous Test cricketer had managed more than three), all while averaging an impressive 47.6.

'He changed the way countries would look at wicketkeepers,' India's captain Anil Kumble wrote when Gilchrist retired. 'Once he started playing for Australia, he forced cricket boards across the globe to have a rethink on how they wanted their 'keepers to be. People only picked 'keepers who could bat really well.

'When you look around international cricket now, most of the top wicketkeepers are good bats ... That change will forever be Gilchrist's legacy to the game.' Of the 15 wicketkeepers to average the most in Test cricket, from a minimum of 25 Tests, only three made their debuts before Gilchrist.

Being a specialist wicketkeeper – however brilliant – is no longer enough. As Kumar Sangakkara said, 'He's done something very bad to the traditional wicketkeeper. He's ruined their careers.'

* * *

But while the era of Gilchrist and Waugh's Australian side changed Test cricket, there was also a dog that didn't bark: T20, which was launched in 2003 and became the dominant form of the game after the creation of the T20 World Cup in 2007 and the Indian Premier League the following year.

For all the talk of how T20 has disorientated batters' approaches in Test cricket – and multi-format players do face unprecedented challenges – it is impossible to discern any effect of T20 at all in the rate at which batters are scoring. This speaks to how different the formats are: as England learned when using World Cup winner Jason Roy as a Test opener in the 2019 Ashes, the modern limited-overs game and Test cricket require completely different approaches. Increasingly, countries are responding to this reality by selecting more specialised teams, reducing the overlap in personnel.

It is a myth that the rise in run rates in Test cricket was influenced by T20. Instead, the surge in Test scoring rates foreshadowed the invention of the new format.

8

LEAGUE CRICKET – THE GAME'S GREAT MISSED OPPORTUNITY

'The horse is here to stay,' the president of the Michigan Savings Bank told Henry Ford's lawyer in 1903, 'but the automobile is only a novelty – a fad.' The banker must have known that most innovation schemes fail. But Horace Rackham, the lawyer, took his chances and bought 50 Ford shares anyway.

In hindsight, all successful innovations appear inevitable, and we all like to believe we would have been Horace Rackham, not the banker. But it's hard to predict the future, and nobody could be sure about T20 when it first appeared. When Adam Hollioake of Surrey won the toss on the night of the first professional T20 game in 2003, he decided to bowl first 'because I haven't got a clue what's going to happen'.

Nearly two decades on, T20's impact has vaulted past what even the most ardent optimists thought possible. It's not just the spectacularly lucrative Indian Premier League: the broadcast contract from 2018–2022 is worth $510 million a year, about double what the England and Wales Cricket Board earn from all revenue sources combined. T20 has become omnipresent in world cricket, with leagues and competitions springing up at every level of the game, from the T20 World Cup to Australia's Big Bash, vibrant at both men's and women's level, to the Everest Premier League in Nepal and beyond.

The profusion of professional T20 leagues around the world attests to the belief that this is a means of raising revenue, a lesson drawn primarily from the IPL. A professional sport only draws more revenue when it attracts more fans – whether that means selling more tickets, growing television audiences, or making a splash on social media. The logic is the same in each case: sports revenues are mainly driven by the number of followers. When T20 created larger audiences, all levels of the games benefited, including the clubs who have competed in the County Championship since the 19th century. Stuart Robertson, former head of marketing at the ECB, put it this way in 2017, 'It was a proper cash cow to those smaller grounds and a life saver. Without Twenty20 at a professional level the domestic game in this country would be in a very precarious state by now.'

Naturally, not everyone approves. Matthew Engel, the former editor of *Wisden*, blames T20 for ruining the sport. 'Everything worthwhile about it is being destroyed,' he wrote in 2017, greeting the desire to create a new T20 competition in England with despair. 'My only interest – in common with many other cricket lovers – is the hope that the damnable thing is a total flop and that we can somehow save the game I once adored, and still love more than the people who have seized control of it.' It could hardly have appeased him that the new tournament was not T20 but rather an even shorter format, The Hundred. Cricketing greats including Greg Chappell, Clive Lloyd, Michael Holding, and Garfield Sobers have all denounced T20. Their reasons differ: Engel is just disaffected by the change, Chappell is worried about batting skills, and Lloyd, Holding and Sobers are concerned that the financial incentives will lead players to desert Test teams.

Is this just a matter of the old guard resisting change while the young ones embrace it? Yes and no. Younger folks in the UK are generally less interested in *any* cricket, though they do prefer the IPL. In 2020, the sports agency Sport MR surveyed a representative panel of around 2000 UK citizens on their cricket-watching habits. In the 65+ age group, 23% followed the IPL, 32% said they followed Test matches in England, 38% watched county cricket. With the 16–24 age group, by contrast, county cricket came in dead last (4%), Tests did barely better (6%), and the IPL was in first place with a still modest 12%. The pattern held across the generations. The older you are, the more interested you are in all kinds of cricket; the younger you are, the more you will lean towards the quicker game. If cricket has a future, it will have to be with the generation TW – that now prefers T20.

The idea of grumpy old men complaining about the demise of the good old days is a standard comic trope, and indeed a Monty Python cricket sketch from 1970 – episode 7, series 2, 'Test Match Against Iceland' – offers one of the finest examples.

Yet short-form cricket is not really so new. Short-form cricket has always attracted crowds, and has generally been more popular for spectators than the long-form games that dominated until the advent of one-day cricket in the 1960s and T20 in the 2000s. In that light, the real question is how long-form cricket came to dominate at all. The answer is a story of a missed opportunity.

Cricket seems to have gained widespread popularity in England in the early 18th century. The first written rules were published in 1744, and they describe a game recognisably the same as today's. The rules are quiet on two aspects that would strike us as fairly important: (a) how many players there shall be in a game, and (b) how long a game shall last. These choices were simply to be made by the contestants rather than predetermined by rigid structures to be adhered to under all circumstances. The number of players on each side could range from as few as four to as many as 22, but the number didn't have to be the same for each team. Unbalanced numbers often helped to create a more balanced contest. Games could be completed in an afternoon, or they could last several days. A collection of scorecards from 1771 to 1791 lists 107 games – 17 were played on a single day, 23 over two days, 35 over three days, 17 over four days and two over five days (the remainder having no dates). Clearly the length of the game was a matter of choice. Typically these games consisted of two innings per side, but many were single innings. A common form of these matches, which still survives today at amateur levels, was the single-wicket game. Here the match was between two players who took turns to bat and bowl, while the fielders were like seconds in a duel.

The most famous single-wicket games in the 19th century were contests for the Championship of England. They were staged three times (in 1833, 1838 and 1846) and described in detail by former prime minister John Major in his history of early cricket. The scores were low – since, as in baseball, a run could only be scored by hitting into a restricted area of the field. The batter also had to get to the bowler's end *and back* in order to score one run. The 1846 Championship match was played between arguably the greatest cricketer of the era, the all-rounder Alfred Mynn, and a well-known batter, Nicholas Felix, in front of a packed house at Lord's. The game lasted five hours. Only nine runs were scored, ending in victory for Mynn, who was the heavy favourite with the bookmakers.

Money changed hands, and that is what appears to account for the decline of single wicket: not that it was unpopular, but that it was associated with gambling, which the Victorian ruling class progressively sought to eliminate from British life almost entirely.

The beginning of the Industrial Revolution is usually dated to the late-18th century, but the full impact on British society did not become clear until the mid-19th century. By then, Britain had been transformed from a rural to an urban society, and an expanding middle class interposed itself between the traditional classes of labourers and aristocracy. Educated in the growing private-school sector – universal state-funded education had yet to be established – the middle classes took to cricket. The game they constructed in the mid-19th century involved a strange combination of nostalgia and ruthless social exclusion and control. They harked back to an era when cricket was a predominantly rural pastime, conveniently forgetting the gambling that was an integral part of the old game. They thought of cricket as a sport that entailed 22 men playing over three days, forgetting the many variants – and that women played, too. Above all, they decided that the highest form of competition was between recognised counties, run by the upper echelon of the middle class, with a few aristocrats thrown in. Class distinctions were enforced rigidly. Paid professionals were only tolerated if they followed the instructions of their betters and remembered to say 'sir', touching their cap in deference as they did so. The flavour of this cricketing movement can be readily inferred from the first history of cricket, written in 1851 by James Pycroft, 'The game of cricket, philosophically speaking, is a standing panegyric on the English character: none but an orderly and sensible race of people would so amuse themselves. As with the Grecian games of old, the cricketer must be sober and temperate. Fortitude, patience, and self-denial, the various bumps of order, obedience and good humour, with an unruffled temper, are indispensable.'

Derek Birley, in his *Social History of English Cricket*, wryly points out the 'complacent superiority' and 'large doses of hypocrisy' that characterised organisations such as the Marylebone Cricket Club, which ended up running the game. In the 1860s and 70s there was a commercial struggle between the promoters of 'gentlemanly' cricket in rural settings and a more professional version capable of attracting spectators in the expanding urban centres. It is perhaps something of a mystery that the gentlemanly version (sarcastically labelled 'The Authorised Version' by Birley) won out at a time when the newly codified sport of baseball was turning professional in the United States: in 1871, the world's first recorded sports league was established at a meeting in Greenwich Village, New York, the National Association of Professional Base Ball Players. Perhaps the English professionals lacked organisation, and perhaps the growing cities were still chaotic and largely lacking in open spaces and sports facilities that would be created in the ensuing decades.

There was certainly no lack of entrepreneurial spirit. In the 1870s a version of the game known as 'clown cricket', where troupes made up of clowns, acrobats and cricketers toured the country providing entertainment at country houses, briefly flourished. One such troupe even undertook a successful tour of America. But this period was also the zenith of British economic and political power, both at home and abroad. The middle classes, equipped by elite schools to run an Empire, flexed and imposed their elitist and bureaucratic prejudices on the domestic game.

Counties themselves evolved in piecemeal fashion. In the 18th century, teams had regularly assumed county names such as Kent and Surrey; some had even organised formal clubs. But the clubs that survive today were only established during the 19th-century revival – Sussex in 1839, Nottinghamshire in 1841, Surrey in 1845. Lancashire, Yorkshire and many others followed in the 1860s and 70s. Around the same time football was codified and organised, by many of the same people behind the organisation of cricket. Charles Alcock, the secretary of Surrey County Cricket Club from 1872 to 1907 and the architect of the first Test match played in England in 1880, was also pivotal in the development of football. As Secretary of the Football Association from 1870 to 1895, he is credited with creating the FA Cup in 1871 and organising the first officially recognised international football match, played between England and Scotland in 1872. Yet in 1873, he resisted the creation of an equivalent to the FA Cup for county cricket teams. While the County Championship is often dated to 1873, it was actually not formally organised until 1890.

Football quickly spread as a spectator sport, helped by the introduction of the weekend. Previously, the working week had consisted of six full days. But between 1860 and the end of the century, employers gradually gave their workers Saturday afternoons off – this is why football matches in the UK traditionally start at 3pm on Saturday afternoon. The working class could never have found time for a whole three-day cricket match.

Like cricket, football had been around in some form for centuries – and, also like cricket, it appears to have experienced a kind of decline at the beginning of the 19th century. It had never enjoyed the same level of organisation as cricket, and was actually somewhat disreputable. It was revived in English schools in the same way as cricket; *Tom Brown's School Days*, published in 1857, lauded both cricket and the Rugby version of football. The first rules were written down in Cambridge in 1848, yet it was the rules created by the FA in 1863 that stuck. The FA Cup, together with the other cup competitions that it spawned, played a significant role in the growth of football clubs. But the crucial development was the creation of the Football League in 1888, probably in imitation of baseball's organisational structure.

As 'league fever' grew in England, imitators of the Football League sprang up almost immediately. In 1889 the Football Alliance and the Northern League were formed as rival leagues; the following decade saw dozens more spring up. The clubs entering these leagues were themselves only a few years old, but the new competition format quickly attracted a large following, and the larger clubs decided to put themselves on a sounder business footing by adopting limited liability status. Most clubs were in the industrial North or the Midlands, where commercial practices were deemed more respectable. While the FA had recognised County Associations in the early days, expecting the game to develop along the lines of cricket, instead clubs organised into leagues. The Football League co-opted its most successful rivals through the creation of a Second Division in 1892 and added two further divisions after the First World War. One particular innovation differentiates the structure of football from American sports leagues: the adoption of promotion and relegation which forced the lowest-performing teams at a higher level to move down, purely on sporting merit, while giving the best teams on the lower level the opportunity to move up.

League fever also came to cricket. The Birmingham and District Cricket League was founded at a meeting held in November 1888 – two months after the first Football League fixtures – the Bolton and District League in 1890, the Huddersfield and District League, the Lancashire League, the Accrington and District Cricket League and the Ribblesdale League in 1891, the Central Lancashire League and the Leeds League in 1892. These leagues were formed in the same Midlands and Northern industrial centres that produced the first professional football clubs. Many clubs founded in the 1870s were both football and cricket clubs, intended to maintain fellowship of the players all year round. League cricket was intended to do for cricket what league football had done for football.

While there are numerous histories of county cricket and county cricket clubs, the literature on league cricket is sparse. Still, the spate of brief local histories that emerged in the 1990s, celebrating the centenaries of the leagues, attests to their resilience. League cricket was a significant enterprise from the late 19th century to the mid-20th century. Jack Williams, who in 1990 wrote what is probably the only economic analysis of league cricket, points out that in at least 15 seasons between 1919 and 1939, the number of paying spectators at Lancashire League cricket exceeded the number of paying spectators at Yorkshire County Cricket Club, the era's pre-eminent county side. In this period, the annual home attendance of Nelson, one of the Lancashire League's biggest clubs, was larger than for Essex County Cricket Club. The figures for the Bradford League were not far behind. 'The cricket in these leagues provides rare excitement on Saturday afternoons – the cricket is invariably fast and thrilling, with great feats performed to force a finish,' John Arlott wrote in 1949. 'Nowhere else in England are such crowds to be found at Saturday afternoon matches – many a county club would be glad of such a gate in one day.'

League cricket did so well in part because it employed some of England's best professional cricketers. Sydney F. Barnes, considered one of the greatest bowlers of all time, spent much of his career in the Lancashire League in the years leading up to the First World War – he did not play regularly for a county team because the pay was better in the leagues. Jack Hobbs, one of England's greatest batters, briefly played in the Bradford League. Cecil Parkin and Fred Root, leading professionals of the interwar period, both played league cricket at different stages in their careers.

Overseas professionals further enhanced the quality of play. The most notable was Learie Constantine, who later became Baron Constantine of Maraval in Trinidad and of Nelson in the County Palatine of Lancaster. In the 1920s and 30s, his performances as an all-rounder for Nelson in the Lancashire League boosted the gates not just of his own team but of his opponents: gate receipts were on average 46% higher in games where he played, Williams found. Constantine's batting was aggressive, inventive, and adaptable in the face of the League's sometimes variable wickets. His bowling was quick, and he was lauded as the most athletic fielder of his age. In later life he was instrumental in the achievement of Trinidadian independence and successfully campaigned in the UK for legislation to prohibit racial discrimination. In recognition of this work, he was elevated to the House of Lords, becoming the first Black peer.

Many other notable overseas Test cricketers played in the leagues over the years, including West Indians (George Headley, Garry Sobers, Clive Lloyd, Andy Roberts, Michael Holding, Joel Garner, Viv Richards), Indians (Amar Singh, Lala Armanath, Vinoo Mankad, Kapil Dev) and Australians (Ray Lindwall and Bobby Simpson). Several members of the dominant Australian sides of the 1990s and 2000s played league cricket, including Shane Warne (Accrington), Steve Waugh (Nelson), Allan Border and Paul Reiffel (both East Lancashire) and Michael Clarke (Ramsbottom). Accrington, of the Lancashire League, even came close to signing Don Bradman in 1931. Bradman seriously considered accepting the offered contract since the money was much better than he was earning representing Australia. But a consortium of Australian businesses – sporting goods manufacturer F.J. Palmer & Sons, Associated Newspapers and radio station 2UE – put together a series of offers of sponsorship and work that convinced him to remain playing for Australia.

Nelson is a small town of 30,000 in the heart of the now-defunct Lancashire cotton industry. Yet in the Constantine era the club regularly attracted crowds of more than 10,000. Other clubs in the leagues that spread across industrial Lancashire, Yorkshire and the Midlands could match this level of interest. Like Nelson, the clubs were mostly located in small towns. So how could they attract such large crowds, especially in contrast with the mostly city-based first-class cricket of the counties? Constantine's description of league matches makes it clear, 'Usually these matches are played on Saturdays beginning at two and ending at seven, allowance being made for lost time. The mills finish work on Saturdays at 10.50, so that everyone has time to get home, do a little shopping, have lunch and get down to cricket in good time for the start of the game. Sometimes a league match is played on a weekday because shop-assistants are at work on Saturday afternoons. In Nelson these matches are played on the Tuesday half-holiday, in East Lancashire on the Thursday half-holiday, and so on. These weekday matches begin at 3 o'clock instead of 2. The mill-hands who leave work at 5.20 pay a reduced entrance fee.'

League cricket was like league football: organised to allow ordinary working people the chance to attend a game and see a result. It was a short-format version of the game, not so very different from games you might have witnessed in the 18th century, and so fully in line with cricket's traditions. It was not limited-overs cricket – an innovation not adopted in the professional game until 1962 – but the rules ensured that teams batting first had an incentive to score runs quickly and, if needs be, declare to leave themselves enough time to bowl out the opposition. The time taken to complete a game was somewhere between a T20 match and a one-day game.

If it was so 'fast and thrilling', and so well suited to attracting crowds, why did cricket not achieve the same level of popularity as a spectator sport that football did in Britain or baseball in the US? Probably the main answer is that those who ran cricket did not want it to, and they used their authority to hobble its spread. Most of cricket's administrators were to be found in the South, around London. They loathed the open commercialism of league competitions. They designated the three-day game as the true version, re-writing history to suit their purposes. It worked. Arlott's apparent endorsement of league cricket is actually taken from a chapter entitled 'The Case Against League Cricket'. The argument boils down to the assertion that the brash version of the game was simply not the 'real' cricket. Some professionals who played in the league would support this view. Here is Cecil Parkin, a former England off-spin bowler, from 1923.

'League cricket is not in the same street as county cricket; it is not the same game. From the bowler's point of view, it is ten times easier in the league than in the county. I don't only mean that in the league a bowler has to play only one day a week. I mean that it is ten times easier to get wickets in the league than against county cricketers. For one thing, the pitches are not perfect in the leagues. Then it must be remembered that the pace league cricket is played at gives a batter little or no chance of playing himself in ... A league batter has to get busy with the runs from the moment he arrives at the crease. Consequently, he is always giving the bowler a chance.'

The gentlemen of southern England opposed league football as much as they opposed league cricket. In 1908, a group of prominent amateur London footballers created the London Football Association with the express aim of keeping commercialism of all forms out of football. They failed miserably because the professional game was already thriving. The cricketing authorities were cannier. They didn't oppose professionalism: the counties employed professional players but kept them in their place. The counties had some standing with the cricketing public because they were already well established in competition before the cricket leagues. That gave them leverage to refuse to play against league clubs. They dubbed their version of the game 'first class' – a fine piece of propaganda – and carefully isolated themselves from competition. In effect they established a cartel at the pinnacle of cricket, and sports cartels are always difficult to overturn. Counties even had the temerity to complain about having to compete financially with league clubs to attract players. In reality, they denied the leagues the opportunity of sporting competition, using their control of the highest level of domestic competition to keep the leagues in their place.

The counties also benefited from the emerging international game, which quickly became the largest revenue-generating source in cricket. Ultimately the counties secured control of the domestic governing body in the 20th century. They used the revenues from popular Test matches, and later from one-day and T20 games, to keep the three- or four-day domestic game alive. A 2019 analysis by Daniel Plumley and Rob Wilson found that Glamorgan was the only first-class county that made an operating profit excluding the subsidy from the England & Wales Cricket Board. Effectively, subsidies from international cricket protect the first-class game.

It was not only the first-class counties that obstructed the development of league cricket in England. The southern elites also prevented the league format from spreading in those areas of the south where cricket was most commonly played – Surrey, Sussex and Kent. As Duncan Stone has documented, the Club Cricket Conference (CCC), created in 1915 as an organisation to promote club cricket in South East England, established Rule 4, which stated that CCC 'shall neither recognise, approve of, nor promote any Cup or League system, and no club connected with a Cup or League competition, or playing a man as a professional, except the groundsman, shall be qualified to attend any meeting of the Conference.' Clubs violating this rule would be expelled. Despite various challenges, CCC held the line on this position until 1968, holding back the development of cricketers in the south of the country; to their credit, the CCC now admits on its website that this was deeply regrettable. Stone has also shown that despite this prohibition, various forms of league competition did exist in the south, but only outside of the cricket establishment; the stories of what were principally workingmen's leagues were largely suppressed. Stone himself has done much to resurrect this lost history.

Yet the northern leagues themselves arguably also missed their opportunity. For league cricket in England to match the impact of the Football League would have required concerted action among the leagues. Had they banded together and created a league divisional structure comparable to football, they could well have succeeded. But there was never the will to do this. Some visionaries did speak out. Learie Constantine, for one, writing with Denzil Batchelor in 1967, proposed a two-day national championship, organised in a league format of four divisions with promotion and relegation, with games to be played on Fridays and Saturdays. He did not prevail.

What happened to league cricket in England is strikingly similar to what happened to baseball in the US. Both in English cricket and US baseball, the elite national level was monopolised by a single league – the County Championship in England and Major League Baseball in the US. In both countries, lesser leagues emerged to provide local entertainment at the end of the 19th century; both thrived until the middle of the 20th century, when the advent of TV and the expansion of leisure opportunities led to a decline in interest. In the US, the surviving leagues were taken over by the MLB and their clubs were turned into farm teams to develop talent for the MLB squads. In England, many leagues have folded; many survive with little or no spectator support, reliant on occasional handouts from the ECB and an ageing body of enthusiasts.

Which is where we started. The big difference between the MLB and the County Championship is the interest they create. Before the Covid-19 pandemic, the MLB had had annual revenues of over $10 billion and annual attendance of around 70 million, or about 29,000 per game. The 126 four-day games of the County Championship generated attendance of 577,000 in 2016, an average of 1,145 per day of cricket. Despite significantly higher attendance at the two short-form competitions, which draw around 5000 spectators per game, the revenue amounted to barely £100 million before ECB subsidies. One cartel makes a healthy profit; the other has relied on being propped-up.

For more than 50 years English cricket has been trying to supplement the finances of 'traditional' cricket. The one-day game had some success in attracting crowds, but the new short formats represent the biggest opportunity in more than a century to create a domestic competition that can attract significant numbers of fans. It may also be the means to finding greater acceptance in the urban centres where football dominates. To many this looks like radical innovation. But it is really a return to the sport's English roots.

9

A FAIR RESULT IN FOUL WEATHER

'The present situation is entirely unacceptable,' said Australian Prime Minister Bob Hawke, announcing that at the next Cabinet meeting 'consideration of new rules for rain-interrupted one-day games' would be on the agenda. The occasion was the final of the tri-series at the SCG between the home team and West Indies in January 1989. In the rain-affected game, Australia scored 226 for four off a reduced 38 overs. West Indies were 47 for two after 6.4 overs when it rained again. When play resumed, the total number of overs for their innings was reduced to a total of 18 with a revised target of 108, meaning they needed to score their remaining runs at a rate of 5.4 an over to win, which they did, comfortably.

Hawke was kidding, but the irritation was very real. At the rain interruption, West Indies needed to score 180 from 31.2 overs – a run rate of 5.7. To maintain this run rate over that many overs would have been far more demanding than the revised target. Australians felt cheated. The anomaly arose out of the method used to calculate revised targets after rain interruptions, which had been in place since the 1960s, when the short form game was introduced. It was called the Average Run Rate (ARR) method and is simple enough. Take the average run rate of the team batting first and then multiply that rate by the number of overs allowed for the team batting second – that number is the target. The anomaly arises when the team batting first has many more overs than the team batting second – maintaining the same rate over a longer period of time is harder. The rule is biased in favour of teams batting second.

It may not have led to legislation, but it did cause the Australians to change the rain rules. They developed the 'Most Productive Over' (MPO) method and persuaded the ICC to adopt it in time for the 1992 World Cup. The idea, an obvious reaction to the tri-series debacle, was to set the target based on a fraction of overs scored at the highest run rate. For example, suppose a team batting first scored 200 in 40 overs, half at a rate of four per over and half at a rate of six, and then 20 overs were lost for the team batting second. The 20 most productive overs were scored at six, and so the 20-over target would be 120, not the 100 implied by ARR.

The flaw in this method was instantly and spectacularly exposed. The 1992 World Cup was the first to see South Africa readmitted to international cricket, and they succeeded in reaching the semi-finals against England, knocking out hosts Australia on the way. England batted first; South Africa bowled slowly, apparently deliberately, causing the number of overs in the game to be reduced from 50 to 45. Set a target of 253, South Africa batted steadily; near the end of the game, they needed 22 runs with 13 balls left. With rain coming down, the umpires asked the batters if they wanted to come off – they said no. Then they asked the England captain, Graham Gooch; naturally, he immediately said yes.

It was late, the crowd was angry, but within minutes the rain stopped. At first the umpires said that one over had been lost. Using the MPO method, this meant deducting from the target the runs scored by England in their least productive over (hence leaving the score from the most productive overs) – which was a maiden. So with one over lost, the target remained unchanged at 22. If that sounds unfair, what happened next was really crazy. The umpires decided that with the game required to end at 10.10pm, two overs had been lost. So now the score from the second least productive over had to be deducted – but that was also a maiden!

As South Africa's batters re-entered the field, they were greeted by a scoreboard that read: 'South Africa to win: need 22 runs off 1 ball'. The text was actually wrong – although no runs had been scored with the bat in the second least productive over, there had been one extra – so South Africa actually needed a no less impossible 21 from one ball. Brian McMillan, the bewildered South African batter, tapped a single from the required ball. England left relieved. 'I think we would have lost if we hadn't stopped for the rain,' England's Allan Lamb later said.

What looked like being a thrilling finish was reduced to a farce. The crowd was furious, the South Africans were disgusted. The representative of the Australian Cricket Board who opined at the press conference that this was 'an act of God' did nothing to improve the reputation of cricketing officialdom. It was no act of God – but an act of administrators who had not thought through all the possible scenarios. This game was not the only one affected – the inequities of the MPO rule had interfered with two World Cup games involving India, one against Zimbabwe, the other against Australia. In seeking to redress an unfair advantage for the team batting second, they had created a manifestly unfair advantage for the team batting first.

* * *

Rather than being scrapped immediately, the rule limped on for several more years. In an attempt to address the bias, the Discounted MPO was developed as an alternative; it didn't really work, either. The Parabola method, which used a quadratic equation to calculate the adjusted target, was employed during a game played in 1990 in Sharjah between India and Australia – that time, play was interrupted not by rain but by a sandstorm – and then used at the World Cup in 1996.

There are endless possible ways to adjust the target score in limited-overs cricket. The website Cricket Archive lists no fewer than 17 different methods, all of which have been used at some time. But the one that everyone knows today is the Duckworth-Lewis (DL) method, first introduced in 1997. It is so famous that an Irish pop band christened itself the Duckworth Lewis Method. At the same time, it may be both the least understood rule in all of sport (*pace* baseball's infield fly rule) and also the most important application of statistical theory in sporting history.

To understand the DL method, ARR is a good place to start. The implicit assumption of the ARR method is that each team proceeds at the same rate, regardless of the stage of an innings. A team that scores 100 runs in 20 overs, for example, can be expected to score 200 runs in 40 overs, and vice versa. Instead of assuming that an innings proceeds linearly, the Parabola method allows for the way that an innings tends to progress, with teams accelerating over the course of the innings. The problem with the Parabola method is that it takes no account of the underlying batting strategy that dictates the way in which an innings evolves. The beauty of the DL method is that it has a theory.

The theory is this: teams have only two resources to build a score, overs and wickets. Teams manage their resources over the span of an innings. At the beginning of a 50-over game, teams tend be conservative in their batting, recognising that if they quickly lose wickets, they might not end up using all of the 50 overs. As teams near the end of the 50 overs, they tend to bat very aggressively – with every passing over, the value of a wicket decreases. The DL method identifies a mathematical equation that converts the combination of overs and wickets left into a single number – the percentage of resources left. At the beginning of the innings this is 100%; at the end it is 0%. The calculation of the exact percentage of resources for any given number of overs and wickets left is estimated, based on actual games played.

The DL method makes it possible to calculate how many resources are left following any given rain interruption. To give an example from the DL Standard Edition: a team that has lost two wickets after 20 overs of a 50-over match is deemed to have 67.3% of its resources left. Now suppose 10 of the remaining 30 overs are lost to rain, so the team now has, according to the table, only 52.4% of its resources left – it lost 14.9% of its resources due to rain. If this happens to the team batting second, the DL method revises the target down by the amount of the lost resources – 14.9%. The beauty of this method is that it can be applied to any number of different situations. Typically, it comes into play whenever the team batting second loses overs due to rain, but it is also applicable to situations where the first innings of the game is shortened due to weather.

* * *

Frank Duckworth has a PhD in nuclear physics from the University of Liverpool, and he spent most of his working life at the Central Electricity Generating Board working on mathematical models related to nuclear power stations. He developed his skills in statistical analysis when it was discovered that nuclear fuel rods in some UK power stations were leaking uncomfortably large amounts of radioactive materials; it was his job to develop the model to understand the problem.

Once he had started down this professional path, he developed an amateur interest in statistics and sport. His first foray, in the 1970s, came when he modelled attendance at Football League matches based on the form of the home and away teams. He forwarded his findings to Alan Hardaker, the opinionated secretary of the Football League, who promptly ignored them. This was by no means the first time that a sports administrator spurned friendly statistical advice from a well-meaning academic, and certainly not the last.

In the summer of 1988, Duckworth was sitting in his garden listening to radio commentary on a one-day match interrupted by rain when the commentator, Christopher Martin-Jenkins, complained that the application of the ARR method was turning an exciting run chase into an entirely predictable one. Surely someone could do better? Martin-Jenkins read out some proposed alternatives, and Duckworth thought to himself, 'Nobody seemed to realise that it was a mathematical two-factor problem.' He quickly wrote a solution to the problem in outline and sent it to Martin-Jenkins. Alas, once again, there was no interest.

After the South Africa World Cup debacle, he decided to write a paper, and he tentatively outlined his solution at a conference of the Royal Statistical Society. Someone in the audience told Tony Lewis, a lecturer at the University of the West of England who was interested in cricket and the estimation of theoretical relationships using statistical models. The two decided to collaborate, and they produced a version of the model that identified the resources available at any point in an innings with any number of wickets down, based on data from actual games played. In 1995, they finally found someone willing to listen and got the ECB to hear them out. Within a year, they were asked to present to the ICC. Ever since, Duckworth and Lewis have become part of the fabric of modern cricket.

* * *

On 3 March, 2003, South Africa played Sri Lanka in the World Cup at Durban; they needed to win to progress to the next stage. Sri Lanka scored 268 in their 50 overs, but as the South African innings progressed, it became apparent that rain was likely to shorten the game. As the first drops came down, both sides carefully studied the DL scoresheet provided for them. For any number of overs and wickets down, it told them what the par score would be – that is, the number of runs equivalent to Sri Lanka's score. As the rain bucketed down, South Africa got word to the batters that the par score at the end of the 45th over, when the game seemed certain to be abandoned, was 229. With two balls remaining of the over, South Africa's score was 223. Wicketkeeper Mark Boucher slog-swept Muttiah Muralitharan for six over deep midwicket, reaching the par score with one ball remaining. Boucher nonchalantly blocked the final ball of the over, not even attempting a run, and punched the air in triumph as the umpires indicated that play would stop. Boucher walked off convinced that South Africa had won.

South Africa had reached the par score. But that meant that their score merely equalled the DL equivalent of the Sri Lankan score – it had not overtaken it. The tie meant that South Africa were eliminated in the first stage of their home World Cup. Once again, the South Africans had been undone by the rain rules – but this time, they only had themselves to blame. They had misunderstood the meaning of the DL scoresheet.

Unlike the ARR or MPO methods, the DL method is a black box – its internal workings are not public knowledge. It comes in two versions – the Standard Edition and the Professional Edition. The Standard Edition is the simpler version, and you can find the table easily enough online. It consists of a single sheet with number of overs left from top to bottom and the number of wickets lost from left to right. Each cell in the table tells you the percentage of resources remaining for each combination of overs and wickets. It's easy to use those numbers to calculate the percentage of resources lost for any number of overs lost and thus to produce an adjusted target.

The Professional Edition, used for games involving professional teams, requires a computer program that is supplied to match officials. Its code is proprietary knowledge. The exact mathematical model has not been published, nor have the data on which the calculations are based. If you want to reproduce the model from scratch to see if they got it right, you're out of luck: you can't. Now, to be fair, Duckworth and Lewis provided a fairly detailed technical explanation in a paper published in 1998, and the new partner in the model, statistics professor Steven Stern, published another article in 2016. Of course, even if they were to set out the exact method in detail, most people would simply lack both the statistical training and the time to implement their own version. By and large, the cricket world seems happy to take the calculations on trust.

This is an extraordinary testament to the DL method – unlike the methods that preceded it, the targets that it produces strike most observers as intuitively sensible. While there are occasional grumbles, there has been no outrage on a scale produced by ARR and MPO. Instead, there are eager wannabe collaborators: in 2004, Duckworth said that they received four or five letters a week with people offering alternative schemes or ways to improve it. There have even been a few academic papers in statistics journals on the subject. But in one-day cricket, the DL method has always produced a target that is widely accepted as reasonable.

No story has done more to get people excited about the value of statistics to sport than *Moneyball*. The book and the film of this name tell the story of Billy Beane, the general manager of the Oakland A's baseball team, and his quest to use statistical analysis to overcome the enormous disparity in resources available to him compared to teams such as the New York Yankees. Statistical analysis, so the story goes, can reveal patterns that team scouts wouldn't notice. This allows you to find ways to hire players whose talent everyone else underestimates. Published in 2003, *Moneyball* accelerated a revolution in professional sport. If they had not done so already, other Major League Baseball teams promptly began to hire maths and computer-science geeks from Ivy League universities. Other North American professional sports – basketball, American football and ice hockey – followed suit, and so did football clubs. In cricket, the growing prominence of statistical analysis is exemplified by the 2021 book *Hitting Against the Spin: How Cricket Really Works*. Nathan Leamon, one of the co-authors, who has been an analyst for both England and the Kolkata Knight Riders in the IPL, has been the nearest to cricket's *Moneyball* man.

Increased computing power, combined with large quantities of team performance data available online, would inevitably lead to the development of what we now call sports analytics. *Moneyball* may have popularised it, but it was not the pioneer. Much of its foundation was laid down by the analyst Bill James, who had been preaching the value of data analysis in baseball since the 1970s. Even earlier, in 1962, the statistician George Lindsey had published a path-breaking analysis that remains the basis for more advanced stats used in baseball today. In the 1950s, the amateur statistician Charles Reep generated probably the first statistical analysis of football, which, while controversial, has had an extended influence on parts of the game.

The DL method, however, is arguably more significant than any of these. Every other contribution to the use of statistics in sport is designed to help any given team to gain a competitive advantage – they are written as strategies. As far as we know, no statistical representation of the game itself has ever been written into the laws in the way that the DL method is. It's not just a theory about how the game is played, which you can choose to follow or not to follow. It actually dictates how every team plays in games affected by rain, and even how they play in anticipation of possible rain. It deserves a book and a movie of its own.

*   *   *

Frank Duckworth and Tony Lewis reached retirement age in the mid-2000s and entrusted the management of their method to another statistician, Steven Stern, a professor of Data Science at Bond University in Queensland. Thus it became the Duckworth-Lewis-Stern method (DLS), associated with the creation of the Professional Edition, which the ICC adopted in 2004. In his 2016 paper, Stern provides background and a fairly detailed breakdown of the revisions to the method, using the opportunity to address some of the academic critics.

In 2002, Ian Preston and Jonathan Thomas proposed an alternative to the DL method. They think that the rain rule should define the target runs after the interruption to preserve each team's winning probability at the time of the break. The insight behind this idea is that batting strategies for the team batting first and the team batting second are different. The DLS method does not differentiate – the model assumes that the three wickets down after 20 overs of a 50-over game has the same implication for batting strategy whether you are batting first or chasing. However, Preston and Thomas showed in another paper that this is not the case, with teams accelerating when setting a target but trying to get ahead of the rate when chasing. The differences are small, but the data supported their conclusion.

It's an interesting theoretical problem. In light of the differences in observed batting strategies, the DL method appears to affect each team's probability of winning, depending on the situation. For example, if the team batting first loses few wickets in its innings and there is a rain interruption that affects the team batting second, the DL method appears to increase the probability that the team batting first will win. This is not ideal – in principle the idea of the rain rule is that your chances of winning should be unchanged. Yet adopting the Preston-Thomas method would not be easy. In contrast to the DL Standard Edition, it would not be possible to produce a simplified version that could be put on a single piece of paper. But the Preston-Thomas proposals are a useful check on the fairness of the DL method. Happily, in the examples they provide, the revised targets Preston and Thomas calculate are not very different from those generated by the DL method. It probably doesn't make a big difference.

More recently, T20 began to pose a new challenge to the DLS method. Should the same adjustment percentages be applied to rain interruptions in the 120-ball version of the game? A paper by Rianka Bhattacharya, Paramjit Gill and Tim Swartz published in 2011 uses data to estimate the quantity of resources used up by balls and wickets in T20 matches. They found that applying the Standard Edition table to T20 could significantly bias the targets. For example, teams in the middle of an innings with four or five wickets lost would have significantly smaller resources left than implied by the DLS table.

In support of their analysis, they cited some T20 games that had been decided by the DLS method. In the 2010 T20 World Cup, England scored 191 batting first against West Indies in Guyana, whose reply was curtailed. West Indies were left with a DL target of 60 from six overs, which they reached with a ball to spare. Many thought that the target was too low, given that the West Indies had 10 wickets in hand for a six-over chase; in effect, it was impossible for them to be bowled out. Paul Collingwood, the frustrated England captain, observed, 'There's a major problem with Duckworth-Lewis in this form of the game … it's certainly got to be revised in this form.'

Some have argued that this is connected to the issue of the Powerplay in T20 – the first six overs where fielding restrictions apply. The rain rules in competitions such as the IPL typically specify a reduced number of Powerplay overs in proportion to the reduction in total overs. There is a view that there's a need to incorporate Powerplay effects into the DLS target calculation itself, since scoring rates are higher in the Powerplay than in the middle overs of the innings. We looked at the average score per ball in the IPL between 2008 and 2020, which gave us about 1700 observations per ball. The average score per ball in the first six overs was 1.234, the average score per ball in the next six overs was 1.197. Over 36 balls this amounts to a difference of 1.4 runs – negligible. Why do people believe otherwise? Possibly because at the end of the Powerplay the run per ball does indeed drop sharply. In the IPL, the average score for the last ball of the Powerplay was 1.30 runs, while the average score for the next ball was only 0.920. But a focus on this steep decrease conceals the fact that, on the whole, there is very little difference between scoring rates in the Powerplay and the next six overs.

In his paper Stern argues that the whole process can't be revised based only on 'a series of specific examples where DL and DLS targets are claimed to be "non-intuitive"' – anecdotes are insufficient evidence. Rather, he says, we need 'a set of principles to which any sensible rain rule should adhere', supported by sufficient data. Duckworth and Lewis had always rejected the idea that there was a need to make a special allowance for Powerplays.

Stern did his due diligence and explored the possibility that T20 might be different. He plotted a comparison of the average number of runs scored from any point in a T20 match to the average number of runs scored from any point in the last 20 overs of a 50-over match, given the same number of wickets lost. He found that the two curves (for a given number of wickets) were almost identical, refuting the claim that there is a major difference in scoring patterns between the two formats. As Duckworth emphasised at the time, West Indies' revised target in Guyana seemed too easy largely because they had already raced to 30 without loss off 2.2 overs when the rain came – 11 runs ahead of the DL par at the time. With all due deference to Collingwood, the data does not suggest that a T20 revision would make any sense.

But Stern did note a development in the short formats that has arisen since the original DL models were estimated. In a high-scoring game, the run rate tends to look much more like the ARR. In other words, the run rate tends to remain relatively stable throughout the innings rather than show a strong tendency to increase, as is the case for innings that produce a more modest total. High-scoring games have become more frequent, enabling Stern to calculate the trend more accurately and to adjust the DL formula appropriately. It may be that some of the criticism of DL in relation to T20 had more to do with the impact of high-scoring games than the format itself. As a result, the formula for calculating the DL targets was adjusted to make the model fit the data more accurately.

Duckworth and Lewis fundamentally changed the way that weather-interrupted cricket matches are decided; the Duckworth-Lewis-Stern method looks set to determine the adjusted run targets for the foreseeable future. Few people can claim to have made a bigger impact on the limited-overs format than the trio of statisticians. As far as we know, the Australian Prime Minister has raised no objection.

PART THREE

CRICKET'S PROBLEMS

10

CRICKET'S CONCUSSION CRISIS

In October 2021, Will Pucovski, long considered one of the most promising young batters in Australian cricket and inked in to play in the forthcoming Ashes series, was training with Victoria, his state side. While in the indoor nets, Pucovski was hit in the head, and concussed. His slow recovery, and the caution in managing his condition, ruled him out of the summer's Ashes series. Pucovski was only 23. Yet it was the 10th known concussion he had sustained.

Pucovski's first concussion came playing Australian Rules football. He sustained another one when he was hit by a door in his home. The other eight have come playing cricket. The list includes some freakish injuries: one concussion after completing a run when he got his bat stuck in the grass and fell flat on the ground, another being hit in the head by a ball from an adjoining net, and another being hit in the head by a ball bouncing up from the ground when fielding. But five of Pucovski's concussions had been sustained while batting and facing short deliveries.

The death of Phillip Hughes, who was killed by a ball that hit the back of his neck in 2014, illustrated how lethal bouncers – balls that go above a batter's shoulders – can be. Pucovski's embryonic career has demonstrated something else: just how common concussive blows are. 'My brain has probably been through a bit more than your average 22-year-old's,' Pucovski said shortly before suffering his ninth concussion.

A month later, Pucovski finally made his Test debut. Three days before, he consulted several neurologists on head injuries to find out whether playing put him at greater risk. Justin Langer, Australia's head coach, said Pucovski told him that he had been assured that his previous concussive blows were 'not necessarily going to have any long-term impact'. How much comfort is 'not necessarily'?

* * *

In 1870, Nottinghamshire's cricketers travelled to London by train. They were there to play the MCC at Lord's, already established as the most hallowed cricket ground in the country, in a three-day first-class match. The game was played under a baking sun.

In the fourth innings of the match, Notts required 155 to win. When they lost their first wicket, George Summers walked out to bat. He had been selected in four Gentlemen v Players matches, considered among the most prestigious fixtures of the day.

Summers' first delivery, as ESPNcricinfo's Martin Williamson has documented, came from John Platts, a fast bowler on first-class debut. A ball, which hit a loose pebble on the wicket, reared up and struck Summers between the cheek and the temple. He collapsed at the crease. W.G. Grace, a medical student at the time, helped Summers stand up, but he was deemed unfit to continue. After observing Summers' calamity, Nottinghamshire's No.4 Richard Daft arrived at the crease with a towel wrapped around his head, covered with a scarf tied under his chin to offer some protection against a similar blow. An opponent promptly mocked Daft's look as 'ridiculous'.

When Summers returned to the Lord's pavilion, he was given a brandy to help him recover; he watched the rest of the game in the sun. Summers declined to stay in London to receive medical assistance, preferring to take the train home with his teammates.

The train was unusually rickety, with carriages shaking. Summers became more ill as the journey progressed. In Nottingham, he returned to his father's house but remained unwell. Four days after being struck by a ball at Lord's, Summers collapsed and died. He was 25. MCC paid for his gravestone and a tablet, which read, 'This tablet is erected to the Memory of George Summers by the Marylebone Cricket Club, to mark their sense of his qualities as a cricketer, and to testify their regret at the untimely accident at Lord's ground, which cut short a career so full of promise, June 19th, 1870, in the 26th year of his age.'

Summers' death is one of the earliest known fatalities resulting from being struck on the head by a cricket ball. The nature of it suggests that the blow led to bleeding in the brain, which in turn caused a fatal subdural or epidural haematoma or haemorrhage.

After Phillip Hughes' death, Peter Brukner, the Australian team doctor, and Tom Gara, a historian at the South Australian Museum, conducted an analysis, funded by Cricket Australia, of how common fatalities were in the sport. Until then, no national boards had ever compiled numbers on how many players were killed while playing the game, either at amateur or professional level. Gara spent weeks labouring over newspaper archives from Great Britain and Ireland, Australia and New Zealand, going back to 1850. Brukner swiftly learned that 'deaths were more common than I thought'.

The authors identified 544 cricket-related deaths in Australia, New Zealand, Great Britain and Ireland: an average of around 3.25 per year. The true figure is likely to be considerably higher: their search only covered three cricketing nations, and the Australian coverage was incomplete. The deaths were split about equally between formal and recreational games.

The macabre list of deaths in cricket the researchers compiled included a spectator being killed by a ball hit into the crowd by his son; a fielder killed by the impact of a bat hitting their chest; and a boy killed by standing too close to a teacher demonstrating a shot. But about 80% of the fatalities recorded were caused by the impact of deliveries striking batters above the waist, with a significant majority of these hitting the heart or higher. Gara, a committed club cricketer 'expected to find perhaps 20–30 deaths' sustained playing cricket in Australian history. Instead, he found 176. 'I am still playing cricket and will continue to do so for as long as I can, but I am much more careful.'

* * *

Batting for Marylebone Cricket Club against the touring West Indians in a first-class match at Lord's in 1976, England opener Dennis Amiss received a blow on the back of the head from Michael Holding, one of the world's most ferocious quick bowlers. Despite the blow, Amiss continued to bat. He hit 203 against West Indies in a Test later that summer, defying Holding and underlining his status as one of the finest players of fast bowling in the world.

Yet he retained uncomfortable memories of being hit. After World Series Cricket – the breakaway competition featuring many of the world's leading players that launched in Australia in 1977 – signed him up, Amiss, who was 34, feared the consequences of suffering another blow.

'I knew that I would be facing a lot of Australian and West Indies bowlers who would be delivering the ball at 90mph,' Amiss recounted to *The Daily Telegraph*. He reached out to a motorcycle helmet manufacturer in Birmingham and asked him to make an adapted helmet to absorb potential blows, using conventional fibreglass with a polycarbonate visor. 'He came up with something lighter than the fibreglass motorcycle helmets around in those days. It had a visor that could withstand a shotgun blast at 10 yards,' he recalled. Initially, the design covered a batter's ears with unforeseen consequences – 'we had a spate of run-outs.' A later model solved the problem by incorporating an equestrian design.

When Amiss arrived in Australia at the end of 1977 with his customised motorcycle helmet, he became the first player to wear a helmet in a professional game. A month into World Series Cricket, the Australian batter David Hookes was struck in the jaw by the Caribbean quick Andy Roberts. He crashed to the ground, dripping blood.

It was the moment the helmet went from eccentricity to necessity. As Hookes had surgery – depriving World Series Cricket of one of its most attractive cricketers for the next five weeks – Kerry Packer, WSC's backer, ordered a batch of Amiss' helmets to be flown out from Birmingham, hoping that they would help protect his other assets.

As word of Hookes' accident got out, Tony Henson, the owner of Sydney and Surfers Paradise, a company specialising in equestrian caps, sensed a business opportunity. Henson asked a colleague, Arthur Wallace, to arrange a meeting with World Series Cricket representatives, as Gideon Haigh recounts in *The Cricket War*. Wallace returned from his meeting saying, 'It can't be done, Tony. They want us to make something that can withstand half a house brick at a hundred miles an hour.'

But it could be done: helmets could at least deflect blows and lessen their impact. In the months ahead, helmets – most initially without visors to protect players' faces – became ubiquitous at the top levels of the game, and rapidly spread through cricket's ecosystem as they became more affordable.

What began as an emergency solution to the dangers of facing the quickest bowlers in the world turned into one of the biggest improvements in player safety in sport. 'Helmets basically wiped out the most common cause of fatality, which was a blow to the head,' said Brukner. 'Since the advent of helmets, I don't think there's been a death from a direct blow to the head. Helmets are very good at protecting you from death. The reason people die when they're hit in the head is that it causes a bleed in the brain, and that's the thing that kills them – that's the thing that you're protected from by a helmet.'

Research conducted by Brukner and Gara shows how much safer helmets have made players. Over the course of the 1970s, there were nine recorded fatalities in Australian cricket – five in organised games, and four in informal ones. Over the following 36 years, from 1980 to 2016, there were only 10 recorded fatalities, with just five in the 26 years from 1990, when wearing helmets became the norm even at recreational level. And so the growth of helmets ought to be acclaimed as World Series Cricket's most important legacy – an innovation that has saved dozens of cricketers' lives since.

* * *

The next catalyst for cricket to take head injuries more seriously was the death of Hughes. StemGuard helmets were developed swiftly after: these have a neck-guard made from foam and plastic that is attached to the helmet.

In an Ashes Test at Lord's in July 2015, eight months after Hughes' death, the Australian opener Chris Rogers was struck by a short ball from Jimmy Anderson. It hit him behind his right ear and landed on his StemGuard. Rogers was one of the few players then wearing the new protection. Peter Brukner, Australia's team doctor, told *Wisden Cricketers' Almanack,* 'We both said to each other afterwards, if he hadn't been wearing it, who knows what would have happened?'

Yet neck guards are still not compulsory around the world. 'It still amazes me that some cricketers don't wear them,' Brukner says. When Steve Smith was hit on the neck by Jofra Archer in 2019, he was not wearing a StemGuard.

Alongside a change in technology, changing the laws of the game can also help to protect players. The introduction of concussion substitutes – first used in Australian domestic cricket in 2016, and in Test cricket in 2019 – may have reduced the number of concussions indirectly. In many cases concussions are thought to be caused not by a single blow, but by repeated ones. Concussion substitutes help to destigmatise a player retiring hurt after a head injury, ensuring their teams aren't penalised. In this way concussion substitutes help to reduce the risk of second impacts after an initial concussion, which could be very serious or even fatal.

Yet, with neck guards and concussion substitutions alike, the puzzle is why safety measures that mitigate risk have not been embraced the world over. Domestic competitions in most Test-playing nations still do not allow concussion substitutes.

* * *

While direct fatalities in cricket remain extraordinarily rare – less than the chances of dying in the car on the way to a game, Brukner notes – death is not the only risk associated with suffering a blow to the head. Across American football, football, rugby and a range of other sports, recent years have highlighted the long-term effects of repeated blows to the head. These may be related to 'sub-concussive' events: blows to the head that do not directly lead to concussions. Repeated impacts to the head – from heading a football to collisions with opponents in American football or in rugby – can lead to degenerative brain injury.

In July 2017, a study examined the brains of 111 deceased NFL players; 110 of them showed signs of a degenerative disease, Chronic Traumatic Encephalopathy (CTE), believed to be caused by repeated blows to the head, of the kind that routinely occur in NFL games. About 20–45% of professional American footballers may be affected by CTE during their lifetime, explains Thomas Talavage, a concussion specialist at Purdue University. In 2015, a class-action lawsuit settlement between the NFL and more than 5000 former players provided up to $5 million per retired player for serious medical conditions associated with repeated head trauma. A range of other sports have also faced lawsuits.

Cricket has been warned. Just because players are rarely killed by bouncers, there is no guarantee that bouncers will not have catastrophic repercussions for these players later in life. A 2020 study by a group of scientists, including John Orchard, Cricket Australia's chief medical officer, identified situational factors associated with concussion in cricket based on video analysis of elite Australian men's and women's matches. It found that 84% of head impacts occurred to a batter on-strike against a pace bowler, with most of the others sustained by close fielders. No deliveries by spinners in the study led to batters sustaining concussion, showing how lower ball speeds reduce risks.

The evolving science has shown that, even as the number of deaths has declined, the ultimate danger of head injuries in sport is greater than previously assumed. The trajectory is unmistakable. 'Concussions have become much more common in cricket over the last 10 or 20 years,' says Brukner. This is not simply the result of increased focus on concussion. 'Since the advent of helmets, a lot more people are being hit in the head.'

There are myriad theories for the increase in head impacts and concussions. Batting technique against short bowling is said to have deteriorated; the protection offered by helmets – and the extra time it takes to move their heads while wearing them – has been blamed for batters being less adept at ducking. Limited-overs formats are blamed for encouraging batters to hook the ball more compulsively. Helmets also may have liberated bowlers to use the short-ball more aggressively. Worldwide, improved strength and conditioning, some believe, has enabled players to bowl up and around 90mph now more frequently than before. And there is simply more cricket played now.

* * *

The experience of Australia suggests that concussions have been systematically underreported. In the men's professional game, there was on average only one concussion per season recorded in the decade until 2014. Following Hughes' death, Cricket Australia commissioned a study by La Trobe University, whose findings were published in 2018. They counted 92 head impacts in men's matches in Australia between 2015 and 2017; 29 of them were diagnosed as concussions. As the authors of the study observed, 'The rate of concussion in cricket is higher than previously appreciated.'

The La Trobe figures equate to a head impact every 2000 balls and a concussion every 9000 balls in male domestic cricket. These figures suggest more than one head impact per Test match that runs the full five days, and more than one concussion for every four such Tests. The table overleaf extrapolates the number of head impacts and concussions in the three international formats for men's cricket over the period 2015–2019. Assuming head impacts and concussions were sustained at the same rate in international cricket as the Australian domestic game, we would have expected there to be 39 incidences of concussions from 2015 to 2018 in Test cricket alone, an average of 9.75 a year. Overall, we could expect an average of 16 concussions and 75 head impacts a year throughout all men's international cricket involving the 12 Full Member nations.

Table 10.1: Estimated number of head impacts and concussions per year in the three men's international formats, assuming rates identified in the La Trobe study

Balls	ODI	T20i	Test	Grand Total
2015	62005	6843	80447	149295
2016	41711	14966	90616	147293
2017	50563	9120	91847	151530
2018	47690	13868	88056	149614

Head impacts	ODI	T20i	Test	Grand Total
2015	31	3	40	74
2016	21	7	45	73
2017	25	5	46	76
2018	24	7	44	75

Concussions	ODI	T20i	Test	Grand Total
2015	6.9	0.8	8.9	16.6
2016	4.6	1.7	10.1	16.4
2017	5.6	1.0	10.2	16.8
2018	5.3	1.5	9.8	16.6

Medical officials argue that, per ball bowled, Australian domestic cricket is likely to produce more head impacts and concussions than the average across the world. There are a number of reasons for this: pace bowlers in Australia tend to be faster, spinners deliver a lower share of overs, and the pitches tend to be quicker. As such, they estimate that, per delivery bowled, the number of head impacts and concussions per ball in all first-class cricket is about one-third of the Australian rate. Using this ratio, and the fact there were 1,012,160 deliveries in all first-class cricket in 2019, implies that there were around 169 head impacts and 37 concussions sustained in men's first-class cricket in 2019.

Brukner does not think that cricket will witness the same prevalence of CTE in retired players as in sports such as American football and rugby, because there are fewer sub-concussive blows to the head in cricket: 'We believe that cricketers are therefore not as much at risk of that long-term issue as those other sports.'

It will be many decades until it becomes clear what damage, if any, Pucovski suffered from his 10 concussions. 'We really don't know whether he's at risk of long-term damage,' said Brukner. 'There's so much we don't know about concussion.'

* * *

Until Shoaib Akhtar broke the mark at the 2003 World Cup, men's cricket was preoccupied by the race to reach 100mph. Pace bowlers in women's cricket are locked in a race to reach their own speed landmark: 80mph. New Zealander Lea Tahuhu has been recorded at 78mph; South Africa's Shabnim Ismail at 79mph, the highest in front of a speed gun. The 80mph mark, experts agree, will not remain unbroken for long. For all of its allure, one less palatable consequence seems inevitable: a rise in concussions.

Across other sports, researchers have found that women incur concussions on the sports field at least twice as frequently as men. 'Women have an increased incidence of concussion in every sport – between two and four times, depending on the study you look at,' explains Dr Michael Turner, the medical director of the International Concussion and Head Injury Research Foundation.

Exactly why women are more susceptible to concussions is unclear. 'The most likely reason is biomechanical,' says Chris Nowinski, the chief executive of the Concussion Legacy Foundation. 'Men tend to have stronger, stiffer necks. Therefore, when a woman is hit in the head with the same force, her head would be expected to move farther and faster, resulting in more deformation of the brain.'

There is no minimum speed of bowling that would make cricketers more susceptible to concussion. But 'faster bowling would be expected to result in more concussions,' says Nowinski. As bowlers reach greater speeds, they will find it easier to bowl bouncers that reach batters at head height, increasing the risks of head impacts and concussion.

The 2018 Australian study into concussions showed that when women are hit on the head playing cricket they are far more likely to suffer concussion. Across the two seasons studied, 32% of head impacts incurred by men led to concussion, but 53% of head impacts to women did so. Though there were only eight recorded concussions in women's matches in the period, compared to 29 in the men's game, the discrepancy reflected the differences in fixtures. Per ball bowled, concussion rates were slightly higher for women – there was one recorded concussion per 6000 balls in elite women's cricket, compared to one per 9000 balls in elite men's cricket.

In the years ahead, the number of concussions in women's cricket seems certain to rise. 'I guess we'll start seeing some more concussions as female bowlers get faster, and use the bouncer more,' Brukner said. If two dominant trends in women's cricket – an increase in the number of fixtures and the speed of bowlers – continue, it may not be long until there are more concussions in women's cricket than in the men's game.

*   *   *

The science is clear. Concussive blows from balls bowled at the head are common; the long-term risks associated with such blows are significant. Imagine if the laws of cricket had always outlawed balls bowled above the chest. It would be inconceivable that authorities, players, fans, or the media would be pushing to make the game more dangerous by allowing bouncers that lead to more cricketers being seriously hurt or incurring traumatic brain injuries. If the bouncer didn't exist, it wouldn't be invented now.

Cricket already has a precedent for dealing with deliveries deemed to be dangerous. Beamers are balls that reach a batter at waist height or higher before they bounce. Law 41.7, which deals with beamers, provides a potential template to implement restrictions on bouncers. If a delivery reaches a batter in line with their head or higher, and it is ruled to be dangerous (which, in practice, is the case for any beamer from a fast bowler), the bowler receives a warning, and the ball is called a no-ball. If they bowl a second beamer, they are banned from bowling for the rest of the innings. The law could conceivably be refined to treat bouncers in the same way as beamers are now.

Brukner advocates banning bouncers, but only for those under the age of 16, as a way to make the sport safer for children. Such a step would reduce the number of concussions in cricket. Yet it would risk leaving players who progress to professional level without experience of dealing with such deliveries, making them more vulnerable to injury from bouncers. It is a difficult trade-off: giving young batters exposure to short deliveries in training – perhaps against softer balls – could help them prepare to receive bouncers in the future. On balance, outlawing bouncers from youth cricket, with a graduated increase in how the best young cricketers are exposed to bouncers, may be one way in which the sport can be made safer.

Yet, this step wouldn't address the area where concussive blows are most dangerous: the professional game in men's and women's cricket. One approach suggested by Brukner is to adopt a standard head injury assessment across all international, and ideally also domestic cricket, to reduce the risk of a second blow to the head. This would also help to address a perceived conflict of interest that arises when away teams do not bring a doctor and the home team doctor has to treat players on both sides. In a Test in December 2016, Brukner conducted concussion tests on Pakistan player Azhar Ali after he was struck on the head. 'I was put in a very uncomfortable position,' Brukner said later. 'Clearly, there was a perception of conflict of interest because if I had ruled him out of the match, that would have benefited Australia.'

Improving batting techniques against short bowling is often cited as a way of lowering the incidence of concussion, and it could have a small impact. But if it were simple for batters to make themselves safer, they would already have done so. Greater enforcement of Law 41.6.1 might also help. The law allows umpires to stop bouncers being bowled if they judge that 'taking into consideration the skill of the striker, by their speed, length, height and direction they are likely to inflict physical injury on him/her'. This rule is used to protect tailenders from bouncers. While greater enforcement would be welcome, it would be unlikely to reduce the number of concussions significantly – tailenders, after all, face the fewest deliveries.

Beyond these ideas, there appear to be few other suggestions on how to make the bouncer safer. Which leaves us with the nuclear option – apply the beamer rule to the bouncer and outlaw it entirely. Clearly, this would change the game irrevocably. 'If you really wanted to reduce concussions, you'd ban the bouncer,' Brukner says. 'But I wouldn't advocate that, because that changes cricket.'

There are two main arguments against banning the bouncer. The first is that the delivery is intrinsically part of the fabric of the sport and the cause of many of the most memorable moments in cricketing history. Because of its potency, the bouncer is omnipresent when pace bowlers are bowling. Even when they do not deliver a short ball for some time, batters know that one might be coming, discouraging them from getting forward to the ball. Pace bowlers have also long used the tactic of using bouncers to push batters back in the crease, and then dismissed them with a fuller ball. All of this would be lost in a sport without the bouncer; it would be disingenuous to pretend otherwise.

The second argument is that banning the bouncer would destroy the essential equilibrium between bat and ball that sustains the sport. Without the bouncer, the fear is that cricket would move irrevocably to being a batter's game, leaving bowlers disarmed.

This argument is much easier to answer. It is true that removing the bouncer would hand an advantage to batters. But there are many ways to compensate bowlers. For example, the Dukes cricket ball, which has a more pronounced seam and so gets more lateral movement, could be used in all Test cricket, rather than only in England, Ireland and the West Indies. The second new ball could be taken sooner. Applying some substances to the ball to encourage reverse swing – as the MCC suggested before the sandpaper affair in 2018 – would also empower fast bowlers. The Decision Review System could be tweaked to rule that any deliveries found to be clipping the stumps were given out lbw. There is an abundance of ways in which bowlers could be compensated for the loss of the bouncer.

Banning the bouncer could mean an enlarged role for spin bowling, and it would probably place greater emphasis on swing and seam bowling. The quickest bowlers would be the ones most affected, but they might even be reinvigorated by being forced to place more attention on the stumps. The yorker, which vies with the bouncer for the quick bowler's most thrilling weapon, could enjoy a welcome renaissance.

These are the conversations that, in its duty of care to players from the grassroots to the apex of the sport, cricket will not be able to avoid. Are the concussions sustained at all levels of the game an acceptable price to keep the bouncer alive? We don't know the right answer. But we are sure that the time for cricket to have this conversation, openly and honestly, is long overdue.

11

STEREOTYPES

The Hundred competition, which launched in England and Wales in the summer of 2021, was intended as an aggressive break with tradition: the 100-ball format, the equal status of men's and women's competitions, the emphasis on entertainment.

Above all it was a break with the traditions of English domestic cricket. Instead of representing counties, the newly formed teams represented cities – eight teams based in seven cities, with two in London. The aim, the ECB announced optimistically, was to 'help The Hundred reach younger urban audiences'. *The Financial Times* reported that 'the ECB says its shift is justified by research, which shows that the growing urbanisation of modern Britain means people now associate more closely with cities than with the "shires".'

Innovations in cricket are often greeted with ridicule. When it was introduced, one-day cricket was considered an abomination. T20 cricket was, and to some traditionalists still is, sacrilegious. The Hundred has generated much opprobrium. We don't want to take sides. Entertainment has always been central to sport, and entertainment that appeals to the intended audience can reasonably be considered an end in itself. Let the people decide.

Our interest in The Hundred concerns the assumptions the competition reveals. Those whose job it is to promote interest in cricket must act on the basis of beliefs: who is interested in the game, why are they interested, and what would make them more interested? Beliefs can obviously be informed by research to uncover the facts – but beliefs about the future must always come down to a matter of judgment. When launching The Hundred, the ECB asserted that it had conducted extensive market research into their audience. That research had revealed, they said, that the new competition would significantly expand their fanbase. They knew that their current audience was ageing, and that short-form cricket was the format most appealing to a younger crowd. And they wanted to make a play for urban fans – on the assumption that county cricket didn't do it for them.

The seven cities selected for The Hundred were London, Manchester, Birmingham, Leeds, Nottingham, Cardiff and Southampton. This adds up to a population of more than 12 million, about 20% of the total population of England and Wales. These teams play on the same grounds that are the homes of county clubs – Surrey (The Oval) and Middlesex (Lord's) in London, Lancashire (Old Trafford) in Manchester, Warwickshire (Edgbaston) in Birmingham, Yorkshire (Headingley) in Leeds, Nottinghamshire (Trent Bridge) in Nottingham, Glamorgan (Sophia Gardens) in Cardiff, and Hampshire (Ageas Bowl) in Southampton. What, then, is the difference between, say, a match that pits Manchester Originals against Northern Superchargers (Leeds) and the historic Roses fixture between the Lancashire and Yorkshire County Cricket Clubs? The composition of teams is a bit different, with more international players or players drawn from other counties. There may certainly be novelty for Yorkshire fans seeing Joe Root, their most famous current player, playing for Trent Rockets in Nottingham.

The message behind the presentation of the teams to the public is very clear: county cricket is boring and stuffy, but The Hundred is brash and exciting. If it goes well, the ECB will expand their audience; if it goes badly, they will alienate their existing fans. The ECB calculates that the benefits will far exceed the costs precisely because the existing audience for traditional cricket is small. Since its introduction in 2003 – an introduction opposed by many traditional fans – T20 has demonstrated short-format cricket's potential to attract new audiences. In that light, the ECB's plan is not crazy.

But the emphasis on 'urban' fans deserves some unpacking. If some traditional first-class counties play their games in cities like London, Leeds, and Manchester, why is there a need to develop new teams with new names? Would, say, Manchester United be a less attractive proposition as a football club if its name was Lancashire County Football Club? The ECB says that the name matters, that it carries different associations, and that potential fans would much prefer to associate with urban Manchester than with (partly) rural Lancashire.

If true, this would be a good example of stereotyping. Stereotyping is a generalised belief held about a particular category of people. If someone holds a stereotype about the kind of people who watch 'county cricket', then the term will generate particular expectations and assumptions about anything associated with it. The same might be true of someone who sees team names such as 'Superchargers' or 'Originals'.

Stereotyping was once considered to be something uniformly negative – a means to dismissing someone out of hand, without giving due consideration to the individuals themselves. But stereotyping need not always be negative. It's quite possible to entertain a positive stereotype about someone. 'County cricket' carries negative associations for some, positive ones for others.

The 'stereotype content model' developed by Susan Fiske at Princeton University and collaborators highlighted two dimensions of stereotyping – warmth, related to trustworthiness and friendliness; and competence, related to capability and assertiveness. Fiske has suggested a causal chain: if you think of a group as cooperative and high in status, you will assign warmth and competence to them. That, in turn, dictates your emotional response, such as pride or admiration, and the entire sequence predicts whether you will be disposed to discriminate against or seek to support and cooperate with them.

Warmth relates to rivalry – are you in competition with the other group? The less competition, the greater the warmth extended to members of that group, since they are not a threat. Conversely, if you believe a group seeks to impinge on your resources, you will think of them with little warmth, you will distrust them, you will be ready to discriminate against them. Immigrants, for example, often suffer unjustifiably from negative stereotyping, because they are both perceived to have low competence and be potential rivals for jobs, romantic partners and so on.

By and large, members of one's own community typically benefit from high warmth and high competence assumptions, creating a sense of admiration.

What, then, would be the stereotype of 'county cricket'? In terms of competence, it would seem to be positive – the format is recognised as the highest level of the English domestic game. What the ECB is concerned about is that it has low warmth. Many people associate the counties with elitism – that's not a positive stereotype. The phrase 'the county set' is a synonym for upper class, upper crust, plummy, tweedy, not to mention huntin', shootin' and fishin'.

The stereotype of who attends a county cricket match is probably quite inaccurate. Most county grounds are in towns and cities – and the vast majority of people in the UK live in urban areas.

Another stereotype is that cricketers are less urban than footballers. The phrase 'county cricketer' conveys a sense of a rural environment, and not a gritty inner city. To discover if this stereotype is based on truth, we looked at all Test players and England men's international footballers born after 1945, and identified their place of birth. Our data included 392 footballers and 234 cricketers.

The data seems to tell a fairly clear story. The median Test player was born in a town with a population of just under 100,000, the median England men's footballer in a city of almost 250,000. Only 11% of cricketers came from Greater London, while 24% of the footballers did. Outside London, the next four major urban areas are Manchester, Birmingham, Leeds and Liverpool. Less than 2% of Test cricketers were born in these cities, compared to 14% of footballers. Compared to football, major metropolises are markedly absent from cricket.

Since we used current data, and there have been demographic changes in the UK in the past 75 years, the analysis can only be approximate. To identify the characteristics of the players' birthplace, we used data from the website citypopulation.de for urban areas with populations larger than 20,000; for the remainder, we used Wikipedia. Of course, 'born in London' is not the same as 'grew up in London', and we have no way to control for family mobility. Also, many villages and towns have expanded over the centuries to the point where they merge with adjacent villages and towns, rendering their identity ambiguous. For example, we treated everyone from Greater London as born in one city rather than counting the separate towns that the city absorbed. Still, the pattern does seem clear.

Phil DeFreitas is one of the few England cricketers who went to school in London. After moving from Dominica at the age of eight, DeFreitas attended Willesden High, a state school. One of his school teachers, Ellis Williams, recognised his potential and helped him join a local club. There, Charlie Myers wrote a letter to MCC that got DeFreitas a trial on the groundstaff – following the path trodden by many professionals – when he was 16. He has no doubt that the two men changed his life, helping him embark on a career that saw him represent England in 44 Tests and 103 ODIs.

'If it wasn't for those people – one my school teacher and secondly, the one person at the club – would I have played professional sport? The answer would have been no, because I wouldn't have been given the opportunity.'

DeFreitas was an unusually talented athlete: he excelled at football and cricket, and he was offered an apprenticeship at Luton Town FC before signing with the MCC groundstaff and later Leicestershire. But he believes that it is far easier for children from inner cities to develop in football, as there are few barriers to entry.

'It's easy – just go to the park and kick a football. That's what I did. So football was easy for me. Cricket was totally different, because you need the facilities. If it rains, where do you go? How many indoor facilities are there? There's not a great deal of them, and there's a certain charge for using indoor facilities. So football is an easy one, you play outside, you play in all sorts of weather. Cricket is different.'

In 2018, DeFreitas became head coach for the London Schools Cricket Association after teaching at Oakham, an elite independent school that is Stuart Broad's alma mater. He is well placed to comment on the starkly different environments.

'Cricket is a very expensive sport, people in the inner cities – some can't afford it. Some of these kids – their parents don't have a car, so they won't be able to travel. I don't think it's just London, I think it's all over. Unless your parents can afford the kit and can get you the gear or you are involved with a good club where they can support you in that way, I think you're struggling.'

The cost of equipment comes up frequently in these conversations. It costs more to get started in cricket than in football, and equipment costs can be a real barrier for families at the lowest end of the income spectrum. At the same time, cost alone cannot explain the general lack of professional players produced by cities. The median household income in the UK is £29,900 – £575 per week. A reasonable quality set of bat, pads, gloves and helmet would set you back around

£260 – not a negligible amount but certainly not a prohibitive one, either. Suppose you had to do this three times, at the ages of 11, 13 and 15. The combined costs amount to an average equipment spend of £2.50 per week per year, or 0.43% of median weekly family income.

Of course, kit is not the only expense. The cost of travelling to coaching and matches is another barrier cited by DeFreitas and Dr Sarah Fane from the MCC Foundation, the charitable arm of Marylebone Cricket Club. It is also often alleged that youth coaches may – consciously or unconsciously – be more inclined to pick players who they coach privately, benefiting those from wealthier families.

Travelling distances in junior cricket tend to be greater than for junior football; because there are fewer grounds in urban areas, travel is more expensive and more time-consuming, especially for those whose families do not have access to a car. While these financial barriers will not affect families near or above the median income, they are a real obstacle to participation for the poorest segment of the population.

Another common argument is a lack of space to play, but there are grounds for scepticism here. UK cities are blessed with more open space than cities in most other countries. Hackney Marshes in East London, close to some of the most deprived areas in the city, is a good example. It is a vast open area that accommodates 80 sports pitches, mostly grass – but a full 69 of them are devoted to football, three to rugby, and eight to cricket. If city dwellers were to clamour for more cricket facilities, those could easily be created – but they prefer football, and public space is arranged accordingly.

Stereotyping may be conscious or unconscious – sometimes you know you are over-generalising, sometimes you're not even aware that your assumptions are biased. Either way, stereotypes, which are often the root of significant discrimination and injustice, are hard to eradicate.

They are particularly prevalent in sport. In America, Black athletes were subject to sporting apartheid and excluded from competition for most of the country's history. The moment the colour bar was broken, Black athletes quickly rose to prominence in many professional sports, most noticeably in basketball. So one stereotype was replaced with another one: now, Black people were 'natural athletes'. Once again, then, they were reduced to their bodies in pernicious ways, since the 'athletically gifted' often came with an unspoken assumption that they remained intellectually inferior to white Americans. Shockingly, the National Football League concussion settlement we discuss in Chapter 10 short-changed Black players on the racist assumption that their cognitive abilities had been lower to begin with, hence they were entitled to less compensation. Only in October 2021 did the NFL agree to discontinue the practice.

The concept of race is itself a cultural construct, largely invented by European thinkers in the 18th century. The Human Genome Project, which completed the mapping of the entire sequence of human DNA in 2003, enabled scientists to conclude without any doubt that there is no scientific basis for traditional racial classifications: two people of European descent can easily be less similar to each other than either of them is to a person of Asian descent. There simply isn't enough genetic similarity among members of an alleged 'race' for the classification to be scientifically meaningful. Race is not a scientifically credible way to sort humans, who share 99.9% of their DNA.

Sadly, the lessons of modern biology are only slowly sinking in, and belief in race as a meaningful scientifically grounded category persists across the world. This in turn feeds stereotyping, prejudice and discrimination. English cricket markedly lacks racial diversity, especially if you compare it to football. The sport's restricted urban presence is almost certainly part of the explanation: according to the 2011 UK census, 81.5% of the UK population lived in an urban location, but almost everyone who described themselves as Pakistani (99.1%), Bangladeshi (98.7%) and Black African (98.2%) did.

Across the men's county game, the number of Black professional cricketers, excluding overseas players, fell from 33 in 1994 to just nine in 2019, according to research by Thomas Fletcher from Leeds Beckett University. As of 2020, only 1% of players in the recreational game, according to the England and Wales Cricket Board, are Black, African, Caribbean, or Black British, compared to 3.3% of the national population in the 2011 census.

'In the area that I'm from, South London, I knew a lot of people – whatever colour they were – in the state system,' Kent's captain Daniel Bell-Drummond, a former England Lions player, who has Jamaican parents, recalled in 2019. 'They didn't really have a clear pathway into cricket.' Bell-Drummond won a sports scholarship to Millfield. 'There's a lot of issues – a lot of them are socioeconomic, and a lot of them are to do with what people see in front of them. They see Raheem Sterling or whoever is playing football.'

In 2020, Lonsdale Skinner told *The Guardian* that the treatment of Black cricketers amounted to 'undocumented exclusion'. Skinner, who moved to London from Guyana as a child, played for Surrey in the 1970s and later became chairman of the African Caribbean Cricket Association: 'The county academies are a system dreamed up by the middle class for middle-class children.'

Cricket is vibrant among British Asian communities: 30% of recreational players in England and Wales are British Asian, even though they make up just 3.2% of the population. Yet, excluding overseas players, only 5% of professional players are British Asian. This means that a young white recreational player is about eight times as likely to become a professional cricketer than a young British Asian player. The number of British Asian cricketers in the men's county game declined from 30 to 22 between 2014 and 2020, according to research by the South Asian Cricket Association.

The broader reasons for the lack of British Asian professional cricketers were exposed by the testimony of Azeem Rafiq, the former captain of Yorkshire, at a parliamentary select committee in November 2021. Rafiq alleged that cricket was 'institutionally' racist as he documented an appalling litany of abuse that he had suffered in the English game. Rafiq described being held down and forced to drink red wine aged 15, even though he is a Muslim, and constantly receiving racial slurs in the Yorkshire dressing room, with British Asian players called terms including 'P*k*' and 'elephant washers'.

While Rafiq's words exposed the ugly reality of racism within the English game, it was already well established that British Asian players often faced extra hurdles to white players. 'Asian cricketers do get judged quicker than others and people do write you off quicker than everybody else,' Moeen Ali, a World Cup and Ashes winner who grew up in Birmingham, told the *I* in 2020. 'I do find it surprising that more Asian cricket talent is not coming through from places such as Bradford, Birmingham, London and Manchester.

'Sometimes the issue of culture comes into it. Just because as a coach you have Asian cricketers who don't relate to you, that should not mean you cannot handle them. You have to develop and learn about other people's cultures and understand how people work, which I think some coaches fail to do.'

The number of British Asian and Black British coaches in the professional game has also been small. In 2019, just seven out of the 118 managers or coaches employed by counties were from either Black or British Asian backgrounds, Fletcher's research found.

Vikram Solanki, who was appointed Surrey head coach in 2020, was the first British Asian head coach of a county. Until 2021, there have been only three Black British head coaches of men's first-class counties. The most recent was Mark Alleyne, a former England ODI cricketer who captained Gloucestershire to an unprecedented five one-day trophies in two seasons. Despite winning two trophies in his four years as Gloucestershire head coach from 2004 to 2007, Alleyne did not even get to the interview stage for four county jobs he applied for since, he said in 2020. And they weren't all head-coach positions.

'The normal line was, oh we've had a lot of quality candidates and you just haven't made the cut, basically,' he said. Alleyne thinks that 'unconscious bias' rather than explicit discrimination is to blame; many positions are not even advertised but filled through informal networks.

The paucity of Black coaches at all levels of the game contributes to racial stereotyping of Black players, Alleyne said. 'A lot of Black guys get a lot of kudos for the physical attributes, but not a lot for their strategic and mental attributes. And that's the thinking that needs to change.'

Gulfraz Riaz, the chairman of the National Asian Cricket Council, also identifies a link between the dearth of British Asian coaches and professional players. 'Over the years, the South Asian player coming through the pathway has got certain labels put against him. For example, they could be a very good fast bowler or a spinner or a very good batter, but they seem to have always tripped over on the fitness and the fielding, and the discipline side,' he said. Riaz argues that more British Asian coaches could make a 'real difference' to the chances of young British Asian players coming through.

In 2021 research from Tom Brown, a performance cricket coach at Warwickshire County Cricket Club and researcher into talent ID, found that, among players in the county academies between U-10 and U-19 level, White players were three times more likely than British South Asians to become professionals. There were also huge inequities along class lines. Among White British players in county academies, those who went to private schools were 13 times more likely to become professional cricketers than those who attended state schools – even when those who received sports scholarships to private schools were excluded from the study. Those who were both state educated and from a South Asian background faced a double disadvantage: they were 34 times less likely to become professionals than White British children who were privately educated.

If the English game is to better represent all the nation's talent, it will need to harness the strengths that exist in inner cities and among Black and British Asian cricketers. Ensuring greater diversity among coaches would be a start.

* * *

The highest level of competition in domestic cricket is the County Championship, which is designated 'first-class'. County clubs that are not designated first-class compete in the Minor County Championship, renamed the National Counties Championship in 2021. These designations, so pregnant with connotations of status, did not just emerge spontaneously – somebody made these decisions, however haphazardly.

By 1873, England had 13 county cricket clubs; the nine largest of them met to establish rules for player qualification. Previously, players could play for whichever team offered the most money – or 'expenses' in the case of the gentlemen. The counties agreed to restrict qualification to either birth or a residency of at least two years – a very effective way to restrict pay as it eliminated competition. Around this time, the press started to publish league tables for the top nine counties. But since each county decided how many games to play and against whom, including counties not in the elite group, the classification was not entirely reliable.

While this version of the County Championship achieved a great following in the press, the counties themselves were ambivalent. In 1885, when the number of county cricket clubs had risen to 21, *The Times* reported on a meeting of county secretaries preceded by a meeting 'of the so-called minor counties'. The quote clearly reflects a certain unease with the distinction. The meeting was to determine the fixture list for the season, and the 'minor counties' wanted to play more games against the 'first-class' counties. This was about status, but it was also about money – higher-quality teams meant more gate revenue.

In 1887, 18 counties formed the County Cricket Council, with a view to regulating competition. Part of their rationale was concern that weaker counties seldom got to play stronger counties. They were right to be concerned. At the end of 1889, the secretaries of the eight counties listed in the championship table privately agreed to recognise the County Championship, which led to a new competition that was officially ratified by the Council on 11 August, 1890. At this meeting, it was agreed that there should be three classes of county for the 1891 season, with teams required to play a fixed number of games against teams in their class, though they could also play teams in other classes. At the Council's next meeting, on 8 December, 1890, William Ansell, the secretary of Warwickshire, who had minor status, made a revolutionary proposal: 'At the end of each season, in the month of August or September, the lowest county in the first class shall play the highest of the second class for right of place; one game only shall be played, and upon a neutral ground to a finish, the winner being placed in the superior class, and the loser in the class below for the following year.' In plain language: promotion and relegation.

The credit for this idea traditionally goes to the Football League, which created a Second Class (later renamed Division) in 1892, with 'test matches' played at the end of the season between teams at the bottom and top of each division to determine status for the next season. Promotion and relegation, as it evolved, became a central feature of football league structures around the world, and the principle that teams should qualify for participation in competition on the basis of 'sporting merit' is enshrined in the FIFA Statutes. When 12 of Europe's largest clubs threatened to create a European Super League in 2021, the proposal led to uproar from fans and threats of sanctions by government, so central to the very soul of the game was the system that William Ansell originally proposed for cricket.

Back in 1890, Ansell's plan met with uproar. Unsurprisingly, the eight first-class counties voted 'nay', joined by only two of the second-class ones. The rest of those – Warwickshire, Hampshire, Derbyshire and Durham – voted in favour. Middlesex, Surrey, Sussex, Gloucestershire, Kent, Yorkshire, Lancashire, and Nottinghamshire, all first-class, knew what they had to lose, but it is perplexing that Leicestershire and Norfolk voted down their own chances of promotion. The segregation of the classes had been decided. The meeting descended into chaos and ended with a vote to suspend the Council *sine die* – without setting a date to resume. The vote passed, and the County Cricket Council was dead. First-class status would now be controlled by the elite.

County cricket clubs continued to form throughout the 1890s; by the turn of the century, there were 31. The lower-class counties now accepted the term 'minor county', which had been used informally by some since at least 1879, and they created their own championship in 1895. Ansell's Warwickshire recovered from the setback of 1890 and were granted first-class status in 1894, along with five others. Durham, formed the same year as Warwickshire, also had a good claim to first-class status. They actually won the first Minor Counties Championship in 1895; under the failed promotion and relegation scheme of 1890, they would have been eligible to compete for entry to the first class. In *Summer's Crown: The Story of Cricket's County Championship*, Stephen Chalke contrasts the decision to ignore Durham with the 1905 decision to admit Northamptonshire, a club with a membership of only 600. Purely on sporting merit, it made little sense to leave Durham marooned as a minor county.

Admission to the first class required a vote of two-thirds of the clubs. After 1905, when the number of first-class clubs reached 16, 87 years passed with only one new club admitted, Glamorgan in 1921. The case of Devon illustrates the lack of interest in expanding the County Championship: when they applied to become a first-class county in 1948, they did not even receive an official response.

Even as a minor county Durham maintained a vibrant club. In 1973, they became the first minor county to defeat a first-class team when they toppled Yorkshire in the Gillette Cup. From 1975 to 1982, Durham went 65 games unbeaten in the Minor Counties Championship. This record eventually led to a renewed attempt to win first-class status. In the early 1980s, a Durham committee member approached Northumberland about a joint bid for first-class status. The idea collapsed in 1985, with Northumberland unconvinced that the County Championship would ever admit a new side.

Some of the Durham committee thought the same. 'The biggest problem was convincing the committee to even attempt first-class status,' said Tom Moffat, a former Minor Counties player for Durham who served as treasurer. One financial expert told them it would be 'lunacy' even to attempt it.

But Durham's dreams remained alive, with local businessmen and the county council undeterred. In 1988, Durham's committee assembled a three-man working group, including Moffat, to explore whether the idea was plausible. In March 1989, Moffat and the group completed a comprehensive feasibility study, convinced that Durham could sustain a vibrant first-class side. The full committee agreed, and Durham promptly submitted their application to the Test and County Cricket Board (TCCB) to become the 18th first-class county.

In response, the TCCB, the forerunner to the ECB, formed a working party of its own to liaise with Durham. 'The working party used to put hurdles up for us to jump,' Moffat said. Most draconian was the stipulation that Durham had to build a ground capable of hosting Test cricket, even though only six of the existing 17 counties had such a facility.

Durham's committee spent much of the next two summers cajoling county chairmen and chief executives. Their arguments traversed diverse terrain, arguing that a team would be recognition of the game's popularity in the North East and help lift it up further, while having an even number of teams could help rationalise the fixture schedule. Durham also had to prove that their entrance would increase the county game's funds rather than spread more thinly the money that the TCCB divided up among the counties. Durham's working group even produced a study from Durham University that showed average annual rainfall in the county to be lower than in many counties with first-class teams. Most importantly, Durham needed to prove that they had £500,000 they could call upon if they became first-class. The first £100,000 came from Newcastle Building Society; support soon followed from Scottish and Newcastle Breweries, and then the local business community pitched in.

On 6 December, 1990, the vote on whether to admit Durham took place at Lord's. Not being a first-class county, Durham's representatives weren't allowed to the meeting. Durham needed 12 counties to vote for the resolution to pass; in the event 16 did, with Sussex abstaining. At the Racecourse Ground, Durham, on 25 April, 1992, they finally played their first County Championship game.

Durham's initial seasons were years of struggle. They came bottom of the County Championship in their first two seasons, 16th in 1994, 17th in 1995 and then bottom again in 1996, when they failed to win one of their 17 games. It was Durham's worst season, yet also a pivotal year. Left-arm quick bowler Simon Brown became the first cricketer to make his England debut while at Durham. Not only was he locally raised in Cleadon in South Tyneside, but Brown had Durham to thank for reinvigorating his career: he had been released by Northamptonshire in 1990, after 15 first-class games.

Most importantly, 1996 was also the year Durham created their academy. This helped make good on the wider ambitions they held when the club was formed: they wanted to be a team not merely *for* the North East but *of* the North East. The academy was led by Geoff Cook, a former England cricketer from Middlesbrough – 'the greatest signing Durham ever made,' according to Tom Jackson, who would serve as Durham chairman.

In the years ahead, academy graduates underpinned Durham's transformation on the pitch. With a squad largely hailing from the area, Durham won County Championship titles in 2008, 2009 and 2013. Products of the Durham academy would also be a common thread in many of England's finest modern teams. Steve Harmison and Paul Collingwood played in both the 2005 and 2009 Ashes. Graham Onions, another academy graduate, was also in the 2009 team; Collingwood also played in the 2010/11 Ashes victory. Ben Stokes, who was born in New Zealand but moved to Cumbria aged 12, and Mark Wood combined in the 2015 Ashes. In the summer of 2019, three academy graduates – Wood, Stokes, and Liam Plunkett – were part of the first England XI to win the 50-over World Cup. Five weeks later, Stokes' 135 not out inspired one of England's greatest Ashes victories.

Allowing Durham to play first-class cricket may have helped to grow talent from the North East that might otherwise have been quashed. Only 18 of England's first 580 Test cricketers were born in the historic counties of Durham or Northumberland, four in the 19th century. During the 97 years of Durham's second-class status, the counties produced seven England players. In Durham's first 29 years as a first-class county, they produced another seven. In the 21st century, the county has arguably been England's pre-eminent source of fast bowlers; Harmison, Onions, Wood, Plunkett and Stokes have all graduated through Durham's academy into the England Test team.

You can make a strong claim that some – perhaps even most – of these players could have been lost to the sport if Durham had not become a County Championship side and developed their academy. Without Durham acquiring first-class status, 'there's not a cat in hell's chance I'd have played professional cricket,' Harmison later said.

This all suggests that English cricket could have been stronger had Durham not had to wait almost a century to join the County Championship. Just as Durham are now credited with helping to unlock cricket talent in new areas of the country, it is possible that, one day, The Hundred could be viewed as having had the same impact in urban areas.

* * *

A crucial figure in Durham's first decade was David Boon, who captained them for three seasons and helped secure their place in the top flight in the first season in which two divisions were introduced in 2000. Boon had already been a beneficiary of a new team's elevation to a first-class competition: his native Tasmania, which joined the Sheffield Shield in 1977. In Australia, Tasmania had been stereotyped as too small and too remote to be a cricket power; just like Western Australia, they were not included in the competition when it started in 1892.

English counties are small, and it's easy to move between them. That can make it difficult to assess the exact impact of any county becoming first-class. But what is true for Durham in England also appears to be truth for Boon's Tasmania and for Western Australia: as new areas gained teams in the domestic first-class competition, the number of international players produced by these areas increased.

Tasmania played its first Sheffield Shield games in 1977. Of cricketers born in Tasmania in the century between 1854 and 1953, just seven went on to represent Australia at Test level. In less than half a century since, Tasmania has produced 11. That means that 61% of all Test players born in the state were born after 1953. The corresponding figures for NSW, Victoria and South Australia are 34%, 32%, and 37% respectively. Tasmania's ability to produce Test players seems to have increased significantly since it won Sheffield Shield status.

The Tasmanian experience replicated what was true of Western Australia – the most geographically isolated first-class side in the world – a generation earlier. When Western Australia entered the Sheffield Shield in 1948, only one of the 182 Australian Test cricketers had come from the state. Of the next 280 players to play Tests for Australia, 48 were from Western Australia. In the years since, Australian cricket has been enriched by cricketers such as Dennis Lillee, Rod Marsh, Kim Hughes, the Hussey brothers, Terry Alderman, Stuart MacGill, Simon Katich, and Justin Langer.

Like so many other forms of stereotyping, regional bias can be a significant source of both positive and negative discrimination. In selection for the Australian national team, many Australians believe there is one particular form of bias at work. 'When they give out the Baggy Blue cap in New South Wales, they give you a Baggy Green one in a brown paper bag as well to save making two presentations,' David Hookes said in the 1980s. Hookes hailed from Adelaide in South Australia, a state which has produced only one-third as many Test cricketers as New South Wales, unfairly in his view.

Batter Brad Hodge made a similar claim in 2009. Hodge is from a suburb of Melbourne in Victoria – the state that has produced more Australian Test cricketers than any other bar New South Wales. In 2006, Hodge was dropped five matches into his Test career, while boasting an average of 58.4. Australia were about to tour South Africa, and he had hit a double century against them just three matches earlier. Yet he was dropped not just from the team but from the squad altogether because of a perceived weakness against the short ball. Western Australia's Damien Martyn and New South Wales' Michael Clarke came in. Hodge played only one more Test, two years later in the Caribbean; he made 67 and 27, yet was never picked again, despite scoring 51 first-class centuries and averaging 48.8 in the first-class game.

Hodge later blamed being dropped from the Test team on New South Wales selection bias. 'Every time that I was on tour, I was a threat to someone else from a different state,' he said. 'So they had allies and friends in that particular squad. For example, in 2005, Simon Katich [originally from Western Australia, but playing for New South Wales at the time] was struggling. So the chances were, if I was to bat, I was going to take his spot in the middle order. But the reality is that it was only me as a Victorian, apart from [Shane] Warne, but we also had five or six, seven or eight New South Welshmen in that squad ... When you're not high up in the ranks, these people speak volumes about you in training and around the selection table and with the selectors.'

We wanted to see if the data supported the belief in New South Wales bias. We can't read the minds of selectors, but we can make an inference about bias. You would suspect bias when players of lower ability are chosen above those of higher ability simply because they are members of the favoured group; in this case, New South Wales players would be chosen ahead of better players from other states. If that were the case, the team would perform worse the more New South Welsh players were in the team.

We used regression analysis to calculate the probability of a win, a draw or a loss, contingent on the proportion of players born in New South Wales, Victoria and South Australia. What we found might surprise Australian fans outside New South Wales. On average, the Australia men's Test team contains 4.4 players born in New South Wales. When the side contained four or fewer New South Wales players, the probability of winning was 43%, the probability of a draw was 27% and probability of defeat was 30%. But when the team contained five or more New South Wales players, the probability of winning was 51%, the probability of a draw was 25% and probability of defeat was only 24%.

New South Wales is indeed over-represented: they are 30% of the country yet 40% of the national team. But alas for the rest of Australia, the data does not support the notion that New South Welshmen get a leg-up: Australia do better when there are more New South Wales players in the team. But stereotypes have never been about the numbers. If you're convinced that New South Wales get an unfair advantage, probably no amount of statistics will dissuade you.

12

WHAT WILL THE FUTURE OF WOMEN'S CRICKET LOOK LIKE? AND THE CASE FOR REPARATIONS

In January 2020, the Associação Brasileira de Cricket – Cricket Brazil – took a remarkable decision. They would introduce professional cricketers for their women's squad before they had done so for the men's. It was a tantalising glimpse of a future in which the women's game will not replicate the structures of the men's but will instead chart a different path.

The calculation made by Matt Featherstone, the president of Cricket Brazil, was simple: 'There is a gap in the market. Women's cricket is still fairly open. Even the top 10 countries that we see playing are not a million miles away in women's cricket as they are in men's cricket. So we decided that this was the market we would go for.'

When Featherstone, a PE teacher from Bromley who played for Kent's second XI, moved to Brazil to be with his wife in 2000, the country did not even have a cricket association. Featherstone helped form one in 2001; the following year, Cricket Brazil joined the ICC, opening up a small source of funding.

Featherstone lives in Poços de Caldas, a spa town in southeast Brazil with a population of 160,000. In 2009, he began working with the local government on growing the game, focusing on taking cricket to disadvantaged communities. 'We started with 26 kids in an orphanage that we used to visit once a week. We realised that the kids loved it – why wouldn't they? We know it's a great game, so why wouldn't other people?'

They might have needed a bit of persuading, given football's dominance in Brazil. But Featherstone has a handy shortcut when he introduces the game:

taco, also known as 'bats' or 'Bete-ombro', is a popular Brazilian street game, played by both sexes. The author M.J. Dees, who calls it 'son of cricket', notes that cricket itself 'is completely eclipsed by the popularity of a game which owes its genesis to Cricket but which has evolved and devolved into the game which is popularly known as Taco.'

Here is how Dees describes the game: 'Taco is played by two pairs, a batting pair and a fielding pair. The stumps [or cans or bottles] are placed either end of the wicket [though the term wicket is alien to the average Brazilian]. Around each set of stumps is the crease [again, this is not called a crease and is a circle drawn a full 360 degrees around the stumps]. At each end a fielding/bowling player stands behind the stumps and the batting players stand with their bat grounded inside the crease. The bowlers attempt to hit the stumps and the batters try to hit the ball as far as possible. Like cricket, on hitting the ball the batters are able to run to the opposite end and accumulate runs.'

You have a winner when one team accumulates enough runs to reach the pre-agreed total – 10, or 12, or 25, for instance.

Like cricket, taco includes stumpings – players are either bowled or run out when their bat is not within the crease. Yet there are some important differences: you can get batters out if you hit them with the ball while they're making a run. If a ball is hit behind, or catches an edge, the batter is not allowed to run. On the third occasion of the ball touching the bat and going behind, regardless of whether runs have been made in intervening balls, both batters are out and the two pairs exchange places.

Taco is thought to have developed out of the cricket clubs that the English established in Rio in the 1860s – the English game didn't catch on, but the home-grown version is common enough that even Prince Harry found himself playing it when he visited a favela, only to get stumped.

* * *

What began as an experiment now sees 5000 locals play cricket in Poços de Caldas. Ten of them are centrally contracted women's cricketers; all 10 started playing through Cricket Brazil's outreach schemes. One of them, Laura Agatha, was first spotted playing taco on the street.

Cricket Brazil's central contracts are tailored creatively to the needs of the players and the local context. Players train for four hours, five days a week at Cricket Brazil's high-performance centre in Poços de Caldas, which has four nets, a fielding area, and bowling machines. They must also spend time coaching in the community. The contracts include free access to doctors and scholarships, which Cricket Brazil negotiated in a partnership with the local university. As of 2021, two-thirds of contracted players are 20 or younger.

Off-spinner Lara Bittencourt is considered a rising star. She first heard of cricket at the age of nine, when her elder sister at Colégio Municipal School was introduced to the sport. 'She told me that it was a sport with a bat and a ball that needed to be thrown with a straight arm,' Lara recalls. 'That was all I knew about the sport, and it already aroused a curiosity in me. Three years later, I joined the project at the same school and fell in love with the sport.'

Lara had always been sporty, but with other games, she would quickly lose interest. 'It was different with cricket. I started out of curiosity but I didn't stop like the others. I think a lot of that was due to the training environment that was always very welcoming, the people that I met who made me not want to miss a training session.'

Lara followed the structured path for young Brazilian cricketers: she started at school in the community projects, moved on to a local club, and then joined the national squad. At 16, Lara was in the first group of Brazilian players to receive contracts. 'Cricket has brought me many opportunities, and it has changed my life in many ways. The professional contract gave me a direction that I didn't have before, of what I want to pursue as a profession. It showed me that making a living from sport is a reality.' Lara believes that Brazil can qualify for a World Cup.

The package that Cricket Brazil offers ensures buy-in from families who have never heard of cricket. 'It was difficult speaking to parents who've not only not seen women's sport being talked about very much but definitely not women's cricket and now suddenly their daughters have been offered full-time professional contracts in this sport,' Featherstone says. He tells parents that cricket offers 'a chance to change people's lives.' Most players are the first in their family to go to university, and the first to receive passports, too.

Cricket Brazil's decision to introduce central contracts – only seven years after Australia introduced what are regarded as the first central contracts in the women's game – reflects how far the US dollars of ICC funding go in the country. The total cost of each player's contract is 2000 reais a month – around £260. Such low costs allowed the organisation to create a contract system despite Brazil's meagre $120,000 a year of ICC funding.

While women's cricket offers Brazil the best routemap to rising rapidly within the sport, Featherstone believes that a successful women's team could also galvanise the men's game: 'If women's cricket starts taking off, that would also then rub off on our under-17 and under-19 boys – seeing that pathway and thinking, "there's a chance for us".'

Some have credited Brazil with being the first nation to centrally contract women before men, but they were beaten to it by a few years. In 2015, Thailand introduced professional contracts for leading women players – albeit not as many as Brazil. As of 2021, they have seven full-time contract players.

As with Cricket Brazil, the Cricket Association of Thailand's investment was driven by pragmatism: thinking about where their limited funds could have the greatest effect. 'Men's competition level is significantly higher – making it more difficult for Thailand, with no cricketing background, to compete at such a high level,' explains Shan Kader, the development manager for the Cricket Association of Thailand. 'Comparatively, the women's game is still in its infancy. Most Associate teams have come out of the starting blocks at the same time.'

In 2007, Thailand made their international debut with a team mostly comprising converted softball players: they were bowled out for 40 by Nepal, extras top-scoring with 16. Thirteen years later, Thailand made their debut in the T20 World Cup. At the time, their men were not even ranked in the world's top 50.

* * *

In April 2021, the Australia women's team set a new record for the longest winning streak in one-day international history, in the men's or women's game. When they defeated New Zealand by six wickets in Mount Maunganui, Australia clinched their 22nd consecutive ODI victory, beating the record set by Ricky Ponting's Australia men's team in 2003. By the end of the series, they had extended that streak to 24 straight victories. Yet even this headline number perhaps understates quite how dominant Australia have been. During this run, Australia scored 2.5 times more runs than their opponents for every wicket they lost, while scoring 50% faster.

More than anything, the streak was a testament to Australia's commitment to women's cricket – administratively, financially and culturally. Since the 1980s, women's cricket in Australia has been supported more vigorously than anywhere else. In 2013, Cricket Australia ushered in a new era of professional contracts for international women players. In 2015–2016, with the launch of the Women's Big Bash, Australia created eight semi-professional teams, mirroring the men's competition. In 2017, under the memorandum of understanding agreed between the players and the board, domestic players achieved semi-professional status. The minimum retainer for players holding both a state and Women's Big Bash contract was set at A$36,000 (£20,000), while the average salary for a women's national team player was increased to A$180,000 (£100,000). Australia doesn't just have an unmatched coterie of female superstars; it also has a depth of talent that is the envy of the world.

Yet Australia's dominance poses a conundrum. It is clearly good for promoting interest in women's cricket in Australia, but is it good for women's cricket globally? The richer cricket nations – Australia, India, England and possibly New Zealand – might pull away on the field, making many matches uncompetitive. With the finances of most Full Member, let alone Associate, boards tight even before Covid-19, most have prioritised their men's team, stunting the development of their women's team.

At the age of 23, Kim Garth, the best Irish player of her generation, stopped playing international cricket for Ireland and moved to Australia to play as a local; it was the only way she could be a genuinely professional cricketer. The same was true of Kirstie Gordon and Leigh Kasperek, who both represented Scotland before switching to England and New Zealand, respectively, for the good of their careers.

In 2016, West Indies won the T20 World Cup, a few hours before their men's side did the same. It seemed to herald a new dawn for women's cricket in the Caribbean. Instead, the side has disintegrated, weighed down by a lack of a local infrastructure to develop the game. The women's game is in danger of replicating the least desirable aspects of the men's game: a big three, widening wealth inequality, and a system that almost compels leading players from emerging nations to switch countries if they are to fulfil their potential.

*   *   *

Clare Connor, the chair of the ICC women's committee, acknowledges the risk of merely replicating the inequalities in the men's game. 'There's no point those three just getting better and better and investing more and more,' she told us. 'That's not a truly global sport. So how does the ICC counter that?'

Connor suggests that all boards could be mandated to ring-fence a certain percentage of their ICC funding for the women's game. This could raise standards among emerging nations and among those Full Members who have historically paid little attention to women's cricket. But it would still mean that, in countries where the men's game is not well-developed, funding for women's cricket would be scarce: a national board that generated little from its men's side would inevitably have relatively little to spend on its women.

Cecelia Joyce, a former Ireland women's player who is now on the board of FICA, advocates a global approach. Rather than make women's cricket depend on the financial strength of the men's game in any given country, she suggests that the ICC give each of its members in the region of $500,000 a year, explicitly ring-fenced for women's cricket. The money could be used to enable players and a few support staff to turn professional, develop infrastructure and grassroots facilities, and fund fixtures. For Ireland and many teams, 'If you gave 500 grand a year to professionalise, you'd have a good team in two years.' This would be similar to FIFA's policy, which shares out the revenue of the men's World Cup to the national associations, the only difference being that the money would be explicitly committed to the women's game.

The plan would cost around $50 million a year, depending on how many national associations were granted funding. Some richer countries would top-up the ICC funding – $500,000 a year would only cover the contracts of a handful of Australia's leading cricketers – but the scheme would ensure a minimum spend on women's cricket in all countries. For Bangladesh, Ireland, West Indies, Papua New Guinea and beyond, it would be transformative, raise professional standards, and give the best cricketers some semblance of security. Players such as Garth would no longer need to move across the world to become professionals. Women's national teams would no longer depend on the wealth of the men's sides to have a chance of receiving significant investment.

Joyce argues that the investment would pay for itself through the increase in quality of teams, the greater global competitiveness, and the development of the sport in new markets. 'You can pump money into the women's game at a much lower rate than the men's game and get a much higher rate of return.'

Women's sport is developing rapidly. In women's football, the growth in recent years has been exponential. Before 2000, Germany had one professional women's league, the US was just starting one, and there was very little else. Today, there are professional women's leagues across Europe and on every other continent. Much of this has been achieved with very limited financial support.

Similarly, relatively small investments today could produce large dividends for women's cricket in the future. And the ICC could afford it: ring-fencing $50 million a year for the women's game would amount to $400 million over an eight-year ICC cycle – barely one-fifth of the ICC's broadcasting rights revenue from 2016 to 2023.

* * *

As we explored in Chapter 6, women were involved in the early days of cricket only to find themselves excluded by men at the beginning of the Victorian era. They struggled to develop their game in the 20th century – men tended to be either apathetic to the women's game or, often, active opponents.

Misogyny has not only affected cricket. In 1921, the FA banned women's football in England. A comparable ban in cricket would have been fatal, since it would have left the women without a ground on which to play. Women were careful about how strongly they advocated for equal rights – even as men limited their access to facilities, women cricketers tried to maintain friendly relations with the male authorities. Lord's did not let women play at the ground until 1976 (the 50th anniversary of the founding of the WCA), perhaps motivated by Rachael Heyhoe Flint's widely publicised threat to sue MCC under the Sex Discrimination Act. Women were not allowed to play again at Lord's until 1987. It took even longer for MCC to grant women the right to become members of MCC – after failed votes in 1991 and February 1998, the members finally consented to accept women members in September 1998, 211 years after the club was formed.

What were the grounds for this male obstructionism? It's tempting to fall back on the idea that it was just the fault of a few reactionary old men. But there was an entire system that held women back, including theories that were paraded as scientific.

Men and women share some traits more or less equally; in others, they differ. The technical term for clear-cut significant differences by sex is sexual dimorphism. It would be hard to distinguish a man's ear or nose from a woman's ear or nose, but men do tend to have larger hearts, and women tend to produce antibodies at a faster rate. In humans, the differences are not nearly so great as those between, say, a peacock and a peahen. In other animals, the ratios are reversed: the female little white-shouldered bat is so much larger than the male that she was for some time considered a separate species. The history of humans provides endless examples where women have been able to pass for men, and vice versa. Scientific consensus is now moving away altogether from the idea that all humans belong to one of two sexes.

Darwin's Theory of Evolution, published in 1859 just as the sports culture in England and America was booming, provided ammunition for those wanting to claim that women are somehow ill-suited to playing sport. The idea that women were too frail for vigorous exercise had been 'established' for some time before Darwin. As an influential guide to women's education put it in 1836, 'the constitution of women bears only moderate exercise'. But combining this prejudice with Darwinism endowed it with special power. If purported differences between the sexes were the product of millions of years of evolution, how could the science be gainsaid?

While women's frailty was a standard trope of the 19th century, the 20th century changed emphasis, basing its claim on measurable differences – in essence, a statistical approach. The undeniable fact that *on average* women are shorter and have less upper-body strength and lung capacity than men was used to suggest a physiological unsuitability for sport at the highest level. But it emerged over the course of the century that the effect of these differences had been exaggerated. It is true that there is a gap between world record measures for men and women, but these gaps narrowed significantly between the 1950s and

1990s as women's participation in sport increased. Clearly, the gap could not have been hardwired in its entirety.

More importantly, the difference between men and women *on average* is in most dimensions statistically insignificant. In 2005 Janet Shibley Hyde of the University of Wisconsin reviewed dozens of studies and reported gender differences for 125 different traits. She found that in the overwhelming majority of cases, the differences within each gender were so large that they dwarfed any difference between genders. For example, there was no significant difference in measures of balance, grip strength, vertical jump, sprinting, and flexibility between men and women, although the differences in throwing velocity and distance were significant. Science was long used disingenuously to justify a lack of support for women's sport. In reality, it provides no such justification.

But culture is hard to change. It is still frequently argued that the small average differences between men and women translate to a significant difference in the quality of competition at the highest level. Men's sports, then, are said to be more popular because men are simply better at sport. The obvious counter-examples are women's tennis and golf. After a long struggle for recognition, female tennis players now earn the same prize money at Grand Slam tournaments as men. Just as importantly, women's tennis is almost as popular with viewers as men's. In golf, women have not quite reached parity; US TV ratings suggest that the leading women's tournaments reach an audience that is about half the size of the men's. Still, that is a very large audience, and the numbers justify the multimillion earnings that the top women can generate.

* * *

The history of women's sport is a history of exclusion. Apart from a few cases, women have been actively and continuously either discouraged or simply barred from participation. Men's cricket may not be the worst offender, but women have struggled to gain recognition by the male administrators of the game, as scholars such as Rafaelle Nicholson and Philippa Velija have documented.

Today's cricket authorities will point to extensive programmes, initiatives and commitments that are intended to change matters. But there is also evidence that, in some respects, the greater involvement of male-dominated governing bodies in women's cricket has not helped. In 2014, Velija, Aarti Tatna, and Anne Flintoff argued that the merger of the WCA and the ECB in 1998 might have undermined women's progress in English cricket. They acknowledge that the merger in theory gave the women greater access to resources, but they point out that men dominate the joint administration. As of 2021, the ECB board has 12 members and only four are women – all are non-executive, while the three executive directors are all men. It took 16 years after the ECB took control of the women's game to introduce professional contracts.

If women are to be treated equally, it is necessary to recognise that their current disadvantages are the direct or indirect result of a history of unequal treatment. The case is clearest in football: the official ban on the woman's game was not overturned until 1971. For half a century, women were excluded from the world's most popular sport. The ban was initiated precisely because women's football threatened to become popular – so the men's Football League lobbied the FA to get rid of the competition. Were such a thing to happen today, it would be a clear violation of competition law, and the FA and Football League could be punished with a substantial fine. By law, such fines can amount to up to 10% of total revenues (not profits). For Premier League clubs today, that would be around £500 million.

Here's the kicker: banning women's football was probably illegal in 1921 as well. It was, after all, a restraint of trade, and these have been illegal in England since at least 1711. But since women had only just won the vote, they were scarcely in a position to mount an extended legal campaign. And by now, the statute of limitations has long expired.

But you can and ought to right a wrong even if you are not legally required to do so. Without the ban, women's football in England might have developed like women's tennis or golf did. Justice requires not only that wrongs be acknowledged but also that amends be made: women's sports, in other words, are due reparations.

The concept of reparations for past wrongs has a long history, however vociferously their opponents protest against the idea. The British were deeply involved in the slave trade, Australian settlers committed egregious crimes against

Indigenous Australians, and we are all familiar with apartheid's poisonous legacy. Clearly, it is not possible to go back and set right every wrong, but it is possible to develop a programme that seeks to address and reverse at least some of the adverse consequences of historic wrongs. The cricket authorities could begin with the necessary first step: acknowledge responsibility. The second step, reparations, would be a matter of negotiation. But $50 million a year would not be a bad start.

13

WHY DOESN'T SOUTH AFRICA PRODUCE MORE BLACK BATTERS?

In 2012, Thami Tsolekile was South Africa's No.2 Test wicketkeeper, behind the veteran Mark Boucher. Tsolekile had played three Tests in 2004 but at the age of 31, he was a different cricketer. His wicketkeeping had long been regarded as outstanding. Now, Tsolekile was scoring runs prolifically too.

In 2011/12, Tsolekile averaged 53.00 in 11 games in South African first-class cricket. While he had dipped the previous season, averaging 25.54, Tsolekile had also excelled in 2009/10, averaging 58.10. He had also starred for South Africa A, the national second-string: as captain, Tsolekile made back-to-back centuries against Bangladesh A in 2010. He performed impressively against the full-strength Australian touring side in 2011, hitting 27 and 58 – the second top score in both innings – against a bowling attack including the Test trio Mitchell Johnson, Peter Siddle and Nathan Lyon.

Tsolekile was picked for South Africa's tour to England as back up to Boucher, who planned to retire after the series. It was widely assumed that Tsolekile would become Boucher's long-term replacement, a role that seemed his after securing a national central contract in April. 'We think he is ready to be a successor,' declared Andrew Hudson, the national convener of selectors.

In a warm-up game against Somerset, Boucher was keeping wicket when a ball from Imran Tahir hit the stumps. The bail ricocheted into Boucher's left eye, lacerating his eyeball. The injury forced him to retire immediately.

Tsolekile had been groomed to take over the role: a wicketkeeper-batter coming in at No.7. Yet when Boucher was injured, South Africa immediately changed their structure. The tour management – captain Graeme Smith, head coach Gary Kirsten and the touring selector – gave star batter A. B. de Villiers the gloves instead. Kirsten announced the decision before consulting with the other selectors. The change of tactics, with De Villiers acting as wicketkeeper while batting at No.5, allowed J-P Duminy – a batter who could also bowl useful off-spin – to come into the side at seven. South Africa won the series 2–0 in England to become the No.1-ranked Test side in the world. They promptly triumphed in Australia, too.

Tsolekile was present throughout those trips – but did not play a single Test. According to him, chief selector Hudson had promised him a slot against New Zealand in the subsequent home summer. Instead, South Africa retained De Villiers as wicketkeeper, although he preferred to play as a specialist batter. Tsolekile's year ended being told that he was not good enough to bat at No.7, he was dropped from the Test squad altogether.

In 2013, Tsolekile scored 159 for South Africa A against an Australia A attack that included Josh Hazlewood, Fawad Ahmed and Nathan Coulter-Nile. His final game for South Africa A came one month later; Tsolekile never secured a fourth Test cap.

In 2020, Tsolekile called his non-selection 'pure racism'. He publicly challenged Smith live on TV, 'There were red flags and you weren't aware. Were you not aware that I was the best keeper-batter in the country from 2010 to 2015, but was continuously overlooked … Were you also not aware that during my time with the Proteas under your leadership, A.B. de Villiers said, "I don't want to be a keeper, I want to become the best batter in the world."'

The controversy over Tsolekile's South Africa career has focused on the way he was shunned after Boucher's retirement. But Tsolekile already had a compelling case to be selected in the previous two years: in Boucher's last 15 Tests, he averaged 22.23, mustering just two half-centuries. Yet all the while – helped by his seniority and playing pedigree, and perhaps by his close relationship with captain Smith – his suitability to bat at No.7 in Test cricket went unquestioned.

* * *

Tsolekile believes that he suffered from discrimination, and that he was ultimately not selected because of his race. Starting in 2020, a social justice committee set up by Cricket South Africa revealed shocking levels of racial abuse in the national team set up. There's no doubt that such a toxic environment is likely to adversely affect the development of players who suffer racial prejudice. But here we address a slightly different issue – was there evidence of prejudice in selection based on the statistical performance of Black players?

The economic analysis of discrimination in sport has a long history. Sport is a fertile area to analyse systemic patterns of this kind. In most jobs, it's hard to obtain productivity data. Not so in cricket: productivity is measured in runs and wickets.

In this case, we wanted to ascertain whether there was evidence of discrimination in the selection of players for South African cricket teams by looking at past performance. If selection is based purely on merit, and if merit is demonstrated by performance, then performance statistics *alone* should determine selection, and a player's racial background should be irrelevant.

The data was supplied to us by Shaun Rheeder, the director of 12th Man Analytics, and Gustav Venter, the head of the Centre for Sport Leadership at Stellenbosch University. The data reports annual performance statistics: innings batted, runs scored, balls faced and not outs for batters, balls bowled, wickets and runs conceded for bowlers in all South African first-class and international cricket from 2004/05 until 2019/20.

At professional level, cricket remains an overwhelmingly white sport in South Africa. Although three quarters of the population describes themselves as Black, Black South Africans constitute only 22% of all professional players. About 9% of the population identify as 'coloured' (this is the term commonly used by the South African government to refer to people with multi-ethnic heritage), and another 9% as white, with 2.5% describing themselves as Indian. Yet 27% of professional cricketers over this period were coloured or Indian, and 51% were white.

This disparity intensifies at international level. Only 11% of Test players in our data were Black, and 61% were white. In ODIs and T20Is the figures for Black players were 12% and 13%; the share of white players was 63% and 64% respectively.

This distribution is a legacy of the segregation practised first by British rulers and then under apartheid. Since the end of apartheid, Cricket South Africa

(CSA) has embraced a commitment to diversity. Its current mission statement describes a 'Transformation Philosophy', which seeks both transformation and redress – that is, restitution for the imbalances created by the old regimes.

Since CSA is also committed to winning games, equitable player development strategies are crucial; otherwise, the team's composition will continue to reflect two centuries of racist structures. Selectors also need to face their own biases, both open and unconscious. After all, even people who consider themselves to be completely free of prejudice can exhibit systematic, unacknowledged racial preferences in their choices. Is there evidence of bias, either conscious or unconscious, in the selection of players for South Africa?

To answer this question, we developed a statistical model to predict international selection in a given season, based upon the players' cumulative performance over previous seasons. Players were divided into three categories. Wicketkeepers could be identified directly; classifying a player as a batter or a bowler was based on the number of balls faced in a season (more than 1000), or the number of overs delivered (more than 400). On this basis, 45% of players in the database were specialist batters, 13% wicketkeepers, and 32% bowlers. The remaining 10% of unclassified players were discarded from the analysis.

Our statistical model relies on regression analysis – the data analyst's weapon of choice. Regression analysis reduces the relationship between the variables measured to an equation, and identifies the best fit by calculating the minimum possible error. Devised mainly by the mathematician Carl Friedrich Gauss over 200 years ago, the method and its variants has become the mainstay of data analysis in social science. Its attraction lies in its capacity for a causal interpretation – 'if X increases by 1%, then Y can be expected to increase by Z%' – although correlation is not causation. We use a particular type of regression, called a logistic regression, to estimate the probability of selection for the national team based on batting and bowling in *previous* seasons.

The regression analysis shows that the statistics that are most important for determining selection in any given season reflect previous performance at international – not domestic – level. Once selected, performance in the national team dominates the likelihood of staying in the national team. Maybe this is as it should be, but it is also Tsolekile's tragedy – had he been given the opportunity, there was a good chance he could have kept his place.

To illustrate the power of this incumbency effect, we ran the model using performance across all formats to predict selection and then ran the model separately including only domestic performance. The model for Test match selection predicted 190 cases where a player had a greater than 50% chance of selection; in 151 of these cases the player was selected – an 80% success rate, with some cases where players were not selected relating to injury or retirement.

A number of factors not in our model might reasonably be expected to contribute to a call-up: for instance, current season performance, quality of opposition in games, fielding and wicketkeeping success, personality and leadership qualities. Despite not controlling for these factors, the 80% success rate suggests that the full model is quite powerful. But when we restrict the model, allowing for selection to be determined by domestic performances only (omitting the influence of international performance), we find just 78 cases where the model's predicted probability of selection was over 50%, and of these, not all were selected. There are 277 players who played for the national team in the data; based on domestic performance only, the model gave a probability of over 50% to only 43 of these players. When the data does not fit the model closely, then not only does the model's success rate fall, but also the ability to assign a probability of over 50% to any player falls. The model results for ODI and T20I selection were similar.

What did the model say about the selection of Black players? We produced several versions, depending on which factors were included. As a rule of thumb, we included only those variables that were 'statistically' significant at the 5% level or better. This is statistical jargon for the idea that the results capture real differences, not random fluctuations.

We did not find evidence in any of the model variants we looked at that being Black made it less likely that you would be selected for an international team. This applied to the Test, ODI and T20I sides. In the versions of the model that we preferred, because they appeared to provide the best fit for the data, we found no evidence of bias one way or the other. Setting aside individual cases, the data does not suggest that there is measurable discrimination in the selection process. The data for coloured and Indian players endorses this conclusion.

At the same time, the analysis undermines one common refrain in South African cricket: that Black cricketers, especially batters, have needed to perform less well than white players to be selected since the team's readmission to cricket. There is a case for discrimination in favour of Black cricketers, to redress the historic injustices they have faced. Opponents of the policy argue that this has been at work in the selection of players for the national side. 'The transformation policy, I can see what they are trying to achieve, but whether they achieve the end goal of a merit selection at [Test] level remains to be seen,' prominent former South African batter Barry Richards said in 2017. Whether positive discrimination would be right or wrong, we found no evidence of it in the data, any more than we found evidence of systematic discrimination against Black players.

It is certainly very possible that specific Black South African batters were overlooked on account of their race. But, in general, we were unable to prove that systemic discrimination against Black batters vying for national selection has occurred. And so, to understand why, as of the start of 2022, there had been just a solitary Test century scored by a Black African batter – by way of comparison, there had been 214 centuries scored by white batters since readmission – it is necessary to look beyond the national team.

* * *

Since South Africa's readmission to international cricket in 1992, Black African batters have performed starkly differently than the bowlers. As of the start of 2022, Temba Bavuma's hundred against England at Cape Town in 2016 is the only Test century by a Black African batter, but there have been 30 five-wicket hauls taken by Black bowlers.

This contrast in the output of Black African batters and bowlers has been mirrored at domestic level. In 21 out of 22 seasons between 1999 and 2021, there were more Black African bowlers among the top 50 wicket-takers in domestic cricket than Black African batters among the top 50 run-scorers.

In 2004/05, CSA undertook a fundamental reform and created six entirely professional 'franchises' across all three formats at the pinnacle of the domestic game. Operating below the franchises were 15 semi-professional provincial teams which functioned as the nurseries for the franchises. A study by Rheeder and Venter found that, from 2016 to 2020, the median batting average of Black African batters selected for their franchise debut was 23.4 at provincial level; the median for white batters was 41.9. Black African batters also tended to have played fewer matches. Black African batters batting in the top six in franchise cricket – excluding nightwatchmen – averaged a combined 27.48. In the same period, white batters averaged 37.65, while players defined as Indian or coloured averaged 35.20. Cricket South Africa were slow to act upon the underrepresentation of Black African cricketers. In 2015, Haroon Lorgat, then the chief executive, said that the board got 'complacent' after the emergence of Makhaya Ntini as a leading fast bowler.

Franchises have tended to select more Black African bowlers than batters. Rheeder and Venter found that there were more than 50% more Black bowlers than batters selected since 2004/05. This is despite there being more batting than bowling slots in a team, and so more opportunities in theory to select Black batters. The franchises would no doubt point to the differences in performance: the Black African bowlers took 65 five-wicket hauls – 13% of all five-wicket hauls. The Black African batters scored only 42 centuries – 6% of all centuries.

CSA have become markedly more ambitious in their transformation efforts in recent years. From 2004/05 to 2012/13, each franchise had to pick four players classified as being of colour, but there was no compulsion to select any Black African players. That changed in 2013/14, when sides had to pick one Black African player. With the board frustrated at the slow pace of transformation, from 2014/15 the target increased to five players of colour, including two Black Africans; from 2015/16, it increased to six players of colour, including three Black Africans. Any franchises who fail to meet these requirements must ask CSA for special permission; the board launched an inquiry after Cape Cobras missed transformation targets in a game in 2019. So what was the impact of the increase in the quota?

Table 13.1: A comparison of batting and bowling performance of Black African players in franchise cricket before and after the changes to the compulsory selection rules

Bowling performance for all players in the Franchise era broken down into Black African players and others before and after the 2013/14 transformation change:

Player category	Overs bowled	5 wicket hauls	Bowling average	Bowling strike rate
Pre 2013/14				
Black African	10391	37	30,77	57,62
Rest	68526	243	31,11	60,55
Post 2013/14				
Black African	13977	25	37,96	65,47
Rest	43657	182	30,28	57,28

Batting performances for all players in the Franchise era broken down into Black African players and others before and after the 2013/14 transformation change:

Player category	Innings batted	Centuries scored	Batting average	Batting strike rate
Pre 2013/14				
Black African	399	10	26,59	46,51
Rest	5939	367	34,74	49,84
Post 2013/14				
Black African	919	30	26,63	46,95
Rest	3766	293	38,22	51,54

*Only batters who batted in the top 7 and who did not have an average batting position lower than 8 over their career were considered.

Source: Rheeder and Venter (2020), 'Transformation Success in South African Franchise First-Class Cricket: A brief statistical analysis'

The results are perhaps surprising. With an increased share of appearances, the average performance of Black bowlers has deteriorated slightly. Yet the average performance of the Black batters has remained steady and actually improved on some measures. This is illustrated in Table 13.1. The upper panel shows the number of five-wicket hauls, bowling average and strike rate for Black African players and the rest before and after the reform. The share of five-wicket hauls is roughly unchanged, but the average runs conceded per wicket and the number of balls required to take a wicket has increased noticeably for the Black bowlers while being largely unchanged for the rest.

The lower panel of Table 13.1 shows that Black batters increased their share of centuries, from under 3% to more than 9%. Batting averages and strike rates, while remaining lower than other ethnic groups, do not appear to have been affected by the quota reform. It is true that the batting performance of the rest has improved somewhat, but the changes are not large. Imposing a requirement to increase the number of Black batters does not appear to have led to a decline in the overall average of Black batters. For batters, at least, the results seem to support the use of quotas. While the returns of Black batters continue to lag behind other players in domestic cricket, there is cause for optimism.

* * *

To many, it was the greatest symbol of how far South Africa had come. On the evening of 2 November, 2019 in Yokohama, Siya Kolisi lifted the World Cup: he was the first Black South African captain in rugby union, traditionally a bastion of white privilege.

Two months later, Kolisi was welcomed to Newlands Cricket Ground. While he basked in the crowd's acclaim during a Test against England, CSA was deep in crisis about its own lack of racial progress. Four years earlier, at the same ground against the same opponents, Bavuma had scored the first Test century by a Black African for South Africa. It was also a symbolic moment. 'When I made my debut I came to be aware of the significance; it was not just me making my debut but also being a model for Black African kids,' Bavuma said. 'In achieving this milestone, it will strengthen that example.'

As Kolisi was being lauded at Cape Town, Bavuma was digesting being dropped from South Africa's side, which now featured only one Black African. Ironically, a couple of hours before Kolisi took to the field, CSA had issued a press release reiterating their commitment to transformation.

'This is something that goes far beyond the game of cricket,' CSA's president Chris Nenzani said. The paucity of Black batters is best understood as reflecting the socioeconomic conditions most young Black people grow up in, a point emphasised by Ashwin Desai in *Reverse Sweep*, his history of post-apartheid South African cricket. Eliminating all traces of racism would, he argues, 'mean a massive investment in the grass roots of the game'. Sport is intrinsically related to the political economy at large. 'If there are no pitches, no decent schools, no decent health care, that's government's problem, not cricket's problem,' says Omphile Ramela, the first Black African to score a first-class double century.

Elite batters tend to come from wealthier backgrounds than bowlers. The root cause of the paucity of Black batters in South Africa and of the disparities in the performance of Black batters and bowlers is the economic inequalities between ethnic groups.

Economic disparities are 'fundamentally the crux of this problem,' says Ramela, who has a master's in economics from Stellenbosch University. 'Where we are as a country, socioeconomically, cricket is not going to be any parents' first investment. Unfortunately from a government perspective, the programmes are not as strong as they should be. So there's that element where if you don't have a strong government, your decline in GDP per capita also precipitates a decline in sport.

'When South Africa's GDP per capita increases, we will produce more cricketers across the different groups because more middle-class people can take up the game, and more Black people can take up the game. Most importantly, when your GDP per capita improves, the working class can actually take up the game because there's just a bit more resources floating around.'

In 2018, The World Bank declared South Africa to be the world's most unequal society, with the top 10% owning 71% of the nation's assets. Inequality remains intertwined with race: the bottom 60% of the population controlled only 7% of the country's net wealth. Remarkably, inequality in South Africa, as measured by the Gini coefficient (the standard economic measure of inequality), has actually increased since the end of apartheid in 1994. Data compiled in 2015 found that 55% of South Africans lived on less than $83 a month, which is classed as being in poverty; 25% lived on less than $37 a month, below the food poverty line.

* * *

Growing up in Durban, Lungi Ngidi's parents were maintenance workers at Kloof Junior Primary School. As the family also lived at the school, Ngidi became familiar with cricket early on. 'Kids would come with their fathers and play every Saturday and I would just sit and watch,' he recalls. 'One day I was invited down to play. I think I was about seven at the time. That's just where my love for cricket took off.'

Ngidi secured a sports scholarship to Kloof, and then another to Highbury Preparatory School. At the age of 14, he won a sports scholarship to Hilton College, one of South Africa's elite schools: it charges pupils more than US $20,000 to attend. 'Now I had facilities where I could actually grow my skills and could practise and play,' Ngidi says. 'Without those facilities, I wouldn't be where I am today.'

The data emphatically suggests that Ngidi is right. The South African sports scientist Habib Noorbhai has calculated that 40 schools have produced the majority of Proteas cricketers since readmission: either boys' private schools or the so-called 'Model C' schools that were open to white children only under apartheid and remain predominantly white.

These schools have also produced many of the leading Black African cricketers since apartheid ended. Kagiso Rabada, the son of a doctor and lawyer, attended St Stithians College, which has produced many international cricketers and rugby players. Andile Phehlukwayo won a bursary to Glenwood High School, a boarding school in Durban. Lutho Sipamla, the son of an insurance broker, attended Grey High School – perhaps the most famous sports school in South Africa. For all the focus upon race, another interlinked divide runs through South African cricket: a class structure that has made the country dependent on a tiny number of schools for the bulk of international players.

'It's different when you don't have any of those facilities and are then asked to go to trials and then perform at the same level as someone who's been training the whole week,' Ngidi says. Improving access to such facilities would, Ngidi thinks, both help the transformation process and help the national team.

'I don't think it's fair and I don't think it's a fair representation of the kids' skill or talent – and therefore that's why we need those facilities to be put in place to make it equal for everyone. It is different if someone can wake up, have a full breakfast and get driven to the trials yet another kid wakes up and has two pieces of bread and has to take public transport the whole way there. By the time he gets there he's probably walked close to 5–10 kilometres. I don't think they're starting at the same level.'

In 2001 the *Star* newspaper described the world of one aspiring Black cricketer, Khotso 'Sonnyboy' Letshele:

Nineteen-year-old Sonnyboy lives in the Kagiso township in Johannesburg's West Rand. While talented in many sports, Sonnyboy took to cricket because of 'food', the orange juice and biscuits provided by coaches were welcome because of the dire financial circumstances of the family. When he was chosen for various representative teams Sonnyboy's teammates remarked on the large amounts of food that he ate. His reply was that he was eating for the following day because he could not be guaranteed a meal. This was only half in jest because his parents and elder brother are unemployed. Sonnyboy has to take three taxis and travel 45km on a two-and-a-half hours journey to get to training. The Gauteng Cricket Board provides him transport fares because he cannot afford this.

A majority of government schools in South Africa do not play cricket. Indeed, some government schools do not have a budget for sport at all. 'The key thing is the education system in South Africa,' says Max Jordaan, the transformation and stakeholder relations executive of CSA. 'The location of the best facilities are still in and amongst those who were previously in privileged positions ... The main thing is about facilities in disadvantaged areas, coaching and regular competition at school level.'

These disparities disproportionately affect batters from underprivileged areas. 'Batting is a resource-intensive exercise,' says Ramela. He believes that producing batters essentially requires three resources. The first is cash – it can cost perhaps 5000 rand to buy a good set of equipment to bat, including a bat, gloves and pads. 'That's way above the minimum wage, if we can call it that in South Africa,' he laments. For bowlers, or those playing football or rugby, a 500-rand pair of boots is likely to suffice.

The second resource is facilities. As a boy in the Johannesburg township of Soweto, Ramela began playing on sand before graduating to play on tennis courts and then concrete nets at Soweto Cricket Club. All that changed when he secured a scholarship to the private schools St Peter's Prep and St John's College in Johannesburg.

The third resource Ramela identifies is time. 'To produce a batter you need someone who's going to be devoted to throwing to the kid – whether it's their parents, whether it's somebody at their school. Young kids need the volume to just hit the ball, learn hand-eye coordination, and just to get ingrained in the finesse of batting.'

All of this explains South Africa's dependence on a tiny minority of schools to produce the bulk of the Proteas side. For an underprivileged child, 'given those constraints that you're faced with, then your best bet is actually getting the scholarship,' Ramela reflects.

If the South African team is to be weaned off their reliance on elite schools, 'we require far more investment into cricket facilities of quality standard in our schools in disadvantaged areas,' Jordaan says. 'The preparation of a player doesn't take six months or one year – it's a lifestyle and it's a lifestyle influenced by your environment. The opportunities to pursue positive lifestyles comes from many, many years of preparation and coaching – good coaching, good surfaces, regular competition. Sport is a microcosm of society. If you have inequalities in society you have inequalities in sport.'

With extraordinary talent, hard work and luck, it is still occasionally possible for international cricketers to emerge from socioeconomic deprivation. The story of Ntini, the son of a cattle herder, is frequently offered as proof. He was discovered bowling in torn shoes by a talent development officer in Mdingi, a township in rural eastern Cape, aged 14. Ntini was loaned a pair of trainers to attend a net session 10 miles away, which led to his selection for a junior cricket festival, setting him on his path to play 100 Tests.

Raw talent like Ntini's can occasionally overcome enormous obstacles. But, aged 14, Ntini also benefited from a scholarship to the plush Dale College – at the time, virtually an all-white school. He finally had access to facilities, competition and training time.

South African cricket has essentially picked only players who either grew up well off or, like Ntini, obtained scholarships. Excluding those who later earned scholarships to leading schools, not a single boy educated in townships or rural areas has gone on to represent South Africa since readmission, according to Noorbhai. It is a statistic that highlights the scale of inequality on the cricket field. As Noorbhai writes, 'South African cricketers continue to originate mainly from cricket schools and middle-class families with exceptional facilities and high coaching standards.'

* * *

Those Black players who have succeeded in South African cricket have tended to be bowlers. This seems to apply equally to the men's and the women's game. One explanation is role models: Ntini was the first Black African Test cricketer ever. Before Rabada's Test debut in 2015, Ntini was the only Black African to be a regular member of the side. Another explanation is institutional racism, which drives Black players to focus on pace bowling.

'Positional bias' is a recognised phenomenon in many sports. American football, like most American sports, did not admit Black players until the 1940s. Once the ban was lifted, a steadily increasing number of Black players came to dominate the game. The one position they long struggled to reach was the quarterback – the playmaker of the game. There is considerable evidence that racial bias held back Black quarterbacks. One study found that, when controlling for factors such as performance, age and experience, Black quarterbacks in the NFL were twice as likely to be dropped from the team as white quarterbacks performing equally well.

In American football, players have described their experience of being slotted into certain positions, and discouraged from playing in others, due to their race. 'In football, the "thinking" positions down the middle – quarterback, center, linebacker – were the ones that we weren't allowed to play,' Warren Moon, the first African-American quarterback inducted into the Pro Football Hall of Fame, told the website The Undefeated in 2017. 'There was a stereotype that we weren't capable of succeeding at certain positions. If you played those positions in college and you got drafted, you knew you were probably going to get moved in the NFL. Supposedly, we weren't smart enough or had the leadership qualities.'

Similar racial stereotyping may help to explain the paucity of Black African batters. 'There's a stereotype that Black players should be bowlers,' the promising Black batter Sinethemba Qeshile said in 2019. 'The first thing we're taught is how to bowl. Not a lot of guys actually get taught how to carry a bat until much later. Also, many of us come from disadvantaged areas which makes it difficult to get spotted. For a long time, most scouts wouldn't actually look at the poorer communities which meant you had to stand out even more in order to get somewhere in the game.'

Ramela believes that young batters are expected to play in a way deemed to be technically correct, which may lead scouts and coaches to overlook players from poorer economic backgrounds, who are unlikely to have been coached in the traditional tenets of batting. 'If somebody comes and is somewhat unorthodox, we actually turn that kid away, we don't look at the fundamentals of batting which is hand-eye coordination and the ability to strike a ball … The stereotype has been perpetuated by people who actually fail to understand that you need to look for talent, rather than a particular style of batter, or someone who looks like a replica of the past.'

* * *

There certainly are promising young Black batting talents, such as former South Africa Under-19 player Qeshile, who made his T20 international debut in 2019, shortly after turning 20, and Wandile Makwetu, a wicketkeeper-batter who captained South Africa Under-19s in the 2018 Under-19 World Cup. Yet it is revealing that both Qeshile and Makwetu attended elite schools – Hudson Park and St Stithians College – that rank among the 10 schools to have produced the most cricketers for South Africa since 1994, according to Noorbhai's research.

Even if Qeshile and Makwetu become international regulars, this would merely conceal the deeper issues that prevent more Black Africans from succeeding as batters in professional cricket. Given that the number of South Africans in poverty has actually increased in recent years, rising from nine to 16.6 million between 2017 and June 2020, 'one could argue that this challenge is becoming more difficult to solve,' Rheeder and Venter said.

Damningly, Ramela believes that cricket programmes and facilities in areas like Soweto have declined since he started playing in the 1990s. 'The programmes have diminished in the townships,' he says.

Given the limits of CSA's power, what could they do? The current policy – trying to build the participation base at grassroots level – makes sense. Ultimately, this will increase the chances of more Black children securing sports scholarships to elite schools, where they will be exposed to an environment that allows them to make good on their talents, just as happened with Kolisi, who received a scholarship to Grey High School.

'You have talent factories spewing out a talent distribution which reflects the social inequalities of South Africa,' Rheeder and Venter observe. 'The transformation challenge in sporting codes that have traditionally had a significant class disparity, like rugby union and cricket – not just in South Africa – are essentially a reflection of the socioeconomic situation in the environment within which the sport is being played.' Based on the underlying economic disparities, and recent performances of Black batters in the domestic game, Rheeder and Venter are not optimistic of meaningful change in the coming years.

'At the developmental level it's a socioeconomic problem of opening the game up and creating opportunities,' Ramela says. 'The most important thing to do is to actually make sure that we can sustain programmes in the township – where we have good coaches, decent infrastructure, and the coaches are there to invest in the kids. You need to be investing in really good coaches at youth level primarily for talent identification.' With strategic investment in townships, Ramela says, players from such areas will not need to get scholarships to have a pathway into the professional game. 'The only way we're gonna produce sustainably is if South African cricket sustains cricket in the townships, because that's where the numbers are.'

Ramela is right to stress the necessity of improving grassroots infrastructure. There is no indication that the power of South Africa's elite schools to producing athletes is diminishing. If the objective is simply to produce more Black players in the medium term, a pragmatic strategy would involve searching for talent in the townships and then channelling it through the elite schools. But in the long-term, only much deeper reform, to spread opportunities beyond a tiny minority of schools, will make cricket in South Africa fairer, and ensure the team are representative of South African society.

PART FOUR
PLAYER PERFORMANCE

14

THE VALUE OF BATTING V BOWLING

In 1977, Kerry Packer launched his cricket circus, World Series Cricket, which changed the face of the game. He hired most of the world's top Test talent of the time.

What did it take to lure them away from their existing contracts? Surprisingly little. Generally, the answer was A\$25,000 a year – that's about A\$150,000 (or £85,000) in today's money. That's what Packer paid England captain Tony Greig and his international teammates Alan Knott, Derek Underwood and John Snow, the West Indians Viv Richards, Alvin Kallicharran, Joel Garner and Gordon Greenidge, and the Pakistan star Zaheer Abbas. The top Australians got a little more – A\$35,000 for Greg Chappell and Dennis Lillee, A\$30,000 for Jeff Thomson, who ultimately withdrew, having been paid the first installment of his fee. Players not considered quite as elite got less.

If that all seems modest by today's standards, it was also modest by the standards of the day. In 1977, the average salary of 650 Major League Baseball players was US \$75,000, the equivalent of US \$323,000 or £233,000 in today's money. The top 70 players, the number of World Series cricketers, would have earned quite a bit more: the highest-paid player in baseball at the time was Mike Schmidt, third baseman for the Philadelphia Phillies, who in that year signed a contract for US \$560,000 a year (\$2.5 million in 2021 dollars). Two Mike Schmidts, in other words, would have paid for the entire wage bill of World Series Cricket.

Cricketers have long been badly paid relative to the biggest team sports – the American major leagues and football. The advent of the Indian Premier League changed all that. Franchises bid for the service of players, making many of the stars among the highest in the world of sports, at least on a *per game* basis. If you're not a professional cricketer, you're probably not that fussed about their salaries. But if you're a statistician, your ears perk up: salary data is full of information. Now, we're going to try to see just what kind of insights we can glean from IPL salaries.

Before examining how batters and bowlers are paid in cricket, we start by showing how this logic applies in baseball – another bat-and-ball sport, but one with a much longer tradition of statistical analysis. (Some readers may prefer to skip to page 191 when we apply this analysis to cricket.)

Baseball is a struggle between pitchers and batters in the same way that cricket pits bowlers against batters. It's also a multibillion-dollar business, and teams compete to hire players to win games. Conveniently, we have a lot of economic data about Major League Baseball (MLB) – far and away the most important form of professional competition in baseball, in which 30 teams compete annually. Comparisons are easy both because the teams are playing in just one competition, but also because players are not restricted by nationality rules that limit them to one employer, as is the case with international cricket – historically a crucial factor in holding down cricketers' salaries.

MLB teams have a limit of 25 active players in their main squads. Around half of these tend to be pitchers, reflecting the demands of the role. Few pitchers now complete an entire game, and a starting pitcher needs a week's rest between games. So with teams playing four to five games per week during the seven-month season, pitcher rotation is essential.

To compare batter and pitcher salaries, we consulted the comprehensive online database created by Sean Lahman. Batters always appear to have been paid better. Since 1986, the average MLB salary has risen from around half a million dollars a year to around five million dollars. During this period the average batter earned 10–25% more than the average pitcher. Averages can be misleading – the hefty salaries for the superstars, which account for a large slice of the total spend, skew the numbers. But if we just focus on the all-time top 50 player contracts in MLB (ranging from $130 million to $426 million, typically over a five- to 10-year period), only one-third of these were for pitchers. No pitcher appeared in the top 10.

What might explain this inequality? Because salaries are known quantities in professional baseball, and player performance statistics are easily compared, we can compare the value of batters and pitchers. Pitchers in baseball are typically rated according to their Earned Run Average (ERA), which roughly means the average number of runs a pitcher would give up in an entire game based on the inning in which they actually pitched. We can use regression analysis to estimate the relationship between pitcher salaries and their ERA in the previous season, focusing on free agents who pitched at least one inning per game (there are nine in a game). The salary data covers 1985 to 2016 and includes just over 1000 observations (each observation is one player in one season). The range of ERA in the data runs from 1.6 to 6.8, with a mean of around four; 95% of free-agent regular pitchers have an ERA between 2.2 and 5.7. A lower ERA is better (fewer runs conceded) – unsurprisingly, a lower ERA correlates with a higher salary. ERA can account for around 20% of the variation in pitcher salaries.

To become a free agent, you must complete six years of service in the Major League. To last that long, you have to be a star. On average, free agent pitchers were paid more than three times the average salary. According to the regression model, you would expect this salary level for players with an ERA of roughly 4. But free agents capable of producing a lower ERA get higher salaries, and those that produce higher ERAs get lower salaries. There's a measurable trade-off.

Not only can we calculate this trade-off, we can also identify the equivalent trade-off for batters, using another venerable baseball statistic called Slugging Percentage. This is not actually a percentage but rather a measure of how many bases the player gained per at bat (or per innings, to use cricket terminology). A hit may result in a single (with the batter reaching first base), a double (second base), a triple (third base) or a home run (rounding all four bases to produce a run). Roughly speaking, then, we can equate four bases gained with an extra run, comparable to the earned run of the pitcher. It's a crude comparison, since four singles, say, produced by four at bats, might not turn into any runs. Conversely, if the bases are loaded (a runner already on each base), then hitting a home run not only allows the batter to advance four bases, but also allows the runner on first to advance three bases, the runner on second to advance two bases and the runner on third to advance to home plate. This outcome, known as a grand slam, adds 10 bases (and four runs scored) from one hit.

To make it comparable to ERA, we translate the slugging percentage into a rate per game. On average, a batter comes up to bat 3.33 times per game (or 10 times every three games). We can calculate that a slugging percentage of 0.400 would generate 12 bases per game on average, enough bases to produce three runs. A higher (lower) slugging percentage earns the batter a higher (lower) salary. We can now produce a table to compare the relationship between pitching and batting salaries of free agents using expected runs conceded/produced per game.

Table 14.1: Free-agent salary in baseball as a multiple of the league average depending on runs conceded/produced

Free agent pitcher		Free agent batter	
Runs conceded per game	Salary as multiple of the league average	Runs produced per game	Salary as multiple of the league average
5	2.25	3	1.91
4	3.00	4	3.07
3	3.75	5	4.23

The table suggests an opportunity. Suppose you currently employ a batter who generates five runs per game (one above the average for free agents). If you trade this player for a pitcher who concedes only three runs per game (one below the average for free agents), then you have left your team's expected performance unchanged (one less run conceded makes the same contribution to victory as one more run scored, on average), but you're now paying a lower multiple of the average salary for the new player. Of course, this is a very rough calculation, and many other factors can be relevant. But as *Moneyball* taught us, that's exactly the kind of calculations managers need to make if they want to maximise their chances of winning within the constraints of the salary budget.

* * *

For readers who skipped the section on baseball salaries, the central insight is that the salary of pitchers is less sensitive to performance than batters. As you increase salaries for the two types of players, pitchers' performances improve more markedly than batters' – suggesting that elite pitchers are generally better value than elite batters.

Before the IPL, this type of analysis was impossible in cricket. But now we can see not only what teams spend on players, but also compare their productivity in the same competition to their rewards, just as we can in baseball. Much has been made of the growth in data analytics in the IPL – teams delve deeply into statistics to figure out how best to spend the available salary budget to maximise their chances of winning. What can we learn about the relative value of batters and bowlers if we look at the numbers?

One important difference between baseball and cricket is that pitchers who can bat are much rarer than bowlers who can bat. Pitching is so specialised that in the American League (one of the two leagues in MLB), they introduced the designated hitter rule, allowing the team to substitute a proper batter for the pitcher when the team is batting. Cricket has all-rounders.

For this analysis we used a dataset of (almost) all balls bowled in the IPL from 2008 to 2020, a total of 193,241 deliveries. Of the 595 players who batted or bowled in this period, 388 did both. Of course, all bowlers can be called on to bat, and most batters can bowl an over in an emergency. If we define an all-rounder as someone who both batted and bowled for more than 10 overs (60 balls) in an IPL season, then 97 players (about one in six IPL players) met this standard at least once.

We want to compare the distribution of rewards for batting and bowling. Figure 14.2 on the next page shows the distribution of balls faced and balls bowled by players in the 2020 IPL. The bottom 40% of batters faced fewer than 10 balls each; the top 20% faced at least 200, with the most 655 in Virat Kohli's extraordinary 2016 season.

The panel on the right shows the distribution for bowling. While one-third of players didn't bowl at all, and another third bowled fewer than 100 balls, the top 20% of bowlers delivered between 200 and 400 balls. The pattern was very similar to batting.

Figure 14.2: The distribution of balls faced and balls bowled by players in the 2020 IPL

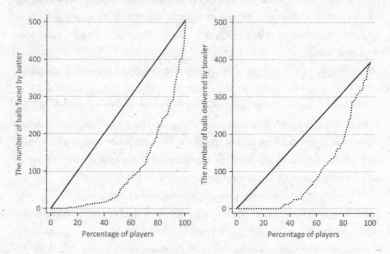

Over a season, the best bowlers tend to bowl as many balls as the best batters face. At every level of ability the pattern is similar. If you ranked all batters and bowlers in terms of balls faced or delivered and picked a particular rank – say, 50th – the number of balls faced or delivered would be very similar, as Table 14.3 below shows.

Table 14.3: Distribution of balls faced and balls bowled ranked from highest to lowest per player in 2020

Band	Batters		Bowlers	
	Number of players	Balls faced	Number of players	Balls bowled
20%	6	398–505	7	345–389
40%	9	284–382	9	299–338
60%	11	227–282	12	197–293
80%	19	113–224	19	126–187
100%	87	1–111	61	1–124
Total	**132**	**14,146**	**108**	**14,146**

All this might seem a little surprising, since bowlers are restricted to only four overs in the IPL, while batters have no limit. It is also puzzling at first glance that we make no allowances for where players bat. Yet a paper by statisticians Tim Swartz, Paramjit Gill and Saman Muthukumarana created a model to simulate runs scored depending on batting order; as an example, they simulated the Australian batting order in the 2007 ODI World Cup. They found that the average number of runs predicted by their model using the actual order was 272, very close to their actual average (273). When they completely reversed the line-up and placed No.11 and 10 as openers, No.9 coming in third and so on, they found that the expected number of runs scored fell by only 38, just 14%. If a radical restructuring of this kind has such a small effect, it's hard to believe that smaller differences could matter all that much. Before the 2020 IPL the Rajasthan Royals modelled the quality of their batting order under two scenarios. In the first, Jos Buttler opened the batting; in the second, he was used at No.4. The Royals estimated the strength of their batting line-up to be almost identical in both scenarios; indeed, they used Buttler in both positions during the season.

Our IPL data suggests that the ability distributions are very similar for batters and bowlers. This is cricket's version of the 80:20 rule: 80% of balls in the 2020 IPL were faced by 28% of the players, and 80% of the balls bowled were delivered by 30% of the players.

So what about the distribution of rewards? For a simple comparison, let's look at the salaries of the players who account for 80% of balls faced and balls delivered. Of the $86 million of salaries reported for IPL 2020, the 44 batters who faced 80% of balls delivered received just under half of all salaries (49.7%). The 47 bowlers who delivered 80% of the balls received just 35% of the salaries. So the top bowlers were paid about 30% less for delivering rather than facing balls. Given that some of these players are true all-rounders (the top batters delivered 13% of balls bowled and the top bowlers faced 16% of balls as batters), this probably understates the premium paid to batters.

This picture is also borne out if we consider just the top 10 batters and bowlers, shown in Table 14.4 on the next page. The top 10 batters faced 13% more balls than the top 10 bowlers delivered, yet were paid 38% more.

Table 14.4: Top 10 batters and bowlers in 2020 IPL by balls faced and delivered, ordered by salary

Batter	Salary (US $)	Balls faced	Bowler	Salary (US $)	Balls delivered
V. Kohli	2656250	400	P.J. Cummins	2214300	321
D.A. Warner	1953130	423	R. Khan	1406250	387
K.L. Rahul	1718750	505	J. Archer	1125000	345
M.K. Pandey	1718750	349	J.J. Bumrah	1093750	372
S.S. Iyer	1093750	400	Y.S. Chahal	937500	338
I. Kishan	968750	361	K. Rabada	656250	382
S. Dhawan	812500	431	S. Sharma	468750	317
Q. Kock	437500	365	T.A. Boult	460000	348
S. Gill	281250	382	T. Natarajan	62500	389
D. Padikkal	28600	398	A. Nortje	28600	346
Total	11669230	4014	**Total**	8452900	3545

This pattern is repeated across previous IPL seasons. Between 2008 and 2020, the salaries paid to the top 20 batters by balls faced added up to $24.7 million, with 9,744 balls faced. By contrast, the top 20 bowlers delivered 7,987 balls (19% fewer) but were paid almost half (47% less).

What explains the premium for batters? Each event in cricket requires both a batter and bowler. In this sense, the contribution of the bowler is the equal and opposite image of the contribution of the batter.

But if that is so, why would a star batter be paid more than a star bowler? In the history of economic thought, there is probably no better account of why different jobs attract different rates of pay than that of Adam Smith in *The Wealth of Nations*, published in 1776, when Hambledon was still the leading cricket club in England and 11 years before Thomas Lord opened his first cricket ground. 'The wages of labour,' he wrote in Book I, Chapter 10, 'vary with the ease or hardship, the cleanliness or dirtiness, the honourableness or dishonourableness of the employment ... the easiness and cheapness, or the difficulty and expense of learning the business ... the constancy or inconstancy of employment ... the small or great trust which must be reposed in the workmen ... (and) ... the probability or improbability of success.'

Looking at Smith's list, who should we expect to be better paid? Bowling certainly *looks* harder than batting: from a purely biomechanical point of view, there is more work in bowling than batting. Yet batting involves more hardship in the sense that it is more dangerous, potentially even fatal, which would tend to favour a premium for batting.

Bowling is more inconstant; bowlers – especially quick bowlers – are more prone to injury and have shorter careers on average, reflecting physical constraints. These also influence the probability of success.

At the start of a cricket career, the chance of either a batter or bowler competing in the IPL is minute. It would be hard to measure whose chances at success were lower – we would need to identify all aspiring talent at a given age, something which no one has yet attempted to the best of our knowledge. It seems reasonable to conjecture that at 18, there are about as many aspiring bowlers as there are batters. If so, then the probability of success would be about the same for each.

The question of 'small or great trust' touches on a point raised by Ed Smith in *Playing Hard Ball* – the batter more easily lets his side down by a moment of carelessness than the bowler. But batters might also be seen as more expendable – there are normally more of them in a team, and sides tend to rely heavily on their frontline bowlers to deliver success.

This brings us to the two points that probably weigh most heavily. First: the easiness and cheapness, or the difficulty and expense of learning the business. Which is more difficult to learn? As we discussed in Chapter 1, batters can train more effectively at an early age, the necessary skills being less dependent on physical maturity. Identifying bowler potential can only really occur once the player is past puberty. But while batters have a long apprenticeship, which implies greater expense over time, bowlers require greater intensity of training once their talent emerges, which implies greater expense per unit of time. The greater dependency of bowling on objectively scarce physical endowments should lead to higher salaries for bowlers. This has certainly been observed in other sports. For example, professional basketball is reliant on the short supply of extremely tall people; American males aged 20–40 who are 7ft tall or more have a one-in-five chance of playing in the NBA, according to David Epstein, author of *The Sports Gene*. Taller players in the NBA tend to be paid higher salaries, reflecting their scarcity.

This brings us to the last explanation for the batter salary premium: the honourableness or dishonourableness of employment. Now, honour is a somewhat loaded term, and we don't mean to show any disrespect for bowlers. Honour certainly carried different connotations in 1776 than it does today, where we would probably call it status. In our more democratic times, the admiration of the general public is a better measure of honourableness in the sense meant by Adam Smith. Just as with baseball, hitting the ball generally generates more excitement in the stands than delivering the ball. In the IPL there is an obsession with counting the number of sixes – there is no such obsession with recording the number of wickets taken, let alone the number of dot balls.

This is not peculiar to the IPL. The public has always admired batting more than bowling. The half-century and century landmarks have always drawn the applause of the crowd, but it was only during the 2001 Ashes series that Glenn McGrath began to hold up the ball after taking a five-wicket haul, demanding to be honoured. Professional cricket has to survive as a commercial activity; spectators' preferences matter.

Consider two IPL teams in the mid-to-late 2010s: Royal Challengers Bangalore and Sunrisers Hyderabad. Bangalore, who could field a batting line-up which included Virat Kohli, A.B. de Villiers and – for periods – Chris Gayle and Shane Watson too, came to be regarded as the galácticos of the IPL. The hottest ticket in the IPL was to watch Kohli and De Villiers bat in tandem. When it all clicked, it was the most thrilling sight in T20, perhaps even in cricket full stop: uniquely, Kohli and De Villiers have shared two double-century partnerships in T20. There was just one snag. As Tim explored in his book, *Cricket 2.0*, going all-in on batting wasn't a very good strategy to consistently win matches. In 2016, when Kohli and De Villiers were at their best, a brilliant late surge helped Bangalore reach the IPL final. But in their next three seasons, they came bottom, sixth, and bottom once again.

The team that defeated Bangalore in the 2016 final, Sunrisers Hyderabad, adopted the opposite approach – prioritising bowling. It was a strategy that ensured far more consistency over the years ahead: the Sunrisers would reach the play-offs in each of the following three years. Theirs was a style appreciated by connoisseurs: playing on tricky wickets at home, Sunrisers used anchor batters, such as Kane Williamson and Shikhar Dhawan, to reach a score of around 140, and then trusted in their brilliant bowling attack to do the rest. Empirically, it was a more effective strategy for securing victory than Bangalore's employment of galácticos. But when it came to generating interest in the team, Bangalore's method was more successful. Who didn't want to watch Kohli and De Villiers in tandem, even if doing so meant they had to watch profligate bowlers at the death, too? Bangalore's cocktail of flat pitches, brilliant batters, and comparatively weak bowling almost guaranteed that both sides would score freely. To most fans, these high-scoring games were simply more entertaining.

If bowlers are underpaid simply because they don't offer as much entertainment value, would a team that invested more heavily in bowlers improve their chance of winning? The evidence from the IPL suggests that the best bowlers may be underpriced. If that is so, shifting spending from batters to bowlers at the highest level would indeed increase the probability of victory. As T20 becomes more serious and winning becomes more important, we would not be surprised if we saw such a shift take place in the years ahead. But it might still require a cultural change in how bowlers are viewed for them to be paid their true worth.

15

DID THE COLD COST INDIA A TEST SERIES VICTORY IN ENGLAND?

In August 1976, the UK's Minister for Sport, Denis Howell, got a new portfolio: he was now also the Minister for Drought. That summer remains one of Britain's hottest on record; peak temperatures topped 30°C for more than two weeks in June and July. During that summer, a fine West Indies side toured England. Led by Clive Lloyd, the team boasted the imperious batting of Viv Richards, Gordon Greenidge, Roy Fredericks and Lloyd himself, combined with the terrifying pace of Andy Roberts and Michael Holding. By the fifth Test at The Oval, West Indies had an unassailable 2–0 lead. But with the large West Indian population of nearby Brixton making it seem like a home game, there was no question of easing up. Lloyd won the toss and decided to bat. By the end of day one, on 12 August, they were already 373–3, a breathtaking strike rate for the time, with Richards completing his double century just before the close. On day two the punishment continued, and West Indies reached 687–8 before declaring. England bowled 182.5 overs over two days in 27-degree heat. Uncomfortable if you're English, quite comfortable if you're from the Caribbean. Despite posting a creditable 435 in their first innings, England were easily beaten.

In the second Test of the 2007 West Indies tour of England, the story was almost exactly reversed. The match began on 25 May at Headingley, England's second most northerly Test venue. England won the toss and batted, scoring 570–7 before declaring just after lunch on the second day, with Kevin Pietersen posting a double century. West Indies were skittled for 146. By the close of the second day, they were 22–2 in the follow-on. Rain postponed the inevitable, and England secured a record victory over West Indies on the fourth day. On the second day, the average temperature at the ground was 10°C. The ESPNcricinfo summariser observed that 'it really has been wretchedly cold throughout'. Tough if you're English, sure, but almost unimaginable for West Indians.

Does the weather make a difference to team performance? It's not hard to think of examples that suggest that it does. Here are two more. The opening Test of the 2008–2009 England tour of India was played in Chennai over five days from 11–15 December, in temperatures averaging just under 30°C. After a classic Test, Sachin Tendulkar's fourth innings century helped India chase down their target of 387 – the fourth-highest successful chase in history at the time – on the final day, when England seemed to wilt in the heat. By contrast, the second Test of the 1984 series was played from 12 December in Delhi; the average daily temperature was around 16°C. In conditions much closer to home, England recorded a convincing eight-wicket victory on the fifth day.

India's tour of England in 2018 also offers a tantalising example. After baking heat in June and July, the weather cooled by the time the five-Test series began on 1 August. Across the series, the average difference in temperature, compared to Test matches played in India, was more than 5°C. It reached 10°C on 10 August, when England bowled out India for 107 on a miserable day at Lord's. Temperatures were closest to Indian temperatures in the first Test, which India lost by only 31 runs, and the third Test, which India won. India lost the series 4–1. But if the English summer had been a little kinder, there's reason to think India could have been victorious.

Anecdotes should always be interpreted with great care. The 1976 West Indies team was emerging as one of the greatest in history, while the 2007 team was poor. India's batting line-up in 2008 was phenomenal; England's surprise series victory in 1984–1985 also involved a victory in Chennai, where temperatures were more in line with norms in the subcontinent. There are many factors that determine victory. While weather effects *might* be one of them, a more systematic analysis of the data is required. We believe that we have produced the first systematic study of the impact of temperature on Test performance.

* * *

Why might weather matter in sport? Superstar athletes, like the rest of us, are products of our environment. Significant changes in our environment can affect our ability to perform routine tasks. For athletes, this effect can be dramatically amplified. This simple insight has led to major changes in the way that athletes have trained over the past 50 years. Half a century ago, an athlete was by and large just sent on to the field to play, regardless of their physical state. Treatment of injuries was rudimentary; in many sports nobody paid heed to diet and physical conditions; and mental preparation was at best crude. They paid little heed to weather considerations as well, although the impact of altitude, demonstrated at the 1968 Mexico Olympic Games by Bob Beaman's remarkable long jump, showed that local conditions matter.

Elite athletes are now surrounded by entire teams tasked with ensuring that a change of environment does not affect their performance. The main strategies seek to mitigate such changes. A personal chef, for instance, can mitigate the effect of unfamiliar foods or eating routines. But no team can change the weather. Exercise physiologists talk about two approaches to adjust to new climes, which sound infuriatingly alike: *acclimatisation* and *acclimation*. Acclimatisation essentially means getting used to the change in the environment *while it changes*; acclimation is the process of preparing for a change in the environment *before it actually happens*.

There's been a lot of research on acclimation and heat, largely because it is possible to conduct controlled experiments about the effect of acclimation regimes. Such regimes may involve exposure to high temperatures, such as sauna time, or simply putting on an extra layer of clothes. In cricket, teams from colder climes use methods like training in multiple layers or doing 'hot yoga' – doing yoga at temperatures of 35°C – to help prepare for playing at extreme heat. A two-week regime of heat acclimation has been shown to improve performance, measured by indicators such as aerobic capacity in a hot environment. This works in both directions – athletes from hot environments will improve their performance in a cold environment if they acclimate first, and vice versa.

Cricket is a particularly fertile sport to study the effect of climate. The main problem for any data analysis looking for causal effects is confounders – all the other factors that determine outcomes. Excluding such confounders from any data analysis is a real problem – like denying the jury the chance to see all of the evidence. But confounders are also likely to be related to the causal factor you are actually interested in, and so once you include a confounder, the analysis can get 'mixed up'. Think of football. You might think that temperature makes a big difference to team performance, so that Netherlands against Brazil will be a different game on a warm evening in São Paulo rather than a cold night in Rotterdam. But what about France against Brazil? The city of Calais in the north of France is much colder on average than most of Brazil, but the difference between Brazil and southern France is much smaller. Northern France is very warm in summer, even if it can be cold and wet in the winter. And in the very south of Brazil, the climate is more temperate. Such overlaps between different countries would tend to confound the climate effect; conversely, looking only at countries with large climate differences would introduce a bias in the selection of teams studied, which could also bias any estimate of the effect.

Another problem in football is the global player market. You cannot simply compare clubs from, say, Sweden and Portugal without taking into account where the players actually grew up. Much the same problem would affect a study of baseball. There are large climatic differences between cities such as Boston and Miami, but cold-hardy players from Boston will play in Miami's humid heat, and vice versa. Some studies have looked at players' short-term adaptation to temperature differences in American football, such as players from Miami in an away game in Boston in December, but they have not controlled for the experience of players living in different cities.

International cricket, by contrast, usually involves teams from very different climatic conditions whose players have relatively limited experience of the climate in the nations they visit. Test match nations also tend to be climatically homogeneous – India is hot almost everywhere, England is rainy almost everywhere. New Zealand's climate is diverse, but most other nations enjoy a far narrower range of climatic conditions. While top international cricketers from other countries may spend some time playing in some other countries – historically England, more recently India – most players play a large majority of their first-class cricket in their home country. Another advantage of cricket, when studying the impact of climate, is that the game is typically played over several days. A five-day Test allows us to observe performance in different weather conditions during the same game.

* * *

Climate data is usually collected in cities, and records go back a long way. We used data from The Global Historical Climatology Network, available for free online. We identified the average daily temperature and the average amount of precipitation for cities hosting Test matches back to 1932. We have data on daily temperature for 1,810 Tests, covering 8,130 days of play (more than three quarters of all days played to date), and rainfall data for 1,282 Tests, covering 5,321 days of play (just over 50% of all days played).

One aspect of climate on which we don't have data is humidity. It has long been argued that humidity accounts for the tendency of a cricket ball to swing through the air, though scientific research has largely debunked this theory – the temperature, rather than humidity, seems more important. Humidity is also likely to affect athletic performance, and this could well be a topic for future research in cricket. But here, we focus on temperature.

Our data covered games played by the 10 Test nations before 2017, the year Afghanistan and Ireland gained Test status. These are Australia, Bangladesh, England, India, New Zealand, Pakistan, South Africa, Sri Lanka, West Indies and Zimbabwe. If we look at the average daily temperature during Tests, the lowest is England at 18.8°C, the highest Bangladesh at 24.1°C. New Zealand's average temperature is almost identical to England's, and Sri Lanka's is very close to Bangladesh's. The rest fall within what looks like a narrow range between 20.7°C (Zimbabwe) and 22.4°C (West Indies). These differences may not look large at first glance, but the variance in temperature is considerable. For example, on one in five day's play in Pakistan the temperatures topped 26.7°C; on one in six day's play in England, temperatures fell to below 14.4°C. A player brought up in Pakistan will rarely have played serious cricket at 14.4°C, just as few players have had to play regularly at 26.7°C in England.

Cricket is a warm-weather sport, in part because rain is more prevalent in the winters of temperate zones than in summer. But this does not necessarily hold for tropical regions: in South Asia, monsoon season is during the summer. Temperature is probably the more important factor. Cricket is not well suited to cold, dry climates. It is difficult to stand around in the cold for long periods of time, as cricketers must, but the bigger problem may be the impact on bowlers, who find it harder to get properly warmed up in cold conditions and hence are more likely to suffer muscle injuries.

Before looking at the impact of weather on each team's performance, we first looked at the impact of weather on their combined performance. We measured this by runs per wicket. This is a measure of what Americans would call offense. We used a regression model to estimate the best fit between runs per wicket on a given day and the average temperature on that day. The effect is very clear: each extra degree C added 0.32 runs per wicket. This might not sound like much, but the difference in a completed innings played at 10°C and 30°C would be 0.32 x 20 x 10 – a total of 64 runs. Interestingly, a similar result has been found in baseball, where teams score more runs at higher temperatures. There are several possible explanations for this phenomenon. Two of the most plausible are:

- The coefficient of restitution, which measures the proportion of velocity of an object that is preserved when it rebounds (such as when a cricket ball hits a bat) is higher in warmer temperatures. A higher temperature will make a ball more elastic, and therefore rebound, while a cold ball is more resistant.
- Human reaction times are slower in cold weather, a phenomenon that will disadvantage batters more than bowlers.

The impact of rainfall on runs per wicket was negative. One tenth of an inch of rain reduces runs per wicket by 0.9 – nine runs per innings on each day. This may not seem very surprising, given that rain interferes with the batter's ability to react to each delivery, while frequent interruptions for rain are generally thought to work in favour of the fielding team by breaking the batters' concentration and giving bowlers additional rest. Yet at very high levels of rainfall, the advantage to the fielding team starts to diminish, possibly because bowling with a slippery ball and fielding in a slippery outfield become more difficult.

The relationship between temperature and runs per wicket varies. For six countries, the correlation is positive – a higher temperature means more runs. But for Bangladesh, Sri Lanka, South Africa and Zimbabwe, the correlation is negative – a higher temperature means fewer runs. Bangladesh and Sri Lanka are the countries that typically play at the highest temperatures, so it might not be surprising that their batting might benefit from lower temperatures: those would still be high enough.

The cases of South Africa and Zimbabwe may reflect the interaction of temperature with another important factor: elevation. At higher elevations, there is less air resistance, so a cricket ball will travel further when hit, making it easier to score runs. The Wanderers in Johannesburg is 6000 feet above sea level; Newlands in Cape Town is at sea level. Newlands has slightly higher year-round temperatures, but scoring runs has proved more difficult – with an average of 29.05 compared to 30.25 at the Wanderers. Once again, this phenomenon is also recognised in baseball, where hitting is widely acknowledged to be easier at the home of the Colorado Rockies, at an elevation of 5,200 feet, than at lower altitudes.

We should expect that a team's batting performance will be optimal at temperatures that are close to the team's national average temperature. But on any given day, the temperature is unlikely to equal the average. A statistical tool called 'standard deviation' describes how far away from the average the temperature will be. For each country, the temperatures on days of play tend to follow the bell-shaped curve, known as the 'normal' distribution. The value of deviation of temperature (on days when Test cricket is played) for each country lies in the range of 1°C to 6°C. For a normal distribution we expect:

- On about one-third of all days (34.1%) the temperature will lie between the average and one standard deviation *above* the average
- On about one-third of days (also 34.1%) the temperature will lie between the average and one standard deviation *below* the average
- On about one-seventh of days (13.6%) the temperature will lie between one and two standard deviations *above* the average
- On about one-seventh of days (13.6%) the temperature will lie between one and two standard deviations *below* the average
- For all the remaining days (around 5%) the temperatures will be either two standard deviations above or below the average.

This gives a sense of the temperature conditions at which teams normally play. So for example, if the average temperature were 25°C and the standard deviation was 1°C, then the temperature was between 24°C and 26°C on 68.2% of days played. Alternatively, if the average temperature were 22°C and the standard deviation was 6°C, then the temperature was between 16°C and 28°C on 68.2% of days played.

The more interesting question is how the temperature affects the performance of one team against another. To find out, we use the difference between runs per wicket of each team on a given day. For a team that bats all day, its performance is better if it scores more runs per wicket. If both teams bat, then a team performs better if its runs per wicket are higher than its opponent's. Because on some days, a team will score runs and lose no wickets, and we do not want to divide by zero, we simply add one to the wickets total for each team on each day. As we look at individual days rather than the whole game, our analysis enables us to focus on the impact of temperature controlling for the quality of each team, which is fixed across the days of any one game. A winning team can play badly on one day, just as a losing team can play well on another day. We suspected there to be a correlation between our measure of daily performance and the ultimate winner of the game – and indeed there is.

* * *

To measure the impact of temperature, we constructed an index of 'temperature advantage'. Take the midpoint between the average daily temperature of Test matches of the home and visiting team. If the home team has higher temperatures on average – such as India playing England at home – then we measure temperature advantage as the temperature on the day minus the midpoint average. If the home team has lower temperatures on average – such as England at home to India – we measure temperature advantage as the midpoint average minus the temperature on the day. So if the home team has a hotter climate, it has a temperature advantage the higher the temperature; if the home team has a cooler climate, it has a temperature advantage at lower temperatures. This also implies that India in England have an advantage on very hot days, and England in India have an advantage on very cold days. The average temperature advantage, across all days' play, using this measure is 2.5°C, although the standard deviation of 3.8°C implies that in around one-sixth of cases, the home team either has an advantage of more than 6.3°C and in one-sixth a disadvantage of more than 1.3°C. The ample variation in the daily temperature advantage gives a good chance of identifying its impact.

The relationship between the advantage of one team over another and temperature advantage is not exact, and temperature is not the only factor in the relative performance of teams. Many differences other than temperature would affect Bangladesh playing in New Zealand. Unfamiliar surroundings, different cultures, different food, and no doubt much else besides. In response, we use 'country interactions' in our analysis, meaning that for each country pair, we allow for a specific value in differential performance, independently of temperature. This value varies depending on which team is the home team – so that Sri Lanka playing in South Africa can have a different value to South Africa playing in Sri Lanka. Our regression model also allows for the impact of a team's form.

The upshot is this: temperature advantage has a significant impact. The effect is nonlinear – so for small temperature differences, the effect is negligible, but as the differences get larger, the effects become pronounced. (Technically, this effect is measured by the square of the temperature advantage.) Consider the home team batting all day. At the average temperature advantage (2.5°C), the effect is only three runs over an entire innings. But if the advantage is one standard deviation higher than this (6.2°C), the value is a 20-runs advantage for the home team, and two standard deviations (10°C) translate to a 50-runs advantage. Because of the way we defined temperature advantage, this means that if the home country's average temperature is larger than the visiting team's, then 'larger' means warmer; if the home country average temperature is lower than the visitor's, then 'larger' means colder.

We also looked at the impact of temperature advantage in the first innings only: 80% of teams that win have a lead after the first innings, so any weather effect in the first innings is crucial. The temperature effect is even larger in the first innings. If the temperature is one standard deviation above the average (hotter in the hotter country, colder in the colder country), the effect on the first innings total is a difference of 43 runs, and at two standard deviations, a full 110 runs. These are very large effects.

It's probably no surprise that weather plays a role in the relative performance of teams, and that visiting teams underperform if the weather is drastically different from the one they're used to. We expect England to struggle on a very hot day in Chennai, and India to struggle on a very cold day in Durham, and this is what the data confirms. Teams already work on acclimating and acclimatising to local conditions. While the expansion of international travel over recent decades has probably enhanced Test teams' capacity, this effect seems to have been offset by the shortening of tours, with fewer warm-up games before and during Test series. Accordingly, home advantage has become more salient. Cultural differences probably play a much smaller role than in the past, while climate differences may be more important.

It's less clear what effect climate change itself will have. Higher temperatures everywhere do not necessarily shift the differences between countries. Scientists often argue that climate change is leading to much more variability in the weather. If so, this could enhance the significance of weather effects by creating more games with extreme temperature advantages – potentially giving home teams a further boost. But it could also be that greater overall variability in climate will make players more adaptable.

While the temperature effects seem clear, rain is harder to account for. The regressions show a statistically significant benefit of rain for the home team, while the difference in the prevalence of rain in the home and visiting team countries seems to have no effect. A team from a country with a very dry climate benefits from rain when playing at home just as much as a team from a rainy country. Recall that these effects relate to the day of play itself, so that the home team has an advantage in terms of runs per wicket on the day it rains. The home team has an advantage of eight to 11 runs per innings on a day with 0.1 inches of rain, the median amount of rainfall on rainy days.

The home rain advantage logically has the biggest effect in the countries with the most rain, which in the data are Zimbabwe, Sri Lanka, Bangladesh, and the nations that make up the West Indies. Surprisingly, the average amount of rain on Test days in England is significantly lower, and almost identical, to Australia and South Africa. Less surprisingly, India and Pakistan are comfortably the driest. Tropical and monsoon rains are rather different from English drizzle, so that the home team advantage may reflect the peculiarities or rainfall patterns in different countries. Perhaps it's just that players know what to expect from the rain in their own country.

Weather is more than just a perennial talking point in cricket. It also helps to shape the outcomes of matches – and, as we have seen, may have cost India a series triumph in England in 2018.

16

IS THE IPL EFFICIENT?

Richard Wardill took his own life in 1873, having embezzled £7,000 from the Melbourne Sugar Company to indulge his gambling habit. *The Times*' Victoria correspondent wrote, archly, 'Wardill had been a useful and popular officer of our leading cricket club, and many of its members took part in a discreditable funeral procession which ignored theft and suicide in honouring a high batting average.'

This is one of the earliest mentions of a cricket batting average, but not quite the first we know of. The oldest reference we have yet found appeared in *The Leeds Mercury* of 12 September, 1846. It reports that the batting average of one Alfred Mynn for that year was 16 and six-sevenths. Mynn's fame would outlast him: in 1997, John Woodcock ranked Mynn as the fourth greatest cricketer of all time.

Cricket has always had an ambivalent relationship to statistics. Scorecards go back to the early 18th century, yet purists have always stressed that numbers can only tell you so much, that cricket embodies a particular form of aesthetics which reveals beauty and grace, especially in batting. The cricketing raptures of the committed Marxist materialist C.L.R. James illustrate how this ambivalence runs deep. In his autobiography Fred Root, one of the best county cricketers of the interwar period, assures readers that 'there are no tedious statistics here, for averages are an abomination to real cricket.'

The sports media have always been among the greatest promoters of statistics. Stats provide endless talking points for analysts, which was as true in the Victorian age as it is today. From the 1860s onwards, the newspapers teem with batting averages, even if it took *Wisden* until 1887 to succumb. There is an eager audience for numbers: apart from the committed aesthetes, many cricket fans relish using statistics to compare players past and present.

Very few people alive now saw Don Bradman bat. Newsreel images of him are grainy and brief, rendering comparison with modern giants such as Sachin

Tendulkar and Brian Lara difficult. But his Test average of 99.94 – more than 50% higher than the next highest of any Test cricketer to play 20 Tests or more – is usually enough to convince any sceptic that he is the GOAT, the Greatest Of All Time. Statistics are rarely as conclusive, but frequently illuminating nonetheless. For example, the Test batting averages of Tendulkar and Lara are similar (53.78 and 52.88), but there's a stark difference in their home and away stats. Lara averaged 58.65 in the Caribbean but only 47.80 abroad. Tendulkar had a slightly higher average abroad (54.74) than he did in India (52.67) – a testament to his adaptability.

While batting and bowling averages have always been part of the fabric of cricket analysis, the sport was relatively slow to embrace data analytics. In this chapter we delve more deeply into using statistics to analyse cricket, and in particular the issue of efficiency in the allocation of resources in the IPL. But before getting to that, we will need to talk about cricket's statistical debt to baseball.

* * *

Baseball makes for a natural comparison to cricket. Baseball is younger, at least in the sense that its formal rules were not written down until 1845, almost exactly a century after cricket's. Yet many people involved in baseball's development were cricketers; the games look vaguely alike to countries that aren't particularly invested in either. Cricket remained the most popular sport in the US until the end of the Civil War; as late as 1900 it still occupied a good deal of space on the sports pages of American newspapers. Even Henry Chadwick, hailed as 'the father of baseball', was a cricket writer.

Chadwick was born in Exeter in 1824. His family moved to Brooklyn when he was 12 – he would stay there until his death in 1908, and you can still visit his grave in the historic Green-Wood cemetery. He played cricket as a young man, and started out in his writing career covering the game. But by the late 1850s Chadwick was increasingly obsessed with that new sport. He is credited with many innovations in the ways baseball games are recorded – one of the most important ones was the development of the batting average, no doubt inspired by cricket. Baseball is more complicated than cricket since scoring runs requires you to circle the bases, which can be accomplished in stages. The ideal measure, then, needed to capture each batter's contribution to the runs eventually scored.

In devising a statistic, Chadwick grappled with the question of how to weight the number of bases gained by any particular hit. In 1867, he decided on a measure which treated all hits equally, regardless of whether the hit took the batter to first base, second base, third base or even all the way home. The baseball batting average came to be defined as the number of hits that enabled the batter to reach at least one base, divided by the number of 'at bats' (which is the equivalent of an individual innings in cricket). To baseball fans, a batting average is just as informative as it is to cricket fans. An average of .100 (10%) is lousy, an average of .300 is excellent, and an average of .400 is stellar – a feat not achieved over an entire season of Major League Baseball (MLB) since Ted Williams in 1941. Americans like to say, with some justification, that hitting a baseball is the hardest skill in sport.

Possibly the most important contribution to sports analytics in baseball came from the statistician George Lindsey. He invented a completely new method of analysing baseball – and his insight has formed the basis of statistical analysis of most other professional sports, including cricket.

His papers, published in the early 1960s, solved the fundamental problem of identifying the contribution of a batter's hit to the scoring of a run. A game of baseball consists of nine innings. Each inning (singular) has two halves – the top, when the visiting team bats, and the bottom, when the home team bats. Each half inning ends when three batters are out. There are 24 possible states of a half inning in progress, combining the number of possible outs and the number of runners on base.

In a regular baseball season, each of these possible base states will occur thousands of times. A typical MLB season consists of roughly 200,000 at bats (a batter's turn against the pitcher). Each of these has a base state associated with it, making it possible to calculate the average number of runs scored from any given base state to the end of the half inning. This is what Lindsey calls 'run expectancy' – the number of runs you can expect to be scored, starting from a given base state. From here it is easy to generate a measure of the batter's contribution – it is simply the difference between the run expectancy at the beginning of an at bat and the run expectancy at the end of the at bat, plus any runs scored during the at bat.

It's a deeply elegant solution. To calculate run expectancy, Lindsey and his father went through the scores for 6000 half-innings in 1959 and 1960 and assembled the averages by hand. Happily, such dedication is no longer necessary.

Multiple sources online provide the data for each MLB pitch going back decades. Lindsey's method forms the basis for the advanced baseball performance statistics that are widely used today – wins above replacement (WAR), weighted on-base average (wOBA), and win probability added (WPA).

The idea of using expectation, a statistical concept, as a benchmark for measuring player contributions has spread to analytics in other sports – like using the concept of xG, expected goals, in football, expected yards gained in American Football, or expected possession value in basketball. In each case, Lindsey's insight is applicable – work out what happens on average in a given situation, and then compare the performance of individuals and teams to that average.

* * *

Belatedly, cricket has started to move beyond batting average. In the 1980s, the accounting firm Deloitte produced an index of batting and bowling strength for Test players, adjusted for the strength of the opposition, with more recent games weighted more strongly. This rating scheme evolved into the ICC player rankings. Their exact formula remains a secret, but it is probably not so very different from the original formula.

Technical papers on statistical methods can now predict game outcomes, using machine-learning techniques such as Naïve Bayesian, Support Vector Machines, and Random Forest models. In each case the models can generate probabilities that given events will occur based on what has actually happened in the past. Perhaps unsurprisingly, many of these papers come from India. Predicting match outcomes is not just an intellectual exercise. Sports betting is a big industry. Bookies build models, and so do the punters trying to outsmart them.

Sports betting is illegal in India. But fantasy cricket – including versions that allow you to play for money – is not. During any IPL game, you will hear the commentators discussing their fantasy cricket picks, while the broadcast shows how many fantasy points players have earned during the game. Dream11, the leading Indian fantasy sports platform, even sponsored the 2020 edition of the IPL. In 2021, Dream11 claimed to have 100 million registered users.

There is a very simple benchmark against which to test any prediction model: the accuracy of the bookmakers. The odds offered by a bookmaker reflect the weight of opinion of large numbers of people – the wisdom of the crowd. The bookmaker odds are easily translated into probabilities. One way to assess their accuracy is to see how often the actual outcome corresponded to the most likely outcome indicated by the odds. Out of 180 games played in the IPL from 2018 to 2020, the bookmakers got it right in 110 cases – 61%. Since a coin toss would be right 50% of the time, the bookmakers' odds are not that much better than a random call – but good enough to keep them in business.

The academic literature on beating the bookmakers is disappointing. Published papers typically claim to either match the betting odds or outperform them by such a small margin that if you tried to bet using their predictions, you would actually lose money after paying fees and taxes. This is true of all sports with active betting markets, not just cricket. When it comes to beating the bookies, there are believers and sceptics. Believers tend to argue that the truly successful prediction models remain unpublished, but we are sceptical about the secret results of secret models.

*   *   *

One reason the statistical analysis of cricket has been so slow to catch up to baseball is because the game's traditional format is open-ended. Football is an even more extreme example: tens of thousands of unique actions over 90 minutes can amount to the difference of a single goal between two teams. In the statistical jargon, the problem is 'overdetermined' – there are too many factors contributing to too few events of interest, rendering it impossible to assign significance to any single factor. Cricket is at least like baseball in that it consists of a sequence of discrete events – balls. But in a five-day Test, the resources available to each team are more than wickets and overs – they include time itself. Time management is an aspect too amorphous to quantify in ways that can be easily analysed. But a limited-overs game looks much more like a game of baseball: fixed resources that can be quantified and analysed.

The Duckworth-Lewis methodology is a case in point: it reduces each event of the game to a quantum of resources. As we elaborated in Chapter 9, DL was invented for the purpose of fairly adjusting targets following rain interruptions. But we can also use their method to measure individual players' contributions.

212

A batter's performance can be rated by the number of runs scored relative to quantity of resources used – the more the better. A bowler's performance can also be rated by the quantity of runs produced relative to quantity of resources used – the fewer the better. When a batter is out, a large quantity of resource is used up; that counts against their productivity and spreads the runs conceded by the bowler over a larger quantity of resource.

We looked at ball-by-ball data for the IPL from 2008 to 2020, a total of 193,241 deliveries, building on models produced by other researchers. To calculate the amount of resource used up by each ball, we used the Duckworth-Lewis Standard Edition (2002). The table is regularly used in club cricket to calculate revised targets after rain interruptions.

The Standard Edition table allows us to calculate the resources available to the team before and after each ball. At the beginning of an innings, with 120 balls remaining, a team has 100% of its resources; after one ball (119 remaining), assuming the team did not lose a wicket, it has 99.35% of its resources remaining – so the resources used up with that ball equals 100-99.35 = 0.65% of its resources. Had the first ball resulted in a wicket lost, there would only be 96.23% of resources remaining, so the ball would have used up 3.77% of the team's resources. This use of resources can be attributed to the batter – they used up the resource. The question then concerns the return: how many runs were scored in using up that resource? Over a batter's entire innings, we can sum the resources used and the runs scored, and the ratio represents a player efficiency measure – runs produced per unit of resource.

This measure can be understood as an adaptation to cricket of a popular measure of batting efficiency in baseball – runs above average. Runs above average is based on the concept of run expectancy. For this exercise, a single delivery in cricket is analogous to an at bat in baseball. Runs above average measures the difference between the actual outcome of an event and the expected – the average – outcome. The sum of a player's performance above or below average represents a measure of batting efficiency in baseball.

Any measure of efficiency should be relatively stable over time and under different conditions. The DL-based player efficiency measure meets that standard, as we can see from the IPL data. Table 16.1 shows the runs scored, the resources used, and runs scored per unit of resource for the opening and chasing teams in the first 13 IPL seasons. Across a season, teams in the first innings use more resources in aggregate than chasing teams, who do not need to use all of their resources once they have reached the target. Chasing teams also score fewer runs on average, as they either win by a small runs margin – a victory by wickets is by a margin of between one and six runs at most – or lose by a margin of runs that is frequently much larger. This skews downward the total number of runs scored by chasing teams. But when we calculate the runs per unit of resource used, teams in each innings are performing very similarly.

Table 16.1: Runs and resources, Indian Premier League, 2008–2020

Season	Runs Innings 1	Runs Innings 2	Sum of resources used Innings 1	Sum of resources used Innings 2	Runs per unit of resource Innings 1	Runs per unit of resource Innings 2
2008	9336	8601	5728	5099	1.63	1.69
2009	8565	7755	5659	5298	1.51	1.46
2010	9887	8977	6000	5609	1.65	1.60
2011	11123	10031	7191	6539	1.55	1.53
2012	11658	10795	7391	6962	1.58	1.55
2013	11848	10693	7537	7180	1.57	1.49
2014	9784	9125	5982	5564	1.64	1.64
2015	9809	8523	5761	5212	1.70	1.64
2016	9756	9106	5957	5370	1.64	1.70
2017	9781	8988	5900	5348	1.66	1.68
2018	10795	9911	5973	5583	1.81	1.78
2019	10417	9816	5972	5627	1.74	1.74
2020	10006	8868	5898	5475	1.70	1.62

Note: in each game each team starts with 100% of its resources – wickets and balls, and uses them up during the innings. Apart from rain-interrupted games, the sum of resources used by the team batting first will be 100 (%). The chasing team that wins will typically use less than 100% of its resources.

Table 16.2 shows the five most efficient batters in the five seasons from 2016 to 2020. These players produced about half a run per unit of resource more than the average players. It is telling how consistently some names appear: Andre Russell and Sunil Narine show up three times, A.B. de Villiers twice. Going back further, both De Villiers and Chris Gayle crop up several more times. The dominance of West Indies players reflects their unrivalled capacity to produce cricketers who can consistently clear the ropes. Some players in the list faced relatively few balls. Narine, a giant of T20 bowling, converted to opening the batting as a pinch-hitter only in 2017. Both Harbhajan Singh and Jofra Archer are considered bowlers who can bat a bit, but are both capable of producing decisive batting performances. In 2020, Archer hit South Africa's Lungi Ngidi for four consecutive sixes. One obvious conclusion is that batters with low averages who can score very quickly – Narine, Harbhajan and Archer – are extremely valuable.

Table 16.2: The most efficient batters, 2016–2020, facing 60 or more balls in a season

Season	Player	Runs per unit of resource	Balls faced	Salary (US $)	Team	Nationality
2016	A.B. de Villiers	2.23	415	1583333	Royal Challengers Bangalore	South Africa
2016	K.H. Pandya	2.15	127	300000	Mumbai Indians	India
2016	C.H. Morris	2.14	114	1050000	Delhi Daredevils	South Africa
2016	A.D. Russell	2.08	125	100000	Kolkata Knight Riders	Jamaica
2016	H. Singh	2.08	91	1333333	Mumbai Indians	India
2017	C.A. Lynn	2.41	175	216000	Kolkata Knight Riders	Australia
2017	J.C. Buttler	2.09	184	570000	Mumbai Indians	England
2017	S.P. Narine	2.07	135	700000	Kolkata Knight Riders	Trinidad and Tobago
2017	G.J. Maxwell	2.06	186	1000000	Kings XI Punjab	Australia
2017	A.J. Finch	2.03	186	150000	Gujarat Lions	Australia
2018	S.P. Narine	2.35	198	1953130	Kolkata Knight Riders	Trinidad and Tobago
2018	R.R. Pant	2.35	412	2343750	Delhi Daredevils	India
2018	A.D. Russell	2.28	179	1328130	Kolkata Knight Riders	Jamaica
2018	A.B. de Villiers	2.24	281	1718750	Royal Challengers Bangalore	South Africa
2018	K.L. Rahul	2.20	426	1718750	Kings XI Punjab	India
2019	A.D. Russell	2.83	272	1328130	Kolkata Knight Riders	Jamaica
2019	H.H. Pandya	2.40	223	1718750	Mumbai Indians	India
2019	S.P. Narine	2.33	90	1953130	Kolkata Knight Riders	Trinidad and Tobago
2019	C.H. Gayle	2.19	338	312500	Kings XI Punjab	Jamaica
2019	J. Bairstow	2.18	293	314300	Sunrisers Hyderabad	England
2020	T. Curran	2.25	63	142900	Rajasthan Royals	England
2020	K.A. Pollard	2.19	143	843750	Mumbai Indians	Trinidad and Tobago
2020	N. Pooran	2.15	209	600000	Kings XI Punjab	Trinidad and Tobago
2020	M.A. Agarwal	2.05	223	156250	Kings XI Punjab	India
2020	J. Archer	2.02	66	1125000	Rajasthan Royals	England

One nice feature of this measure of efficiency is that a bowler's statistics exactly mirrors a batter's. A bowler who gives up fewer runs per unit of resource leaves the opposing team having to chase more runs with the resources they have left. The standout player in the bowling stats is Rashid Khan, who appears from 2018–2020. Moeen Ali, who was not widely considered a standout IPL player, appears twice in the list, although the first time from bowling relatively few balls. The value of Narine and Archer as all-rounders is confirmed by their appearance in both lists.

Table 16.3: The most efficient bowlers 2016–2020, delivering 60 or more balls in a season

Season	Player	Runs per unit of resource	Balls delivered	Salary (US $)	Team	Nationality
2016	A. Zampa	1.27	103	45000	Rising Pune Supergiants	Australia
2016	M. Rahman	1.28	376	210000	Sunrisers Hyderabad	Bangladesh
2016	D.S. Kulkarni	1.40	297	300000	Gujarat Lions	India
2016	B.C.J. Cutting	1.41	68	75000	Sunrisers Hyderabad	Australia
2016	S.P. Narine	1.43	262	700000	Kolkata Knight Riders	Trinidad and Tobago
2017	M. Nabi	1.21	66	45000	Sunrisers Hyderabad	Afghanistan
2017	P. Negi	1.22	200	149000	Royal Challengers Bangalore	India
2017	A.J. Tye	1.25	128	75000	Gujarat Lions	Australia
2017	K.V. Sharma	1.27	189	478000	Mumbai Indians	India
2017	G.J. Maxwell	1.31	115	1000000	Kings XI Punjab	Australia
2018	M. Ali	1.21	81	[unknown]	Royal Challengers Bangalore	England
2018	L. Ngidi	1.24	163	78130	Chennai Super Kings	South Africa
2018	I. Sodhi	1.29	139	[unknown]	Rajasthan Royals	India
2018	R. Khan	1.37	411	1406250	Sunrisers Hyderabad	Afghanistan
2018	A. Mishra	1.43	226	625000	Delhi Daredevils	India
2019	R.A. Jadeja	1.28	329	1093750	Chennai Super Kings	India
2019	I. Tahir	1.30	389	156250	Chennai Super Kings	South Africa
2019	M. Ali	1.33	152	265630	Royal Challengers Bangalore	England
2019	R. Khan	1.36	364	593750	Sunrisers Hyderabad	Afghanistan
2019	R.D. Chahar	1.37	287	296880	Mumbai Indians	India
2020	R. Khan	1.06	387	1406250	Sunrisers Hyderabad	Afghanistan
2020	A.R. Patel	1.24	134	714300	Delhi Capitals	India
2020	J. Archer	1.26	345	1125000	Rajasthan Royals	England
2020	J.J. Bumrah	1.28	372	1093750	Mumbai Indians	India
2020	W. Sundar	1.30	302	500000	Royal Challengers Bangalore	India

We compared our results with the rankings produced by CricViz, one of the leading cricket analytics firms. They have developed a proprietary measure of player performance called Match Impact Explainer, which is also based on the Duckworth-Lewis-Stern method. They don't publish their model, and it adds several adjustments not included here, such as the measurement of a player's impact as a fielder. But Imran Khan from CricViz shared their top-five rankings for each season; it bore a strong resemblance to our ratings. Yet if you're asking whether these rankings would help you make money in fantasy cricket or betting against the bookies, just remember: we marked ourselves down as sceptics.

* * *

One feature that emerges from this analysis is the relative undervaluation of bowlers, an issue which we have considered in Chapter 14. The average pay of batters was \$982,000, compared to barely more than half that (\$541,000) for the salaries of the bowlers for whom we had data. This is despite bowlers delivering significantly more balls than the batters faced (5885 compared to 5154). It looks like a lot more work for a lot less pay.

The pay/performance relationship is one of the most interesting analytical questions in sport. Stefan showed in his book *Soccernomics* that this relationship is very close in football – team performance correlates almost perfectly with the salaries paid to the players. Players circulate in a market with many buyers and sellers who have plentiful information about their abilities; as a result, players are priced efficiently. The correlation between salaries and performance is also very strong in baseball, albeit not quite as strong as in football. Yet in sports such as American football and basketball, the correlation is either weak, as in the NBA, or non-existent, as in the NFL. Salary caps account for that difference: if each team spends the same amount on salaries, then by definition salaries cannot explain the variation in the performance of the teams. The NFL has a hard cap – teams must strictly meet the same spending limit. The NBA has a soft cap – salaries can vary among the teams, a model similar to the IPL.

Player performance can still be related to salaries. If the market works efficiently, individual pay should accurately reflect performance, and this could well be the case in the NBA and NFL. We used our measure of resource efficiency to examine the pay/performance relationship for 428 players who appeared in the IPL from 2008 to 2020 and for whom we had salary data. We ran a regression analysis.

The results were striking. Most factors we included made no difference – nationality didn't matter, and the team you played for didn't matter. Nor did your efficiency score, either as batter or bowler. Only two things mattered. One was the number of balls you faced as a batter. Each additional ball faced in the IPL was worth another $2500 in salary. The other was the number of balls delivered. Each additional ball bowled was worth just under $1000 in salary.

There are two ways you might look at this result. The first is to say that the market isn't operating very efficiently – teams aren't able to distinguish quality from quantity, which may change as analytical techniques develop. The second is that the model isn't good enough to capture the relevant differences.

Whatever the case, there will be a lot more research in the coming years. For any geeks reading, it is becoming ever-easier to undertake this kind of analysis on a laptop; the software you need, such as Python or R, is open source. If you're looking for cricket datasets to analyse, you can find plenty of them, including the ones used for this analysis, on sites like Kaggle.com; once again, they are free.

The Duckworth-Lewis method may have been cricket's *Moneyball* moment, but in the next decade analytics in cricket is likely to deliver a lot more. The next great leap forward might well come from a teenager in Bangalore or Delhi, or even Boise, Idaho. Spotting it among the flood of research papers might be the biggest challenge.

PART FIVE
THE FANS

17

A DAY AT THE CRICKET

On New Year's Day 2007, a crowd of just over 46,000 turned out for the New Year Test match at Sydney Cricket Ground (SCG), a tradition that can be traced back to 1931. Already 4–0 up and the Ashes safely recovered, they watched England eke out 234–4 on the first day, and returned in similar numbers the next to see England dismissed and the home side reach 188–4. On day three, a little under 42,000 spectators saw Australia reach 393, scored at a rate of more than four per over compared to England's rate of less than three. By the end of that day, Monty Panesar was in as nightwatchman, England had collapsed to 114–5, and the whitewash was all but secure. Still, 37,000 people turned up on the fourth day, even though Australia required just 46 to complete a 10-wicket victory.

Four years later, on 2 January, 2011, 44,000 attended the first day of the New Year's Test, but under very different circumstances. England had already retained the Ashes and had just mauled Australia at the MCG by an innings and 157 runs. At the time, the SCG was under reconstruction, so this still represented a capacity crowd. In a day interrupted by bad light, the hosts limped to 134–4 on a first day that ended when debutant Usman Khawaja was dismissed for 37; the state of Australian cricket at the time was such that home supporters gave Khawaja a standing ovation. The likelihood of a redeeming victory was already remote. On day two, in front of 40,000, Australia were bowled out for 280; Alastair Cook, enjoying the greatest series of his life, ended unbeaten on 61 as England reached 167–3. On day three, England did what they looked likely to do throughout that summer and batted the whole day, reaching 488 for seven – yet 40,000 people were still there to watch. Day four only extended Australia's pain: England's first innings ended on 644 and Australia on 217–7, still 146 runs behind. Although the attendance was down a little, still more than 35,000 were watching. On day five, though, just under 20,000 bothered to come to watch the 17.4 overs required by England to complete an innings victory.

These two games represent something close to the all-time high and all-time low for Australian cricket; in a sense, then, they were very different events. Yet, the attendance figures are remarkably similar. For all the differences in the state of Australian cricket between 2007 and 2011, the spectators' simple reason for being there was the same: they wanted to see the cricket. Here we use attendance data for international matches in Australia, which is recorded more reliably than anywhere else, to explore *why* people want to see the cricket.

* * *

For any sport it is crucial to know what attracts spectators to games. Get this right, and a virtuous cycle begins: more fans, more revenue, more funding, more talent, better games, more fans … Conversely, losing fans can lead to a spiral of decline – fewer fans, less revenue, less funding, less talent, worse games, fewer fans…

Cricket administrators are not unusual in being obsessed with this calculus. What does set them apart is how the game has largely relied on long-distance international competition rather than domestic leagues. Given how significant international games are for the finances of cricket, there is disappointingly little attendance data available.

In other professional sports, it is frequently possible to uncover attendance records going back for decades, often even for a century or more; for English football, records of club attendance go back to the 19th century. Oddly, there is no published research on Test matches attendances before the 1980s, neither for England nor for any other country: except for Australia. Luckily, Richard Cashman, one of the pioneers of sports history in Australia, assembled a collection of attendance statistics for both international and Sheffield Shield cricket for the period from 1887 to 1984. His book about Australian cricket crowds sports has the unbeatable title *'Ave A Go Yer Mug! Australian Cricket Crowds from Larrikin to Ocker*. Using his data (updated to the present using data supplied by Ric Finlay), we are able to take a long view.

Most statistical analysis of sports attendance is conducted by economists. They have long been obsessed with one particular idea: that the attendance at a sporting event depends on the uncertainty of its outcome. Ostensibly, this makes sense: what's the thrill in seeing one team slaughter another? But fans often do like to root for an underdog; a balanced, uncertain contest does not provide that pleasure. Perhaps there's a cost to having too much balance? Other emotions can figure prominently: even neutral fans frequently cherish the opportunity to cheer on the opponents of a widely hated team – such as the New York Yankees or, during their hegemony, the Australia cricket team.

Once you look at actual games played, the uncertainty-of-outcome hypothesis starts to look very theoretical indeed. Bayern Munich won the Bundesliga championship every season from 2013 to 2021, but attendance at Bundesliga games did not fall until Covid-19 drove fans out of stadiums. Leagues that feature highly unbalanced competition frequently have very high attendance levels. While economists often point to the NFL in the US as an example of a successful, highly balanced competition, both the NBA and Major League Baseball have always been characterised by significant imbalance, and yet both remain very popular. The period after the Second World War, which saw the Yankees win six World Series championships in seven years, is even revered as a golden age. Dozens of economic studies have sought to test the uncertainty-of-outcome hypothesis using data; we can draw two broad conclusions.

First, to the extent that balance does matter, attendance will generally be higher when the home team is expected to win. It is possible for the imbalance in favour of the home team to be too great – the research consensus is that, to maximise attendance, the home team's chances of winning should be no more likely than about 66%. That is still unbalanced, just not *too unbalanced*. But perhaps more importantly, the research's second conclusion is that uncertainty of outcome is only one factor among many in determining fans' desire to watch, and often actually quite a minor one. As the Sydney Ashes Tests of 2007 and 2011 showed, attendance levels can be quite insensitive to the competition itself, which brings us back to the question: just what does determine attendance?

As well as uncertainty of outcome, analysis of attendance data generally focuses on factors such as ticket prices, the quality of teams, and income levels.

Almost uniquely, Test match data allows us to examine the decision to attend the same contest on different days. In most sports, the contest lasts only a few hours, and almost never more than one day. The decision to attend the game is necessarily made before the game has been played – and therefore we cannot examine the impact of the state of the game on the decision to attend, in the way that we can with a five-day Test.

Our data analysis is based on all international games played in Australia from 1877 to early 2019. This includes 426 Test matches played over 1948 days, 437 One-Day Internationals, and 37 T20 Internationals, giving a total of 2422 days. The highest recorded attendance is 93,013 for the World Cup final played by Australia against New Zealand in 2015 at the Melbourne Cricket Ground (MCG). For some games, attendances numbered only a few hundred spectators – typically on the final day of a Test, where the losing team was already on the brink of defeat. More than half of all games were played at either the SCG or MCG; the remainder were split mainly between the Adelaide Oval, the WACA in Perth, and the Gabba in Brisbane.

The most striking result of the regression analysis is that attendance appears to be responsive to the runs scored by the home team and the home team's loss of wickets. On average, every run scored by the Australians increased attendance on the following day by seven people; every run scored on the day itself was associated with an increase of 10 in the attendance figure. Conversely, every Australian wicket lost on the previous day reduced the current day's attendance by 315; every wicket lost on the current day was associated with a loss of 333 spectators on that day.

Now, it might seem counter-intuitive to suggest that the accumulation of runs and wickets could affect attendance *on the same day*. After all, what we are measuring here is the number of tickets recorded as sold, not whether or not someone left the ground in disgust, as the bulk of the Australian crowd famously did on Boxing Day in 2010, when England humiliated the hosts. But it seems plausible here to invoke what economists call 'rational expectations'. International cricket matches generate a lot of interest; anyone going to a game is likely to be well informed about the relative strengths of the two teams. At Sydney in 2007, Australians fully expected to complete the whitewash. Four years later, even the most myopic supporters knew that England had overpowered their team. So while fans cannot know what a given day will produce – and no doubt always hope for the best – the decision to attend the game is likely to be influenced by expectations about the most likely course of events. Fans are generally well aware of which days are likely to go well or go badly.

The regression data suggests that cricket fans tend to plan their attendance when their team is doing well, and especially when they expect to see their own team batting. This is not a purely Australian phenomenon. As a general rule, fans prefer to watch their own team score runs rather than their opponents. With the truly great batters, of course, spectators may attend just to watch a master bat. When Sachin Tendulkar was in his pomp, Vaibhav Purandare relates in his biography, Indian cricket fans would cheer whenever the Indian batter ahead of Tendulkar was out.

The 'home team batting' effect may also help explain the wage premium for batters over bowlers in the IPL. Sadly for bowlers, the batters are the ones who seem to produce the larger share of the entertainment value. Don Bradman is a compelling example.

In 2004, Julian Blackham and Bruce Chapman published a study of the Bradman effect. They compared Australian home matches in which Bradman played from 1930 onwards, the year when his legend was born, analysing the difference in crowds between days when he did and did not bat. They found that when Bradman batted, attendance was 25% higher on average – an extra 7200 fans per day. Measured in 2004 dollars, they estimate Bradman's value in terms of additional revenues to Australian cricket at $1 million per season, compared to his salary of less than $10,000. Of course, if England, or any other country, had been able to lure Bradman away from Australia, his salary would have been much higher. The Australian Cricket Board was well aware of the Bradman effect, advertising his name extensively in the run-up to a Test match.

The Bradman effect, then, seems like the most extreme version of the impact we have identified across the entire dataset – fans are attracted by the prospect of the home team batting. We found a number of other factors that contributed to the variation in daily attendance. Perhaps not surprisingly, games staged in the two largest cities, Melbourne and Sydney, tended to attract larger crowds than games played in less populous cities such as Perth and Hobart. Attendance tends to increase as the summer progresses and then declines as the season comes to an end. With games traditionally scheduled around Christmas and New Year, these tend to be the peak of the season. Test attendance tends to drop off on the fourth and fifth days, as the end of the game approaches. Like baseball, and unlike most other team sports, close finishes are rare in cricket; tension tends to dissipate towards the end of a game rather than increase. Family and friends are reluctant to buy tickets to the fourth and fifth days in advance, knowing they might not have much cricket to watch.

We did not find that Ashes games had significantly higher attendance, nor did we find that the day of the week on which the game was played mattered. Over the entire dataset, the average attendance at Ashes games was the highest (20,900 per game), but in general, other teams were not so far behind. This may sound strange, since in recent years the Ashes have attracted substantial crowds and a gap between other matches has opened up, but this hasn't been the case historically.

England have been Australia's opponents in almost half of all Australia's domestic Tests. This is not just because they have been played for longer – they are played more often as well, with England touring every four years, the only team to consistently tour Australia for a five-Test series. Ashes games are always scheduled for the most popular dates in the season, so attendance will be high for that reason alone – many fans go to the Boxing Day Test every year, regardless of who Australia are playing.

The absence of a day of the week effect is also interesting. In England, the staging of Test matches tended to follow a stable pattern. Traditionally, games started on Thursday, played until Saturday, then took Sunday off. Although originally reserved for reasons of religious observance, Sundays became a day for the players to indulge in boozy barbeques. West Indies off spinner Clyde Butts got married on the rest day of his Test debut in April 1985 – and completed the game on the Monday and Tuesday. In the early 1980s, England began experimenting with playing on Sundays; by 2001, the rest day had been abolished entirely. Thursday is still the conventional starting day, but if back-to-back Tests are staged, the first could start on a Wednesday, or the second on a Friday.

In Australia, Friday has been the most popular day for the start of a Test, accounting for just over half of all games, while Thursday and Saturday accounted for another one-sixth each. Just over 10% of all games started on Sunday, Monday, Tuesday or Wednesday. Partly this reflects the scheduling of holiday games. The Boxing Day Test starts on Boxing Day – whatever day of the year that is, and the New Year Test has often started on 2 January (to make matters more complicated, the scheduling has varied over the years). In England, you might expect attendance to be highest on a Saturday: this is not a working day, the Test is usually well poised, and fans who buy tickets in advance can reasonably expect a full day's play. It is hard to make a similar generalisation about Australia, given the variety of weekdays on which games begin.

*   *   *

It is tempting to say that the imminent death of Test cricket is what keeps it alive. Australian Test match attendances peaked in the 1940s, at around 34,000 per day, although this was probably exaggerated by the brief postwar boom; the average of the golden years of the 1920s and 1930s was more like 23,000. By the 1960s, the daily average was 18,000, then 15,000 in the 1970s and 11,000 in the 1980s – though total attendance was much healthier, given the significant expansion of foreign tours. In the era of Australian dominance, attendance skyrocketed, reaching averages of more than 22,000 per day in the 2010s, higher than anything seen since the 1950s.

This effect is illustrated in Figure 17.1 on the next page, which shows the average daily attendance at Test matches from 1960 to 2019. The downward trend is clearly visible in the early years and appears to stabilise, albeit with substantial year-to-year fluctuations, in the 1990s. The recovery seems to begin in the late 1980s or early 1990s and really accelerates in the era of the dominant Test team, which one can roughly date from the mid-1990s until Shane Warne's and Glenn McGrath's retirement from Test cricket in 2007. The peak year is 2006, the year in which the Ashes are recovered. Since then, the Australian Test team has enjoyed mixed fortunes, and attendance levels have moved sideways. Compared to the peak of 2006, there is even some evidence of a declining trend, but it is too early to tell whether this is merely random fluctuations in the data.

Figure 17.1: Average daily attendances at Test matches in Australia, 1960–2019

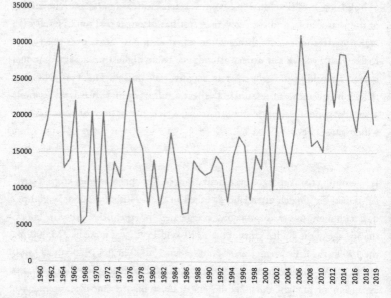

One villain often suspected in the past of plotting the death of Test cricket was television. Indeed, Geoffrey Boycott has argued that, to increase crowds at Test matches, TV coverage should be blacked out within 50 miles of the ground. The notion that the ability to watch the game on TV was reducing the incentive to attend the game may have made some sense in an era when broadcasters paid very little in fees to show games. That nonsense was ended by Kerry Packer in the 1970s; since then broadcasters and Test cricket have developed a close, even symbiotic, relationship. If anything, the argument today is more likely to be that there is not *enough* Test cricket on television, or at least, not enough on free-to-air. Migration to pay TV has increased revenue, while reducing viewership. The broadcast of live Test matches on free-to-air TV in the UK ended in 2005, just as Channel 4 achieved some of cricket's largest ratings for the remarkable Ashes series, peaking at 8.4 million. Since then, the peak for a Test match on Sky Sports is the 2.1 million who watched Ben Stokes clinch the Headingley Ashes Test in 2019.

The other villain typically fingered for the attempted murder of Test cricket is the short-form game. Yet the improved attendances for Tests in Australia coincided with the advent of one-day and then T20 cricket. Limited-overs cricket had already been around since 1962, but not initially as an international game. The first ODI was played when the 1971 Ashes Test at the MCG was abandoned because of rain after four days. On the final day a limited-overs game was hastily arranged – a way of 'making some brass for Australian cricket', England captain Raymond Illingworth grumbled. It was a Tuesday, the game was played at short notice – and yet 46,000 fans turned up. But it still took until the 1983 World Cup for administrators to embrace the full potential of the format. In the 1980s and 1990s, the average ODI in Australia was attracting over 33,000 fans – nearly three times the number attending the average day of Test cricket.

The comparison was not flattering: an entire Test match attracted about the same level of attendance as the average ODI. While many believed that ODIs enabled cricket to reach a wider audience, to Cricket Australia ODIs were simply much more profitable than Tests. Nonetheless, the number of days of Test cricket played in Australia since the 1980s has remained stable at around 26 per year, compared to about 10 ODIs.

In the 2000s, T20 arrived. If T20 has done any harm to other formats of the game, it is ODIs that appear to have suffered most. Average attendance at ODIs in Australia fell to 24,000 in the 2010s; the number of games played also dropped to accommodate the new format. Attendance at international T20s has averaged around 40,000, including a game against India in 2008 at the MCG which attracted 84,000. As T20s thrive, the schedule of ODIs is being rationalised. From 2010–2015, the nine leading Full Members – those part of the World Test Championship – played 2.6 ODIs for every T20I. From 2016 until the end of the 2021 T20 World Cup, they played only 1.2 ODIs for every T20I.

For all the talk about Test cricket being cannibalised by the limited-overs game, the rise of the shorter-form game in Australia has gone hand in hand with the revival of Test cricket. As always, correlation is not causation: it might be, for example, that Test attendance would have risen even faster if there had not been any one-day or T20 cricket. But the evidence that limited-overs cricket is killing Tests is flimsy.

18

HOW THE BARMY ARMY ARE KEEPING TEST CRICKET ALIVE – FROM THEIR SOFAS

It was another typical England Ashes tour: a tale of doom and gallows humour down under. Brisbane and Melbourne had brought moments of English hope, but only fleetingly. The numbing reality was of consecutive thrashings, first by 184 and then 295 runs.

To Australian eyes, the only surprise was that several thousand English fans had come all the way to Australia to witness the 1994–1995 Ashes series. The Australian media had a moniker for the ragtag group of English fans, borrowing from a common football chant: the 'Barmy Army'. The English resolved that the best way to deal with the chant was to own it.

English supporter Paul Burnham turned 30 a few days after England's mauling in Brisbane. He had just quit his job at British Airways and had a new one working in the City of London to begin in March 1995. In between, Burnham resolved to spend several months following his great love. He was accompanied by record numbers of travelling England supporters, reflecting a combination of cheaper air travel and the England football team's failure to qualify for the 1994 World Cup; denied the opportunity to see the footballers struggle in the US, a few months later they watched England get mauled in the first two Ashes Tests instead.

'It was really backs-to-the-wall stuff,' Burnham says. 'A defiant group of people that got bigger and bigger each Test, defying the typical Australian fans in those days who were pretty abusive to England supporters and particularly to our players on the pitch. So it's their fault that we were created really because we just didn't want to sit there and listen to some pretty aggressive comments.'

For the third Test at the SCG, English fans spread the word to buy tickets on Sydney Hill. A group of several hundred decided to put on a show.

Burnham led the constant chant at the SCG, 'Mike Atherton's Barmy Army,' showing the support for the England captain and team. The chants became louder and more frequent as the Test progressed. Perhaps coincidentally – although Burnham would like to take credit here – England produced by far their best performance of the tour, with Australia needing a fifth-day rearguard to salvage a draw.

Burnham and his followers now decided that they needed the attire to match their chant. Before the fourth Test in Adelaide, he offered to procure T-shirts inscribed 'Mike Atherton's Barmy Army' together with the wearer's name and found 100 takers – 'it stopped everyone calling each other mate'. On the first day of the Test, Burnham went to T-Shirt City, a shop in central Adelaide, to place the order. The merchandise didn't arrive until the third day, by which time Australia had established a handy first-innings lead. Over the following two days England turned the game around, with Devon Malcolm and Chris Lewis skittling out Australia in the second innings to seal an unlikely 106-run victory. Don't tell the Barmy Army it wasn't the T-shirts wot won it.

Several thousand England fans now descended on T-Shirt City to get their own commemorative apparel. 'They kept themselves open to 11 o'clock at night, and people were coming in ordering and then they worked through the night putting people's names on,' Burnham recalls. Sensing the demand for more, Burnham and two friends and co-founders, David Peacock and Gareth Evans, placed an order for several thousand to be shipped to Perth. The trio earned a modest mark-up on each shirt, which helped to fund their tours.

During the tour, Atherton's agent had jokingly approached Burnham in Adelaide, 'He said, "Have you asked Michael? Have you asked his permission?"' More pertinently, Burnham did not want the group's focus to be on one man. After the 1994–1995 tour, the embryonic group changed their name from Atherton's Barmy Army to simply The Barmy Army. In March 1995, he trademarked the name Barmy Army in England, Australia and South Africa, the latter being England's hosts in 1995–1996.

* * *

Until 2003, Burnham juggled the Barmy Army with an array of other jobs, including working for the magazine *Cricket World* and for spread betting companies. In 2003, he decided that the Barmy Army was secure enough a gig for him to quit his other jobs and devote himself to working for the travelling group full-time. Today, the Barmy Army Ltd is a successful small business with an annual turnover of £600,000. Burnham has now seen well over 100 England Tests abroad.

'I was able to live the dream,' he says. 'Cricket really does throw up some unique characters. The Barmy Army is very good at collecting all of those.

'It's amazing to have so many people from around the country – all different ages, travelling overseas and having the time of your life, watching the England cricket team. It used to be good when we weren't very good, it's even better now.'

The Barmy Army's reputation as mostly a bunch of middle-aged white men is not entirely undeserved. Only 11% of Barmy Army members are female. There is not yet a breakdown of membership by ethnicity, but to glance at a Barmy Army crowd is not to see a snapshot of Britain's ethnic diversity. The average age of Barmy Army members is believed to be 40–45, though the age of those on Barmy Travel tours is significantly older.

As a business, the Barmy Army has two strands. The first, Barmy Travel, is a travel company that works with airlines, hotels and national boards to develop package tours for travelling supporters, including match tickets. The Barmy Travel business, founded in 2003, is the main source of income.

Yet the more popular strand of the Barmy Army is the umbrella group, open to anyone who is an England fan. The Barmy Army currently has 3500 members who pay £30 a year each in return for priority access to tickets – the Barmy Army has close relationships with overseas boards and all English grounds bar Lord's, which does not recognise fan groups. They also receive emails with travel advice and tips. Around 90% of travelling English supporters make their plans independent of Barmy Travel, but they still use the Barmy Army's advice on hotels, restaurants and how to get tickets.

The Barmy Army has also served as the distributor of tickets for away supporters. On England's Test tour of South Africa in 2019–2020, Cricket

South Africa used them to distribute 1000 tickets a day to travelling England supporters who collected them from Barmy Army representatives in hotels, locking out ticket touts.

While the Barmy Army are best-known for their boisterous chanting, they have used their power as a force for good. Since the tour of South Africa in 1995–1996, they have raised money for charities. On the third evening of every Test, they organise a charity party, featuring a guest speaker, auction, raffle and sometimes a live band. So far, more than £500,000 has been raised for more than 50 charities supported by the Barmy Army.

* * *

Any institution as successful as the Barmy Army will naturally inspire imitators. While Australia's Fanatics, who organise tours across a multitude of sports, were launched in 1997, by far the most significant rival to the Barmy Army is the Bharat Army, the Indian equivalent, which was founded during the 1999 World Cup in England.

India's match with Pakistan at Old Trafford took place against the tense backdrop of the Kargil War and predictions of fights between rival supporters. When 25-year-old India supporter Rakesh Patel, who had travelled up from his home in South London, arrived in the ground, he sought out fellow Indian fans. 'Myself and a couple of friends entered a stadium that was 70% full of Pakistan fans,' Patel recalls. 'We had tickets in different parts of the stadium and decided to come together in one stand rather than sit separately – by the end of the match we had 200–300 Indian fans around us.'

Happily, predictions of unrest during the game proved ill-founded, just as they have done since. 'We won the match but more importantly the atmosphere we created and the camaraderie led me to believe we should have an official supporters group for the most passionate fans in the world – hence the Bharat Army.'

The Bharat Army is routinely called India's equivalent of the Barmy Army, but that undersells it: the Bharat Army is much bigger. While the Barmy Army have 3500 members and four full-time staff – though these can be joined by 25 part-timers for Ashes tours – the Bharat Army have just over 100,000 members and 15 full-time staff, spread between London and Ahmedabad. The popularity of different formats among the two fan groups gives a sense of the different priorities between cricket's old world and its new.

Whereas the staging posts in the Barmy Army's growth have been Ashes tours, the story of the Bharat Army is intertwined with the one-day international World Cup. The World Cup led to the creation of the Bharat Army, and the event does more than any other to sustain the group's growth. For the Bharat Army, the 2003 World Cup in South Africa 'was probably the most important as this is when ESPN Star Sports started covering us as a fan group and started to do segments on us before India's matches,' says Patel, who is now the chief executive of the Bharat Army.

The record number of supporters on a Barmy Travel tour package is the 1200 who went to Australia for the 2017–2018 Ashes. For the Bharat Army, the record is more than nine times higher. During the 2019 World Cup, when the Bharat Army were awarded an ICC Travel and Tours licence, they distributed 11,200 tickets through their official travel programme. While an estimated total of 15,000 English fans travelled to Australia for the 2017–2018 Ashes, an estimated 80,000 Indian fans came to England for the 2019 World Cup.

The two largest fan groups in cricket share a strong rapport. Yet a comparison of Bharat Army and Barmy Army support for their two marquee events – the World Cup and Ashes – with other tours to the same country illustrates their divergent preferences. On the 2017–2018 England tour of Australia, England's prospects were far stronger in ODIs. Yet 35 times more supporters signed up to the Barmy Army's official Test package, only to see England thrashed 4–0, than came to watch England win the ODI series 4–1. For the Bharat Army, the relationship is inverted. The World Cup is unmistakably king. More than five times more Bharat Army members attended the 2019 World Cup than India's Test series in England a year earlier.

*   *   *

On a sweltering afternoon in Cape Town at the start of 2020, England needed five wickets after tea on the final day to seal victory. To get them,

England would need to overcome a pitch offering scant assistance and South African defiance.

Several times during the final day, captain Joe Root could be seen looking beyond the field for an alternative source of inspiration for his players: the travelling Barmy Army, whom Root roused by using his arms to gesture for more noise. When Ben Stokes sealed England's thrilling victory with 50 balls remaining, the Barmy Army were certain that their support had helped secure the win.

'That was one of those Tests where you know you've made a difference,' Burnham says. Of all the England captains in the Barmy Army's history, 'Root is definitely the most proactive' in enlisting supporters to chant. 'He knows if he goes to the crowd and gets everyone going everyone's going to make an effort for him.'

Other England players have also welcomed their support. In 2003, after England won a consolation victory at the SCG, Nasser Hussain led the team on a lap of honour, even though they'd lost 4–1. 'It was a lap of honour to say we've really let you down on this trip, we've won the last game at Sydney and you've stood with us all the way through – we just want to go around and show our appreciation,' Hussain later said. Naturally, the Barmy Army celebrated like they'd won the FA Cup.

The benefit of the support offered by fans is well attested across many sports – it's just that usually it's the home team's support that makes the difference. Whether by intimidating the opposition, intimidating the umpires or simply boosting the morale of your players, fan support works.

Covid provided some startling evidence of what happens when you take away the support for the home team. The most striking example was football's Bundesliga. The 2019–2020 season was interrupted by Covid after nearly three quarters of games had been played; after a break, the rest of the games were played without fans. In the first part of the season, home wins outnumbered away wins by 97 to 78. Without fans, away wins outnumbered home wins by 37 to 26. This reversal may have something to do with specific circumstances in the Bundesliga. But research by the psychologists Dane McCarrick, Meric Bilalic, Nick Neave, and Sandy Wolfson looked at 15 different European leagues encompassing almost 10,000 games in 11 countries and found that the absence of fans due to Covid did indeed reduce home advantage.

Crowd support helps, principally through the mechanism of influencing referees and umpires, as a substantial literature in economics has shown. The phenomenon is called 'favouritism under social pressure'. If the Barmy Army provided more vocal support to England while travelling, we should expect to see an improvement in England's away record relative to its home record in their era compared to the pre-Barmy Army era. But this doesn't appear to be the case. In 314 Tests played before the Barmy Army came together, England's win percentage (treating a draw as half a win) was 51% at home and 45% away. In the 315 Tests played since, up to the 2021/22 Ashes, the home win percentage shot up to 64%, while the away win percentage fell to 43%. This does not prove conclusively that there is no Barmy effect – home advantage in Test cricket has increased generally – but it certainly isn't self-evident in the averages.

The Barmy Army pride themselves on 'intelligent supporting,' as Burnham terms it. 'We tend to sing when the boys are bowling and not when they're batting and we get behind them when it's at the end of the day and they're knackered and they really need to lift.'

Throughout the 2010/11 Ashes, the Barmy Army belted out their song about Mitchell Johnson, Australia's biggest threat, 'He bowls to the left, he bowls to the right, that Mitchell Johnson, his bowling is shite.' Johnson claimed that the chanting damaged his performance. 'I think back then I let it affect me a lot,' he said in 2012. 'It's hard not to when that's all you can hear in the cricket ground – your name being sung, and the songs are very catchy.'

It seems he learned how to deal with it. In 2013/14, Johnson took 37 wickets to help Australia win the Ashes 5–0.

* * *

About a year before each England Test tour, Chris Millard, the managing director of the Barmy Army, visits the relevant country. The trip aims to take in all the hotels and all the venues, sampling local pubs and restaurants and replicating the fan experience as far as possible. 'I go out before to make sure the hotels are great, the transport links are OK and I'm aware of everything,' he says. 'We leave no stone unturned.'

In November 2016, Millard and Burnham visited Australia in preparation for the following year's Ashes. He travelled to all five cities that would host Tests, visiting every ground, meeting every local tourism board, and having two meetings with Cricket Australia. He and Burnham also negotiated plans for the Barmy Army's highly anticipated A$100-per-head Christmas lunch in the Melbourne Crown Casino for 650 travelling England supporters.

Relations with overseas boards have not always been easy. 'Each country in the world has tried to take advantage of the travelling England fans,' Burnham says. Boards including Sri Lanka and West Indies have got into rows with the Barmy Army after trying to charge England fans a separate price to the normal figure for overseas fans – while Burnham accepts paying a different price than home supporters, he sees no justification for charging England supporters more than other travelling fans. In 2006/07, perhaps in response to England's 2005 Ashes victory, English supporters were spread around grounds in Australia rather than allowed to sit together. The Barmy Army's trumpeter, Bill Cooper, was even escorted out of The Gabba after celebrating an Australian wicket.

But economic self-interest has led home boards to embrace the Barmy Army. Even for Cricket Australia, the world's third wealthiest board, they provide a significant top-up of funds. For poorer boards, the Barmy Army's cash can be vital.

'Governing bodies see the value in working with us to make the tour better for the tourists because one, they can make more money out of it and two, they want to put on the best experience possible so people go back,' Millard says. Boards recognise the simple truth that the more members of the Barmy Army they can attract, the more cash they will make.

A year before England's 2019/20 tour of South Africa, Millard met Cricket South Africa. The venues for the series had already been decided, but the board wanted Millard's advice about which order of matches would be most attractive to England supporters to encourage them to stay longer.

'We spoke about what the fixture list would look like to best suit tourists and how they would best leverage the tourism market,' Millard recalls. The series would begin with a Test on Boxing Day in Pretoria – about half an hour on the road or train from Johannesburg, from where most fans stayed – and then the traditional New Year's Test in Cape Town. The last two Tests were scheduled for Port Elizabeth and Pretoria, but it was not clear in which order.

'It made sense for Port Elizabeth to be the one after Cape Town to keep people out there because a lot of people stay in Johannesburg for both the Pretoria Test and the Centurion Test. So they could leverage the tourism market more if they had another venue that wasn't near Johannesburg after Cape Town.' It was a neat encapsulation of the Barmy Army's standing in the game. Starting as a renegade fan group, they now help to decide the tour itineraries.

* * *

The Caribbean is heavily dependent on tourism, and Cricket West Indies likes to say that the game produces a significant economic benefit for the region. But it is easy to exaggerate how much cricket tourism contributes to the local economy. National income accounts don't measure activities like tourism directly – they measure goods and services bought and sold.

Imagine you are sitting at a bar on the waterfront in Barbados and you order a beer. That is money that some might like to call a benefit to the local economy. But before doing that, you have to deduct the cost of growing the ingredients, brewing the beer, bottling and shipping it, and paying for the use of the facilities. If all these activities take place on the island itself, then you are indeed contributing to the local economy. But if the farmer bought farm equipment made in China, the brewing equipment was imported from Mexico, the truck was built in Brazil and the hotel was built by a US hotel chain, how much of that money is really going into the local economy? Worse still, what if you ordered a bottle of imported Budweiser? Think of the popular tourist nations around the world: do you think of them as rich countries? Those who are, like France, aren't rich because of tourism. Nations don't get rich on tourism.

Cricket West Indies retains the consultants YouGov (under the branding of YouGov Sports) to research the economic impact of their tournaments on the local economies. After each event they release figures alleging significant contributions – in 2019, the figures were $126 million for the Caribbean Premier League, $76 million for England's tour, and $60 million for India's. The beauty of making these claims is that no one can contradict you – who knows how much money would have been generated if these tours had not taken place?

Economists have long challenged the credibility of such research. First, even if true, these numbers are trivial. The estimated GDP of the Caribbean islands in 2019 was $82 billion – so the combined cricket events amounted to 0.32% of total GDP. Not nothing, but little short of a rounding error in the national income statistics. Second, just paying someone a lot of money to stage a competition doesn't mean it's very profitable: if the organisers have to import everything, they could even lose money. This is as true for nations as it is for individuals and businesses. Third, most cricket is played in the tourist high season – the northern hemisphere winter, which means that cricket tourists are often just displacing other potential visitors. Fourth, sitting in a stadium all day watching cricket is not especially good for an island's economy. What the economy needs is more spending on services – like renting boats, renting scuba diving equipment or hiring tour guides.

Of course, this is not to say that the islands don't welcome cricket tourists, just that the economic benefit to the economy is not that significant. Much the same analysis has been applied to other sporting events, notably the economic impacts of the Olympics and the World Cup. The pattern is always the same. The paid consultants, such as YouGov, proclaim significant benefits; the economists follow up with a study finding the economic benefits either negligible or even negative. When London hosted the Olympic Games in 2012, tourism to the capital decreased by 6% compared to the same time of year in 2011; those without Olympic tickets preferred to holiday elsewhere instead.

* * *

Even if the Barmy Army's economic impact on the general economy is modest, there is one area where they do make a significant contribution: Caribbean cricket itself. Cricket West Indies struggles to generate revenue from the local population – which is generally relatively poor and only numbers six million. Thanks to the steep costs of hotels and the need for charter flights to take teams between the islands, nowhere is hosting cricket as expensive as it is in the Caribbean.

To gauge the impact of the English and Indian fan groups, consider matches without them. During 2018, the West Indies first hosted Sri Lanka for three Test matches and then Bangladesh for two Tests, three ODIs and three T20Is. The total broadcasting revenue for the two series was less than $1 million. Little additional money came in as gate receipts; Cricket West Indies lost a total of $22 million from the two series – an astronomical figure that highlights the structural inequalities in international cricket. While West Indies is an extreme example, the essential pattern – of mid-ranking teams losing eye-watering sums when hosting each other – is typical.

In 2019, the year after incurring those losses, both England and India toured the West Indies for multi-match series. England came for three Tests, five ODIs and three T20Is; India toured for two Tests, three ODIs and three T20Is. The 2019 England tour generated $3.5 million in direct ticket sales – about 90% of that came from England supporters, as anyone watching the matches could attest. India's tour generated $2.85 million in ticket sales, but the bulk of that was generated in Florida, where the West Indies hosted India for two T20Is. The willingness of England fans to travel to the Caribbean, along with the cash they spend there, allows the board to monetise the series in another way. Cricket West Indies negotiate 'bid fees' – financial support from hosting islands, for England games; this was worth $3.3 million in 2019.

Yet, for Cricket West Indies, the real economic significance of England touring lies in the broadcasting revenue. To understand why, consider where CWI generate their cash. In the four financial years from 2016 to 2019, Cricket West Indies earned total revenue of $168 million, according to the board's accounts. Revenue from the ICC accounted for $47.7 million, just under a quarter. But comfortably the biggest source of cash was media rights: these were worth \$73.3 million, amounting to almost half of CWI's revenue and 60% of revenue excluding money from the ICC. Such a dependence upon broadcasting revenue is in keeping with the norm for most sports governing bodies throughout the world.

While many sports organisations generate most of their revenue from domestic broadcast sales, in the West Indies this pattern is reversed. Cricket West Indies' home market in the Caribbean is only the third biggest market for broadcasting rights, with English and Indian broadcasters accounting for 60% of Cricket West Indies' broadcasting revenue. With visits by all other countries loss-makers, this essentially leaves West Indies dependent on a combination of ICC income and tours by England and India to stay afloat. From generating a puny \$986,000 in media rights in 2018, when Sri Lanka and Bangladesh toured, CWI generated \$33.7 million in 2019, when England and India toured.

'If England or India didn't tour the Caribbean, it would be nigh on impossible for us to be a sustainable cricket organisation,' explains Dominic Warne, the commercial and marketing director for Cricket West Indies. 'I would suggest that might be similar to other smaller cricketing nations around the world. That broadcast revenue is so important for us.'

In 2020, during the height of Covid-19, West Indies endured almost two months in a biosecure bubble so they could maintain their commitments to touring England. It was an act for which the England and Wales Cricket Board were indebted to Cricket West Indies.

To show their thanks, England agreed to play an extra Test on their next tour of the Caribbean in 2022. While England also agreed to play two extra Twenty20 matches, it was revealing that West Indies requested that England play another Test. Against India and most opponents, playing more limited-overs games would be financially preferable; against England, uniquely, it made financial sense for the West Indies to stage an extra Test.

'The Indian market is much more focused on white ball cricket – I would expect that trend to continue,' Warne says. 'England, on a per-fan basis, is singularly our most important tour. The long-term trend is that it will only continue to be our most important tour in terms of fans in the stadium, and the interest.'

The ragtag movement that Burnham formed in 1995 helps the finances of Cricket West Indies and other boards by travelling around the world to follow the England Test team. Yet the economic impact of those who follow England Test tours from home is far more important. You could say that the stay-at-home Barmy Army are helping to keep Test cricket alive from their sofas.

PART SIX

THE FUTURE

19

HOW NETWORKS EXPLAIN
THE RISE OF ASIA

On a drizzly winter's morning in 1993, Alan Smith, the chief executive of England's Test and County Cricket Board, entered the committee room at Lord's. The agenda seemed routine enough: an International Cricket Council meeting to confirm that England would host the next World Cup.

Smith was actually walking straight into an ambush. Pakistan, India and Sri Lanka had hatched a plan to co-host the World Cup together. To get the votes they needed, they offered to pay each Associate member – those who were not Test-playing Full Members – £40,000 more than England offered. It was 'by a long way, the worst meeting I have ever attended,' Smith complained afterwards. 'Fractious and unpleasant.'

After two tumultuous days, England lost the right to host the 1996 World Cup. Instead, it would be staged on the subcontinent. 'They seem not to like their erstwhile colonial subjects coming to London and beating them at what they still consider their own game,' chortled I.S. Bindra, then president of the BCCI, after the meetings. 'We in the subcontinent want to prove to the rest of the world that whatever they can do, we can do better.'

'When the Asian bid won, it was a defining moment for the balance of power of world cricket,' recalls Ehsan Mani, who was Pakistan's representative on the ICC. 'It was clear that things would never be the same.'

Three years later, after the 1996 World Cup had broken all financial records in the sport, world cricket was divided about who should take over the reins at the ICC. On one side was India's Jagmohan Dalmiya, favoured by the Asian bloc; on the other was Australia's Malcolm Gray, the favoured candidate of cricket's old world. Dalmiya ultimately won by repeating the subcontinent's tactics of 1993: promising more funds for emerging countries who were sick of patronising paternalism from cricket's old order. It was a strikingly similar template to how João Havelange had won the presidency of FIFA, world football's governing body, in 1974.

When he became ICC President in 1997, one of Dalmiya's first acts was to launch the Wills International Cup (later renamed the Champions Trophy) – effectively a mini-World Cup. The tournament was explicitly created to drive cricket's expansion: half the £10 million profits from the first competition in 1998 were allocated to develop cricket outside the Test-playing world, and the first two tournaments were even held in Associate nations. The Champions Trophy marked the tentative onset of cricket's first concerted attempts to globalise the game. With hindsight, it also heralded the moment that the ascent of Asia beyond the continent's three oldest Asian Test nations – India, Pakistan and Sri Lanka – began.

'That's when the story starts,' says Tim Anderson, who worked in a series of roles for the ICC, including as head of global development from 2010 to 2016. 'The Asian region has had a good run from that day onwards.'

Cricket has long been tentative about globalisation. But from 2001, the ICC began to make a more concerted effort to expand into new frontiers. The ICC's burgeoning commercial deals led to major increases in the funding that Associate nations received from the governing body, enabling them to invest in facilities and play more fixtures. In the same year, Bob Woolmer, one of the world's most respected coaches, was appointed to the new position of ICC high performance manager, charged with improving the best emerging nations.

During Woolmer's time, the coterie of leading Associates did not include many Asian teams. In both the 2003 and 2007 World Cups, which featured 14 and then 16 teams, no Asian Associates qualified.

In 2007, the ICC created the World Cricket League which, for the first time, offered a formal competitive structure to track the emerging nations' progress. There were only three Asian nations among the top 18 Associate counties when the World Cricket League launched – so, including the Full Member countries above this structure, just seven of the top 28 countries in the world at the time were from Asia.

By November 2021, 13 of the top 28 teams in the men's T20I rankings played in the Asian region, as did nine of the top 28 teams in the women's rankings. Many of cricket's best stories in the 21st century have come from Asia: Bangladesh's transformation from the punch line of jokes to cricket's top table; Afghanistan's 13-year journey from their first official international to being a Test nation and one of the world's top 10 ODI and T20 nations; Thailand's rise to qualifying for the women's T20 World Cup in 2020; and Nepal and Oman gaining one-day international status and reaching the men's T20 World Cup.

While the Continent's four ICC Full Members were the only Asian teams to make the 16-team World Cup in 2007, an average of seven Asian teams out of 16 played in the men's T20 World Cups between 2014 and 2021. Analysis of the World Cricket League (which was reformed in 2019) by CricketEurope journalist Andrew Nixon showed that during the 12 years of the competition, each Asian country was promoted an average of 1.4 divisions (assuming a value of +1 for each promotion and -1 for each demotion). By contrast, the average for teams from the other continents (Africa, the Americas, East-Asia Pacific and Europe) was negative, with relegations outnumbering promotions.

Table 19.1: World Cricket League average promotion and relegation by countries from each region, 2007–2019

Africa	–0.56
Americas	–1.57
Asia	+1.42
EAP	–1.00
Europe	–0.18

For all the attention given to India's sporting and financial rise in the 21st century, there is a bigger story: the rise of Asia. This is a tale of economics, demography and network effects. It reveals much about how and why countries from outside the traditional elite rise in international cricket.

* * *

On Christmas Day 1979, Soviet tanks rolled into Afghanistan, marking the start of the decade-long war between Afghanistan and the USSR. The Soviet invasion also heralded the start of Afghanistan's emergence into the top 10 cricket nations in the world and a lesson in the power of unintended consequences.

The horrors of the war led many thousands of Afghans to flee. Most went to Peshawar, the Pakistani city close to the border with Afghanistan. In Peshawar, Afghans learned the sport, catching glimpses of matches on television and playing – normally with a tape-ball, a tennis ball covered with electrical tape – among themselves or with locals.

Kacha Garhi, a refugee camp in Peshawar, was a hotbed of Afghan talent. Mohammad Nabi, who would later captain his country and become one of the first two Afghans signed by the Indian Premier League, was born in Peshawar on New Year's Day 1985. Like many of his future international teammates, Nabi played club cricket in Peshawar, including with and against Pakistani professionals.

In 1995, Allah Dad Noori, a refugee returning to Kabul, formed the Afghanistan Cricket Federation, which would become the Afghan Cricket Board. During their rule of Afghanistan from 1995 to 2001, The Taliban allowed the sport to exist because of its conservative dress code and because it was viewed as a Pakistani sport. In the last months of Taliban rule, Afghanistan applied for membership of the ICC, which was granted in June 2001.

Three years later, Afghanistan played their first official game. The team, which initially largely comprised of former refugees from Peshawar, then embarked upon an extraordinary rise up the ladder of international cricket – playing in their first T20 World Cup in 2010, their first ODI World Cup in 2015 and then becoming Full Members in 2017, just 13 years after their first official game. Sultan Rana, the head of the Asian Cricket Council, observed that, 'Russia's invasion of Afghanistan was a plus for cricket.'

While Afghanistan's story is unique, emigration has been a common theme in Asia's ascent. Economic migrants from Bangladesh, India and Pakistan have taken the game to countries such as Oman, the United Arab Emirates, Hong Kong, Singapore, Kuwait, Malaysia, Qatar and Saudi Arabia; late-night games in car parks are common. Players from Bangladesh, India, or Pakistan have often accounted for half or more of players in their national teams. In 2019, Oman earned ODI status and qualified for the T20 World Cup, for the second consecutive time; eight of their squad were born in Pakistan, six in India and only one in Oman. In Oman and the UAE, a model of corporate patronage is common. Some companies hire migrant workers to play for the company team based partly on their cricket ability, which in turn can lead to playing on the national team. All this has started to raise interest among the local populations, too, with cable TV and then live streaming enabling both migrants and locals to follow the professional game.

Wider shifts have also favoured Asian nations. In 2019, *The Financial Times* reported that Asia accounted for 38% of economic global output, up from 26% at the start of the 2000s. Economic growth has translated into better diets, increased life expectancy, and more money to spend on infrastructure and facilities – including for sport. Growth has eroded and – in many cases – reversed the competitive advantage of other cricketing countries over Asian teams in facilities and infrastructure. This has allowed the region's existing advantages in playing numbers to be brought to bear.

'You've got this massive fanbase in Asia, and what comes from that is mass wealth,' observes Anderson. 'Once the opportunity to commercialise was born around 2000, the huge fanbase, plus huge wealth now equals greater passion, greater fanbase, which ultimately is going to equal better standards of play. Those two massive fundamentals are so significant compared to, let's call them, the competitors – the rest of the countries around the world.' Even when some Asian nations experienced governance crises – notably Nepal, who were suspended from the ICC for government interference with the board, and Afghanistan – these broader advantages remained.

The ICC's funding policies have also benefited the 21 ICC members who are part of the Asian region. Under the ICC's 'scorecard' model for funding Associate teams, each Associate is ranked on a range of factors, including national-team performance, number of grounds, or numbers of junior players. The rankings translate into a formula that decides how much money they receive. The funds are paid to boards in US dollars. Naturally, this means that it can buy more in, say, Nepal than in Scotland.

'The money that ICC provides goes further in some economies than others – there's absolutely no doubt,' says Richard Done, who was high-performance manager of the ICC from 2004 to 2020. 'Internal costs are the difference.'

While richer countries can make up some of this shortfall – for instance, sponsorship opportunities may be greater – at Associate level the funding distribution generally helps Asian countries to fund far more professional contracts, so their wages are comparatively more attractive to players. From 2015 to 2020, around half a dozen Scotland international players who were close to their prime retired to pursue other opportunities. In 2016 captain Preston Mommsen, who was 29 and in the best form of his life, retired to take up a career in property development. Mommsen's contract was worth around £30,000 before bonuses – slightly above the average wage in the country, but several times the median in Nepal, whose rise was not stymied by players leaving the sport for opportunities outside the game.

* * *

In September 1983, three months after India won the World Cup for the first time, a group of Asian administrators met in Delhi. Representatives from India, Pakistan, Sri Lanka, Bangladesh, Malaysia and Singapore formed the Asian Cricket Conference, later renamed the Asian Cricket Council (ACC). The ACC was the first, and only, regional governing body in cricket to exist entirely independently of the ICC, organising its own competitions and generating its own cash.

The first Asia Cup took place the following year. While it initially only included the existing three Asian Test nations, the tournament gradually expanded. Bangladesh first appeared in 1986, after India withdrew, and the next edition grew to four teams. The tournament now comprises six teams, taking place every two years.

The Asia Cup gives emerging nations fixtures against Test opponents that have been virtually absent for teams in other regions. In the early 2010s, Afghanistan and Ireland were the two leading Associate nations, with Ireland more established after successful 2007 and 2011 World Cup campaigns. Ireland only played nine ODIs against Full Members from 2011 to 2015; Afghanistan played four in the space of two weeks during the 2014 Asia Cup.

Yet, however welcome this extra exposure to Test nations for Asian Associates, even more important is the money that the Asia Cup generates. Some of this goes directly to members, leaving them less dependent on ICC funding than Associate members in other countries. But most of the ACC's income from the Asia Cup bankrolls its wider programme of competitions.

The ACC runs competitions from under-16 level, for both East and West Asia, to an under-19 Asia Cup and sub-regional T20 tournaments. They also organise an Emerging Teams Cup, in which teams of emerging players from Full Members compete with the full teams from Associates. The ACC also runs parallel women's competitions for the Asia Cup, the Emerging Teams Asia Cup and under-19s. Thailand's women participated in all these tournaments before reaching the T20 World Cup. Multi-sport events – such as the Asian Games and Southeast Asian Games – have also included cricket. Asian nations simply have a far more plentiful supply of cricket than their rivals from other continents.

Associate coaches acknowledge these benefits. 'They do the emerging tournaments which is probably unique compared with the rest of the world outside of the qualifying structure for an under-19 World Cup,' says Done. 'So they're getting challenged at a level more regularly than in the other Associate regions.

'I think of the number of times we've had meetings with all of the Associates, sitting down with the coaches and the management trying to figure out how we will do things. And if you ask them, what do you need to be better, the two answers would be having more cricket and more money.

'In the emerging countries, playing enough games competitively is probably the biggest gap for most of the countries. We've faced that for years … We tried to get 40 to 50 days of real quality cricket. Whereas I suggest the Asian sides get that pretty easily.'

The Asian Cricket Council's abundance of tournaments imbued players with experience of playing in events. This went some way to replicating Associate tournaments, in which promotion and relegation between divisions and qualification for world events could be decided in tournaments only lasting a week or two.

'There's more event opportunities in Asia than anywhere else,' Done says. 'The simplest bottom line – if you can play more quality-event cricket, you're more likely to get player improvement. And therefore the teams are likely to improve at a faster rate.'

A few years ago, Papua New Guinea, consistently just below the very leading Associates, made unsuccessful overtures to join the Asia region, realising the benefits this could bring. In the East Asia-Pacific region, they suffer from being comfortably the strongest Associate while being simultaneously denied chances to play the two Full Members in their region, Australia and New Zealand. If they were in Asia, they would have had far more similarly-ranked teams to test themselves against, as well as more chances to play higher-ranked sides and to access the ACC's wider support structure.

'In terms of the development of the game, the ACC is as important as the ICC for Nepal to date,' believes Bhawana Ghimire, the former chief executive of the Cricket Association of Nepal. Other Associates have had one international governing body to help them. Asian countries have effectively had two.

* * *

Shortly after Kenya's semi-final defeat in the 2003 World Cup, Michael Holding – a former West Indies great and later a leading commentator – spoke to Steve Tikolo, Kenya's captain. 'Holding told me that the ICC had earmarked Kenya to be the next Test-playing country,' Tikolo recalled.

In their remarkable World Cup run, Kenya defeated three Test nations and, with the help of New Zealand forfeiting their fixture in Nairobi, reached the semi-finals, where they lost to India. After beating Bangladesh, Kenya had won six of the seven ODIs between the sides; judging by on-field performance, there was no doubt who was the stronger side.

Kenya made a formal bid for Test status in 2000, and made renewed attempts after the World Cup. On cricketing merit, their case for elevation was compelling: Kenya had defeated West Indies in the 1996 World Cup and had twice beaten India as well. But as one ICC official allegedly told a Kenyan administrator, 'You do not have 100 million people.' Bangladesh, now 160-million strong, does not have this handicap. It is also an Asian nation. Their elevation to Test status, and the extra money and fixtures this opened up, played out in committee rooms just as much as on the pitch.

Despite defeating Scotland and Pakistan in the 1999 World Cup, 'I knew that our on-field performances alone wouldn't get us Test status,' observed Saber Hossain Chowdhury, who was president of the Bangladesh Cricket Board at the time. 'We had to do a lot of cricket diplomacy ... Our off-field diplomacy compensated for our lack of playing standards.'

Chowdhury was assiduous in wooing the rest of the cricketing world, touring the globe in search of votes. But being from an Asian nation meant that he effectively started with three Full Member votes, while Dalmiya, who was ICC president, pushed Bangladesh's case too. The motivation was part inclination to promote a neighbour and part self-interest – if Bangladesh became a Test nation that would mean another Full Member vote for the Asian bloc.

The contrast with Kenya's treatment after the 2003 World Cup is instructive. Kenya's attempts to be promoted to Full Member status were not merely ignored; their ODI fixture list against Test nations went from reasonable to almost non-existent. In the 18 months before the World Cup, Kenya played 18 ODIs, including a tri-series with India and South Africa and another with Australia and Pakistan. In the 35 months after the World Cup, Kenya played a meagre five ODIs, by which time the promise of what cricket could become in Kenya had evaporated. Had they been an Asian nation, the cricketing world might not have frittered away their potential.

Cricket's intransigence about admitting Kenya was long replicated in their attitude towards Ireland. In the 2006 edition of *Wisden Cricketers' Almanack*, editor Matthew Engel railed against what he termed 'The expansion menace'. At the time, the ICC's mission statement involved 'promoting the game as a global sport'; Engel claimed that 'it should change its mission statement.' Arguing against expanding the World Cup to 16 nations, he wrote that 'it is time to stop wrecking the game we do have in the vain pursuit of the one we don't,' warning that awarding full ODI status to Associate countries would 'add another layer of distortion to cricket's poor old statistics.'

The notes also mocked Ireland's prospects in 2007, their inaugural World Cup. 'The top two of the five teams who qualified for the World Cup via the ICC Trophy are Scotland and Ireland. Well, whoop-de-doo! In cricketing terms, these are not separate countries. It is just a historical quirk that the England cricket team is not called Britain or the British Isles. Every Scotsman and Irishman who gets good at cricket wants to play for England, and always has done. Of course they do.

'And we have enough form-lines to go on to know how good these teams are: stronger than a Minor County; worse than the weakest first-class county. About where they have always been. The idea that they can provide proper opposition for any genuine Test team is ludicrous. But the World Cup will be substantially ruined to perpetuate this myth.'

Yet in the World Cup, Ireland toppled Pakistan and Bangladesh; they backed up this performance by beating England in the 2011 World Cup and West Indies and Zimbabwe in 2015. This amounted to a greater number of victories over Test nations than any of the other three teams elevated to Full Member status since 1975. But Ireland's paucity of cricket against Test opponents contributed to three leading players – including future World Cup-winning captain Eoin Morgan – switching to play for England.

Many at the ICC privately believed that, had they been an Asian country, Ireland would have been promoted years before. Instead, their elevation had to wait until 2017, until Afghanistan were simultaneously promoted, thereby increasing the Asian representation among Full Members to five out of 12.

From Dalmiya's day, Asian Associates also benefited from more ICC cash than their rivals. As ICC president, Dalmiya argued that Asian emerging countries should receive more cash given the amount of cricket's revenue that came from the Continent. From 1997, when the development programme was launched, until the end of 2015, 6% of the ICC's total commercial revenue was spent on development. Half of this money went to Asia, and half to the rest of the world combined. The playing field was skewed in Asia's favour.

Such financial support was only the most obvious manifestation of how existing Asian Full Members aided emerging teams in the region; Full Members also share knowledge, coaches and facilities. 'There is a much stronger collegiality on a regional basis in Asia than anywhere else,' observes Anderson.

Perhaps the best case study is Afghanistan. In 2002–2003, before their first official international, Afghanistan played in a low level of domestic competition in Pakistan. Afghan players trained at the academy of Rashid Latif, the former

Pakistan captain; Kabir Khan, a former Pakistan cricketer, coached them. Afghanistan's players continued to play games on the other side of the Durand Line, including for clubs in Peshawar. Several players, including future IPL player Nabi, also played professionally for Pakistani domestic teams.

As Afghanistan rose, so the nature of Pakistan's support changed. Afghanistan toured Pakistan in 2011 and 2013 to play Pakistan A. The Afghan Cheetas – effectively the national team – featured in Pakistan's main domestic T20 tournament in 2011. Aptly, in 2012, Afghanistan's first ODI against a Full Member was against Pakistan; so was their first T20I against a Test nation outside an ICC event. In 2013, Pakistan formalised their support, signing a Memorandum of Understanding with the Afghan Cricket Board that allowed the Afghan team access to the national cricket academy.

In the years since, partly due to geopolitical tensions, the relationship between the two boards has broken down. Now, Afghanistan increasingly turns to India for help.

Since 2015, with Afghanistan unable to play internationals in their own country, Afghanistan have used Greater Noida, just outside Delhi, as their home stadium. Afghanistan have also played in Dehradun and Lucknow. All the while, India's government assisted Afghanistan's cricket team, including providing $1 million to build a stadium and facilities in Kandahar. The BCCI has also provided support to Afghan coaches and umpires.

'Today cricket is [a] unifying force for the people of Afghanistan,' read a statement from Prime Minister Narendra Modi when Afghanistan played their first Test match, against India in Bangalore in 2018. 'India takes pride in being shoulder-to-shoulder with Afghanistan in this journey.'

In 2019, the Indian government sent Yuvraj Singh and Harbhajan Singh, two World Cup winners, to the Maldives to play a Cricket Friendship Series. They later signed an agreement to help the Maldives build its own cricket stadium; the BCCI organised coaching courses for those from the island. As the Indian government has increasingly seen cricket's value as a tool for soft power, so it has extended its support to far less advanced cricketing countries in Asia.

* * *

In 2005, the ICC moved its head office from Lord's to Dubai. It wasn't just the promise of paying no tax for 50 years: the move was a symbol of the changing balance of power in world cricket. Four years later, the ICC opened the Global Cricket Academy in Dubai. The centre includes 38 natural turf pitches, with wickets that replicate Australian, Asian and English conditions, six indoor practice pitches, and two floodlit international-accredited venues. Taking the ICC's headquarters to Dubai amounted to a recognition that the centre of gravity of world cricket was shifting, but it also reinforced that shift. Easy access to Dubai's outstanding training facilities gives nearby Asian teams a competitive advantage, especially the UAE and neighbours Oman.

Asia is the best-connected region in cricket, creating networks of knowledge-sharing that emergent teams in the region can latch on to. It's very likely that this is a formula for success. In their book *Soccernomics*, Simon Kuper and Stefan argued that the dominance of European football over the global game could be attributed to its unmatched internal networks. With Melanie Krause, Stefan found statistical evidence that seemed to corroborate this explanation, charting the rise of smaller European football nations such as Portugal, Belgium and even tiny Iceland while smaller nations on other continents continued to struggle.

'The biggest advantage that we have is there are so many Test-playing countries in the region,' says Sultan Rana, from the Asian Cricket Council. 'We have more funds than the other regions. We have more resources, we have five Test-playing countries in one region – it's a big boost. I think the help from Test-playing countries has been amazing. And perhaps that was the major difference between the other regions and the Asia region.'

The power of networks in cricket can also be seen when looking at countries that have lacked them. Just as Asia has benefited from being the best-connected cricket region in the world, so the Americas, a single ICC region, have suffered from being the worst. Their teams have suffered the greatest net decrease in ranking of any region during the World Cricket League. Revealingly, the greatest decrease of all was suffered by Argentina: seven hours by air from the nearest Test team, West Indies, and without any similarly-ranked Associates on the Continent, it is geographically perhaps the country most isolated from cricket's networks. In 2007, Argentina – considered a potential Test nation before the

Second World War – were effectively the 22nd ranked team in the world. By November 2021, they were 53rd on the T20I rankings.

'I believe fluid and close contact with a Full Member is crucial when you want to take your game to the next level. So in that aspect we could say it's harder than for other Associates,' says Esteban MacDermott, a former Argentina international player and the chief executive of the Asociacion de Cricket Argentino.

'You get better when you play better teams,' MacDermott reflects. 'In the past, the Americas Cup was played every two years where we got to play Canada, USA and Bermuda among others. That pushed us to get better – but now that competition has been reduced to only for global qualifying events, which means four years can go by in between events and we get fewer games in.'

Asian Associates, with an abundance of Full Members in the region and a coterie of similarly ranked teams nearby, would not recognise these problems. While the Asian region has done much right to help emerging nations, Asia's network effects can't easily be replicated elsewhere in the world.

West Indies have engaged noticeably with Canada and the United States in recent years, allowing both countries to play in their 50-over competition, but a combination of geography and economics limits what they can do. South Africa's board have had a swathe of internal issues to grapple with, which might help explain why both Kenya and Zimbabwe have not made good on their early promise. Australia have helped Papua New Guinea, who have long played in the South Australian league, but have not gone as far as arranging matches between PNG and Australia A.

Perhaps the most likely source of a rival to the Asian Cricket Council lies in Europe, where England, the second wealthiest cricket nation, have the potential to champion the European game, especially given the ease of travel in the Continent. Yet England have often seemed reluctant friends of their neighbours, and they have not championed the Full Member ambitions of Ireland and Scotland in the way the Asian bloc supported the ascent of Bangladesh and Afghanistan. The England and Wales Cricket Board restructured men's county cricket after 2013 in a way that omitted Scotland and the Netherlands, who both wished to continue playing in the domestic game. The ECB has refused to participate in any European-wide competitions that could provide the Continent's answer to the Asia Cup. Nor have they tried to imitate Asia in creating an emerging tournament between the under-23 sides of Full Members and full-strength Associate teams. At a sold-out Grange Cricket Club in Edinburgh in June 2018, Scotland defeated England for the first time in an international cricket game. England currently have no plans to play Scotland again.

In 2020, Bangladesh won their first ICC global event, toppling India in the final of the Under-19 World Cup. With Pakistan finishing third, the top three sides were all Asian; in 2022, six of the top nine sides were from Asia, including Afghanistan finishing fourth and the United Arab Emirates finishing ninth. Unsurprisingly, the tournament was won by India; from 2006–2022, India reached seven out of the nine finals in the Under-19 World Cup, including all of the last four.

These developments added to the sense that the dominant macro-trend in international cricket so far this century is far from played out. 'Asia will continue to be the strongest region in world cricket – I think forever. I can't see that changing,' says Anderson.

Given a choice about the prospects of two equal-ranked nations in, say, Europe and Asia, his answer was unambiguous: 'If all things are equal, but one country sits in Europe and the other country sits in Asia, yes I'll take the Asian one every day of the week.'

20

HOW AFGHANISTAN IS BRINGING CRICKET TO GERMANY

In December 2009, Arif Jamal and his brother Khalil fled Khonan Village in eastern Afghanistan. Arif was 14, and Khalil only 11. 'Because of war, we left Afghanistan,' Arif says. 'There is no childhood there.'

With the area unsafe, Arif and his brother undertook the hazardous journey to Europe in pursuit of a better life. Their uncle paid an agent to help them. They travelled to Quetta, in Pakistan, where they joined a group seeking to migrate to Europe. They walked for 16 hours to cross the Iranian border. From then on, they either walked or rode on trucks, sometimes crammed into one vehicle with 40 or 50 other refugees. Once they reached the border between Iran and Turkey, they again found a way to cross.

In Turkey, Arif and his brother walked for two days through woods until they reached Izmir, on the Aegean Sea. This time they were packed into a tiny boat with other refugees. 'We crossed that with a small boat. It was about nine-hours journey ... You could have died there. It was the most dangerous part of the whole journey.'

After nine harrowing hours, they landed on the Greek coast. But their journey was not yet over. 'We went on to travel in a gasoline tank. It was just like a coffin. We stayed there with four people, and it was about one and a half or two metres long, this tank. It was just like a fuel tank, but it was very secretly made to put us inside, and we stayed there about 12 hours, and we were taken to Italy.'

Once in Italy, Arif and Khalil had to reach Essen, in Germany's North Rhine-Westphalia. It was the only place in Europe where they had any family: their uncle Matilluh. They travelled by train, using money their family had raised for their trip. Police intercepted them in France, but together with another migrant they met at the hostel where they were taken, Arif and Khalil escaped. Finally, 48 days after leaving Afghanistan, they arrived in Essen. 'We went to the authorities and we claimed asylum here.'

While they waited for their application to be processed, Arif and his brother lived in a centre for minors, both orphans and young refugees who had travelled by themselves. In the youth home, they had internet access – and found out that Afghanistan had qualified for the 2010 edition of the men's T20 World Cup.

The Jamal brothers had learned about cricket in Peshawar, in Pakistan, where their family had fled when fighting had intensified in Afghanistan in 2003. 'We always played cricket there,' Arif recalls. Once their family moved back to Afghanistan in 2006, they brought their love of the sport back with them.

Six thousand kilometres from home, cricket was a piece of childhood. Usually, the computer room closed at 5pm, but a social worker let Arif watch Afghanistan play their first match in a cricket World Cup, against India. 'When I came here I had nothing which would connect me with my homeland, or with my childhood. The language was different. The clothes we wore were different than we wore back home. So it was completely different from what we knew. And cricket was the only thing which reminded us of our childhood and the positive part of our lives. So I think it was just like a small light and enjoyment in our depressed lives.'

The staff in the centre quickly realised cricket's importance to Arif and the other children. 'When they saw the emotions and the tears, how much we enjoyed it, and what it meant to us, they started to find cricket here in Germany for us.' The social workers learned that there was a governing body, der Deutsche Cricket Bund (DCB) for cricket in Germany. After they contacted the DCB, Brian Mantle, the chief executive, who happened to live in Essen, came over to the hostel to talk to the Jamal brothers. He brought a couple of plastic bats and windballs as gifts.

'The only thing which had a positive role in my life at that phase of my life was cricket,' Arif says. 'When I couldn't sleep, and when I was feeling depressed and down, I would just close my eyes and imagine playing cricket.'

The Jamals were the only Afghan children at the home at that point, so the other children were mystified watching them play. But bafflement turned to interest. Gradually, other children at the home joined Arif and his brother. After one broken window too many, the home banned playing cricket inside.

Arif and Khalil were still living at the home when Mantle, whom Arif calls 'my first friend in Germany', took the older boy to trials for the national under-18 team: 'He had a very major role of giving me confidence and hope here in German society.' The trip was a success: Arif was selected for the squad, and went on to play for Germany against Belgium and France. 'It was just like a dream, that I would get a chance.'

Two and a half years after they had arrived in Germany, a period filled with tense meetings with lawyers and numerous threatening letters from the authorities, the government granted them asylum. 'We were always in fear that we would get deported back to Afghanistan, and would have to leave Germany,' Arif recalls. 'We got many letters from the authorities, in which they would give us three weeks to leave.' Arif and Khalil, now 16 and 13, were finally safe from deportation. Getting asylum 'was like freeing a prisoner'.

After meeting Mantle, Arif learnt about the German cricketing scene. In 2011, he was involved in the creation of the Blue Tigers, a team made up mainly of Afghan refugees who were under the aegis of the Essen Club DJK Altendorf 09. To get his cricket fix in the winter, Arif also formed the A09 Mavericks, a team made up of a mixture of players from Asia, Australia and South Africa. In 2020, they won the North-Rhine Westphalia Indoor Championship.

In Germany, sports are normally organised through multi-sports clubs. The DJK Altendorf 09 offerings include tennis, table tennis, badminton, gymnastics, judo and running. The broad reach guarantees facilities, funding and access to sponsors. German clubs have increasingly dedicated themselves to integrating immigrants and refugees. A09 proudly displays photographs of the cricket teams on the section of its webpage that presents its array of sports. Cricket is listed as 'Cricket – der Weltsport' – 'Cricket – The World Sport'.

Arif's work was part of the transformation of German cricket through immigration. For immigrants from Afghanistan and Pakistan, playing cricket is 'a therapy,' Arif says. 'It's something which connects them with their home, and it's something where people forget their sorrows. The problems I had in 2010 and '11, they are facing right now. They're going through the same phase. They have left their family. They don't know the language. They are living in a different culture with different people. The food is different, everything is different, and cricket is something.' He has used the public platform he gained through cricket to highlight the isolation and sadness that characterises the lives of many refugees who have fled mortal danger or extreme deprivation for a life that, despite its relative safety, can be disconsolate.

Today, Jamal runs his own furniture removal company in Essen, in between studying for a sociology degree. But cricket is still central to his life. He continues to play at club level, volunteers for the DCB, and raises funds to buy equipment for cricket-loving refugees. 'Cricket is a game of concentration, and they forget their sorrows. They have no grief, they have nothing. A T20 match takes three hours. Believe me, this is a session of therapy for these people.'

Arif still cherishes his caps for Germany Under-19s: 'When I introduce myself to anyone, it's one of the things I mention, that I have played for Germany. I'm very proud of that. It's something I think I will remember for the rest of my life.'

To Arif, the real meaning of cricket is not measured in runs, wickets or victories: 'Cricket brings you to people similar to you, who are experiencing the same harsh or difficult situations of life. And they would talk about these problems. They would meet people in the club who have experienced all these things. We would help each other to start small jobs.'

For his cricket club, 'We would take food with us, eat on the ground, and just sit out for hours after the match, we would talk about a lot of stuff,' Arif said. 'I think that's the first step to get these people from just like sitting in the dark rooms in their hostels to get them out into the world, to connect them with German society.'

Friendships forged in cricket have given Arif, and other migrants, a greater sense of purpose: 'I had no self-confidence. Through cricket I've achieved a lot of things. The main thing is I got confidence in life, and I got hope.'

Some migrants have progressed to the senior national team. In 2015, Abdul Shakoor left Peshawar in search of a better life in Europe. His arduous journey was similar to Arif Jamal's; he was jailed in Turkey on three separate occasions. Shakoor has opened the batting for Germany in T20 international cricket, and is in the process of securing a German passport.

Migrants have helped cricket's popularity surge in Germany. Since 2015, the number of cricket teams has soared from 70 to 370 – even while playing numbers in club cricket have been trending downwards in many countries, including England. At the height of the refugee crisis, around 2016, 'we were literally getting a call every day, and new clubs were being set up one or two every week,' Mantle explains. At most new clubs, 'we basically get a field, put down a coconut mat, and off we go. We've got about 130 grounds in Germany, but probably 100 of them are just football fields with a coconut mat in the middle.'

There are currently just over a quarter of a million Afghans documented as being in Germany, by far the largest concentration in Europe. Altogether, more than 11 million foreigners live in Germany, a country with a total population of 83 million. Most of the foreign population are citizens of other EU states; most of the refugees are from Syria, thanks to Germany's extraordinary humanitarian effort in welcoming more than one million displaced persons from the Middle East conflict.

Recent years have also seen a marked increase in Indian students, many of whom subsequently settle in the country: around 150,000 Indians now live in Germany. They have brought other forms of cricket with them that thrive alongside traditional hardball leagues. In Hamburg, an IT hub in Germany, there is now a vibrant softball cricket league, with those born in India making up the bulk of players; there are also tapeball leagues, with players predominantly from among the 75,000 German residents of Pakistani origin.

The surge in playing numbers has led to dreams about what German cricket can achieve. After they have lived in Germany for three years non-citizens can represent the country under ICC eligibility rules. Other countries with large immigrant populations are also well poised to benefit from these residency rules. The most obvious is the United States: ahead of the 2023 launch of Major League Cricket, a new professional cricket structure, several former Test cricketers have moved there, including New Zealand's Corey Anderson, Pakistan's Sami Aslam, and South Africa's Dane Piedt.

By 2025, Cricket Germany hope to be ranked in the top 20 in the men's T20I rankings. In the women's rankings, they believe they can rise at an even faster rate and reach the top 15. The women's game has a very different character, with most players at national level born and raised in Germany.

The growth of German cricket is being abetted by some unlikely sources. In Germany, local sports clubs, of which there are more than 90,000, have always received significant financial support from local government, which accounts for about half of all sports-club revenue. For German cricket, another source of financial support is the DJK-Sportverband, the Roman Catholic Church's sport association in Germany. It has donated more than €150,000 to help fund clubs that support refugees.

'I only knew cricket from old movies,' says Stephanie Hofschlaeger, the general secretary of DJK-Sportverband. But after observing migrant communities playing the sport, she 'quickly recognised that cricket was a good way to comfort many refugees. Sport speaks all languages. In Germany, many nations come together in a team at cricket. You play, you laugh, you win and you lose together. And you're happy. Sport is one of the most beautiful things in the world. It motivates and gives impetus, which our refugees need in order to cope in a different culture and find a home.'

German sports clubs play a significant role in local communities that goes well beyond just playing games; they often see it as their mission to promote community values. Membership fees are cheap – around three euros a month for children and six for adults. For many clubs the values include the creation of community for refugees and immigrants.

There's symmetry in the relationship between Afghan and German cricket. Afghans have helped spread the game in Germany, but Germany has also supported Afghan cricket. The German Federal Foreign Office spent €800,000 funding the construction of a stadium in Khost, which also received support from the European Commission, Luxembourg and Norway. 'The most important reason for supporting the stadium was to bring together communities from both Afghanistan and Pakistan,' says Martin Karl Zickendraht, who worked as the first secretary of the German Embassy in Kabul. Sadly, after the Taliban regained control of Afghanistan, the future of the stadium – like Afghan cricket – is uncertain.

* * *

Growing up in Kunduz in Afghanistan, Muslim Yar and his family had a shared obsession. 'Cricket is a popular sport in our family – everyone follows it, and everyone likes it,' he recalls. Yar and his friends and family would play with a tennis ball. In May 2016, at the age of 17, Yar fled Afghanistan: 'There was no protection, there was no peace.' Together with his younger brother, Yar made the arduous journey to Germany.

In Frankfurt, Yar joined his older brother, who had lived there for more than a decade, as well as two of his sisters, 'Life was hard because we don't know how it works here. We could not speak German.'

Yar also missed cricket, which he assumed he would not be able to play in Germany. 'I talked with my brother and he told me: I have a friend, and he's playing here in Frankfurt. Then I said, Okay, well, it's like my hobby. I like cricket – that is good for me. And when I went to the club, I met with the president of the club, and I told him in Afghanistan I play cricket, and I can play well.'

Yar has represented the MSC Frankfurt cricket club since 2016. 'I did not get any money from cricket, but I love this game,' he says. Yar laments that, unlike in Afghanistan, many locals 'don't know what cricket is,' because football dominates the sporting landscape.

One member of Yar's family remained behind in Afghanistan: his older brother Sharafuddin Ashraf. Rather than live with the family in Kunduz, Sharafuddin lived in Kabul in accommodation provided by the Afghanistan Cricket Board to members of the national squad. He made his debut for Afghanistan in 2014. 'It is a proud moment for me, him playing for Afghanistan – it is a big achievement for him,' Yar says.

While Sharafuddin has been in Afghanistan's squad, his younger brother has broken into Germany's national team. In some matches, Yar has played alongside six other players who emigrated from Afghanistan. 'They all just love the cricket – that's why they play.'

Yar played his first game for Germany in 2019, benefiting from the ICC's three-year residency rule. 'I'm happy now playing for Germany,' he says. 'My brother says he is proud of me because you came here, and in three years, you were in the German national team.'

Just like his brother Sharafuddin, Yar is an orthodox left-arm spinner. They both also bat right-handed, but write left-handed: 'We are the same.' Were the Yar brothers to play against each other in an international match it would embody the curious, symbiotic relationship between Afghan and German cricket. 'It will be good to play against Afghanistan,' Yar laughs. 'I will bowl against my brother.' Inshallah.

* * *

Germany provides a glimpse of possibly a seminal moment in cricket's development: Afghanistan is the first non-Commonwealth country to export cricket. Yet emigration has always been central to cricket's growth.

'It's like a cycle of cricket. Everybody has learned it from somebody else,' Mantle says. 'Now the Afghans are bringing it to Germany, and hopefully the Germans will learn from them. That's how cricket grows, and that's always my argument when somebody says it's not a German sport.'

Football and baseball were English inventions as well. But, unlike cricket, they were not presented as the leisurely domain of upper-class British gentlemen. Many nations had an early heritage of both cricket and football, but football – easier to play and without the same stigmas attached – quickly dominated.

For most its history, cricket's spread has been inextricably linked to the British Empire. The first explicitly international organisation was the Imperial Cricket Conference, founded in 1909 at the instigation of South Africa. It included only two other nations – England and Australia. Restricting the organisation to imperial countries stymied cricket's global growth; the missed opportunity was particularly great in the United States and Argentina. Cricket had been the most popular sport in the US up to the 1860s, when it was usurped by baseball, and it was still played to a good standard before the First World War, chiefly in Philadelphia. Cricket also had a strong presence in Argentina, who defeated touring teams from the MCC in 1912 and 1926. It was not until 1965 that the ICC renamed itself as the International Cricket Conference and introduced Associate membership to aid emerging nations. The ICC became the International Cricket Council in 1987.

By dropping the word 'Imperial', cricket administrators signalled at least a passing interest in growing the sport worldwide. The institution of the World Cup, following the template that had worked well in football, was another such step. But it came late: the football World Cup started in 1930, yet there was no cricket World Cup until the women created one in 1973. It would take two more years until the men finally got a World Cup of their own.

Football's World Cup has expanded from 13 to 16, 24, 32 and now 48 teams. Yet cricket's expansion has been tentative – and even gone into reverse. The number of competing sides finally reached double figures in 1996, but in between World Cups, Associate nations remained hampered by a dearth of funding and fixtures. After notable World Cup successes, both Kenya and Ireland found that Test nations became more reluctant to play them. One senior ICC official described Bangladesh and Zimbabwe, at the time the two lowest-ranked Full Members, as 'scared' to play leading Associates, fearing a defeat would make their own Test status come under discussion.

In 2007, the Cricket World Cup was enlarged from 14 to 16 teams. A large part of the rationale for the competition was the broadcasting revenue that it could generate, especially in India. The ICC seeded the competition seeking to ensure that after the initial rounds India would meet Pakistan, and the game would be played at Barbados' picturesque Kensington Oval. But the wrong teams made the Super Eight stage: Bangladesh and Ireland knocked out India and Pakistan in the pool stage, and the lucrative India-Pakistan match never took place.

Broadcasters were aghast. 'Had that not happened, the 16-team World Cup would have become the norm,' one ICC insider said later. Driven by commercial considerations, the ICC contracted the World Cup – first to 14 teams, and then to the 10-team round-robin format used in 2019. David Richardson, then the ICC's chief executive, publicly admitted what was already known to be behind the decision: a desire to guarantee India nine matches. When the authorities announced in 2021 that the competition would revert to 14 teams for the 2027 and 2031 editions, it was a tacit acknowledgement they had not previously been acting in the best interests of the game.

Perhaps cricket is unlucky. The sheer financial clout of India – which is estimated to generate about two-thirds of cricket's revenue – leaves the sport uniquely vulnerable to the risk of one national team underperforming. India's calamity in 2007 could have been tolerated in football, whose men's World Cup has survived Argentina and Germany being eliminated after three games, and

England or the Netherlands failing to qualify, without dramatically damaging broadcasting figures.

Sir Stanley Rous, the FIFA president until 1974 and a patrician Englishman of the ilk who would have been at home in cricket administration, argued that the standard of play in Africa and Asia simply wasn't high enough to allow each continent even one guaranteed representative in the World Cup. The years since have proved Rous wrong: while Europe and South America retain their dominance of the tournament, African and Asian teams have enhanced the World Cup. The expansion of the tournament has grown the sport's global depth, deepened football's appeal – and generated plenty of cash to boot. It is an example that cricket would do well to heed.

Cricket's administrators have largely focused on furthering the interests of the sport's biggest members. Even after the end of Australia and England's veto power in 1993, the ICC's voting structure has meant that Full Members effectively hold all the voting power, with Associates lacking the votes to stop changes or force through reforms. This system has allowed the biggest Full Members to profit handsomely from the cash generated by the ICC: in the 2016 to 2023 broadcasting cycle, India claimed $406 million from the ICC, twice as much as the ICC's 92 Associate members combined.

FIFA, by contrast, has a one-member one-vote system, and distributes funds to member associations on a much more equitable basis. While participating nations receive a share of prize money, the remaining surplus is distributed more or less equally among all member nations; indeed, developing nations have access to special funding for development projects. None of this is to say that FIFA is an organisation without profound problems: the money distributed to poorer federations lacks accountability and frequently appears to vanish, leaving countries as bereft of football infrastructure as ever. Even so, it's hard to argue that the inclusiveness of the World Cup has not been good for football.

* * *

While cricket's efforts to grow have been haphazard, basketball, the sport with a better claim to being the second most popular in the world, has offered another template for how to grow a game.

Basketball was invented in Springfield, Massachusetts, in 1891 by James Naismith, as a game that could be played indoors during New England's long, cold winters. It spread first through the US college system, which gives extraordinary emphasis to athletic competition. A global governing body, FIBA was created in 1932. By this time, basketball was already recognised as an Olympic sport, and a World Cup followed in 1950.

The NBA was formed only in 1946. It did not achieve national prominence in the US until the 1980s when a generation of emerging Black stars came to dominate. For basketball worldwide, the 1992 Olympics, the first in which professionals were allowed to play, was transformative. The US's basketball team arrived in Barcelona with the 'Dream Team': a squad of iconic players, including Michael Jordan. They were there not so much to win the gold medal, which was a waltz for them, as to evangelise. According to Juan Antonio Samaranch, then IOC President, 'the most important aspect of the Games has been the resounding success of the basketball tournament, as we've witnessed the best basketball in the world.'

Unlike chronically loss-making big football clubs, the NBA is a business, meant to generate profits for franchise owners. Led by a commissioner empowered to direct the organisation towards lucrative opportunities, the NBA recognised that they could grow by taking matches abroad and investing in grassroots development overseas. In 1972, there weren't any foreign players in the entire league, not even Canadians. Fifty years on, the NBA has gone from being a US basketball league to a global league that just happens to be based in the US. On opening day in the 2020/21 season, the NBA included 107 overseas players from 41 countries and six different continents. It had also made good on the dreams of sports administrators the world over, by unearthing a superstar from China in Yao Ming, who played in the NBA from 2002 to 2011.

The IPL is cricket's equivalent of the NBA: a domestic league which is really the world's league, overwhelmingly the dominant club competition in its sport. This creates an opportunity for the IPL to replicate the NBA's strategies. Indeed, the structure of the IPL – explicitly modelled on US sports leagues – makes it ideally suited to emulate the NBA. While most of the IPL's attention so far has focused on growing in the Indian market, the NBA offers a template for the IPL to be altogether more ambitious, demonstrating how one domestic league can promote a sport's globalisation. Like the NBA, the IPL could centrally fund a series of academies dotted around the world. Obvious places to start would be the US, Canada, and Nepal. Germany or the Netherlands could act as a hub for continental Europe, Kenya or Nigeria for Africa. Ultimately, just like the NBA, the IPL would benefit from more talent, more global eyeballs – and more cash.

But the most obvious lesson that cricket can heed from basketball is the power of the Olympic Games. For men's and women's cricket alike, the two greatest benefits of featuring in the Olympics are simple. First, the exposure: the chance to see a sport you may never have seen. Second, the Games are a vital source of cash for a sport – expansionism with someone else footing the bill. In 2016, rugby rejoined the Olympics after a 92-year absence; between National Olympic Committees and government funding, this has been worth an estimated £25 million in extra funding per four-year cycle.

There are also broader benefits: in the US, for instance, it is much easier to raise college sports funding for Olympic sports. Collegiate sport in the US is a huge enterprise, generating around $10 billion in revenue a year. Getting a share of this funding for cricket would make a huge difference. US colleges also hand out many scholarships for foreign nationals, helping to internationalise sport. If cricket was played in the Olympics, it's probable that a collegiate competition would start in the US, and even that some colleges would offer scholarships to promising players – just as has happened since rugby rejoined the Games. Since 2009, rugby has also been added to the school curriculum in countries such as Brazil, China and the US itself.

Cricket remains cut-off from these benefits. The only cricket match in the Olympics remains Devon and Somerset Wanderers (representing Great Britain) defeating the French Athletic Club Union (representing France) in the 1900 Games in Paris to win the gold medal.

Until recently the ICC has occupied the curious position of being the one world governing body that doesn't want to be in the Olympics. The interests of a few boards that control the game trumped the interests of the majority: 90% of ICC's member associations, surveyed in 2008, supported the notion of including cricket in the Games. Belatedly, there has been a distinct shift in the attitudes of

England and India – the two richest and most influential boards – who both now support inclusion in the Olympics. In 2024, the US and the West Indies will co-host the T20 World Cup, with 20 games to be played in the US. Cricket hopes to appear in the Olympic Games from the 2028 edition, in Los Angeles.

The possibilities in cricket's new frontiers are tantalising. 'If we become an Olympic sport it's a complete game changer,' says Mantle, the chief executive of Cricket Germany. Like most countries, the German government prioritises sports funding for sports included in the Olympics. As of 2021, the DCB earns around €600,000 a year, with the majority of that coming from the ICC. It does not yet receive any funding from the German government.

In Brazil, the rugby federation received R$10.4 million (£1.4 million) from the Brazilian national Olympic committee from 2017 to 2020. Before rugby became an Olympic sport, the rugby federation was not eligible for any such funding. Brazilian cricket needs the Olympics. 'The golden egg for us is when hopefully the ICC can say that cricket will be an Olympic sport,' says Featherstone.

Like Mantle, Featherstone thinks of the Olympics as 'a complete game changer – not only for Cricket Brazil but for 90% of the Associate world. When you go to a Brazilian company, start talking about cricket, they look at you as if you're the most alien person in the world. They've never heard of it, and the first conversation is, why are you telling me that this is the second-best sport or second-biggest sport in the world but it's not an Olympic sport? And therefore you hit the wall very quickly, in a lot of Brazilian boardrooms. This would change if it became an Olympic sport.'

For most of its history, cricket administrators have celebrated the exclusivity of the sport – like members of a snooty Victorian members' club delighting in their elevated company. The snobbery and the elitism go a long way towards explaining why cricket's attempts to reach a broader audience have been so timid. But globalisation, migration patterns and the economic clout of India have combined to give cricket another chance to grow, and empower people like Arif Jamal and Muslim Yar to spread the sport around the world. Let us hope that, this time, cricket's administrators take the chance.

ACKNOWLEDGEMENTS

Over the years we have both benefited from the advice and inspiration of many people, too numerous to name. However, we should mention the following who made valuable contributions to the writing of this book:

Elizabeth Bott, Nicholas Brookes, Alex Cao, Stephen Chalke, Chris Chiwanza, Adam Collins, David Court, Tracey Covassin, Andrew Fidel Fernando, Ric Finlay, Johan Fourie, Rick Frenette, Daniel Gallan, Keshava Guha, Gidon Jakar, Imran Khan, Jarrod Kimber, Jason Krol, Martin Lange, Neil Leitch, Fay Lomas, Stacy Lynn-Sant, Jono McCrostie, Robin Parris, Ian Preston, Shaun Rheeder, Stephen F. Ross, Osman Samiuddin, Ed Smith, Tim Swartz, William Szymanski, Dale Ulrich, Wray Vamplew, Gustav Venter, Keith Walmsley and Richard Wigmore. We thank them all.

Special thanks to Silke-Maria Weineck, who read the first draft of each chapter and made extensive, valuable suggestions on how to make our prose more readable, without ever succumbing to the charms of cricket. We also thank our diligent copyeditor Richard Whitehead.

We are grateful to our agent David Luxton and to everyone at Bloomsbury Press for their faith in and enthusiasm for this project, especially Charlotte Croft, Holly Jarrald and Katherine Macpherson.

BIBLIOGRAPHY

We have not used footnotes in the main text, but here we provide a guide to the main resources we used. In addition to personal interviews – which we distinguish from second-hand interviews in the text by using the present tense (so 'says' for an interview we conducted ourselves, 'said' for one given elsewhere) – we relied on Cricinfo (and its partner site *The Cricket Monthly*) Cricket Archive and printed newspaper sources, notably *The Times*, and *Cricket* (available through the Association of Cricket Statisticians online), for much of the cricket history. A good deal of the newspaper sources can be found on Newspapers.com and Nexis Uni.

GENERAL

Allen, D. R., *Grand Matches of Cricket Played in England 1771 to 1791* (J. W. McKenzie, 2008).

Altham, H. S., and Swanton, E. W., *A History of Cricket: From the First World War to the Present Day* (Allen & Unwin, 1962).

Birley, D., *A Social History of English Cricket* (Aurum, 1999).

Bowen, R., *Cricket: a History of its Growth and Development Throughout the World* (Eyre & Spottiswoode, 1970).

Jones, B., and Leamon, N., *Hitting Against the Spin: How Cricket Really Works* (Constable, 2021).

Major, J., *More Than a Game: the Story of Cricket's Early Years* (HarperPress, 2009).

Parker, E., *The History of Cricket,* vol. 30 (Seeley Service, 1950).

Stoddart, B., and Sandiford, K. (Eds.), *The Imperial Game: Cricket, Culture and Society* (Manchester University Press, 1998).

Underdown, D., *Start of Play: Cricket and Culture in Eighteenth Century England* (Allen Lane, 2000).

Wigmore, T., and Wilde, F., *Cricket 2.0: Inside the T20 Revolution* (Polaris, 2019).

1. BATTERS AND BOWLERS, NATURE AND NURTURE

Anders, J., Green, F., Henderson, M., and Henseke, G., 'Determinants of private school participation: All about the money?' *British Educational Research Journal*, 46(5), (2020), pp. 967–992.

Belmi, P., Neale, M. A., Reiff, D., and Ulfe, R., 'The social advantage of miscalibrated individuals: The relationship between social class and overconfidence and its implications for class-based inequality', *Journal of Personality and Social Psychology*, 118(2), (2020), p. 254.

Brown, T., and Kelly, A. L., 'Relative access to wealth and ethnicity in professional cricket', *Birth Advantages and Relative Age Effects in Sport* (Routledge, 2021), pp. 184–206.

Bull, S. T., Shambrook, C. J., James, W. I., and Brooks, J. E., 'Towards an understanding of mental toughness in elite English cricketers', *Journal of Applied Sport Psychology*, 17(3), (2005), pp. 209–227.

Cannon, M., Vedel, A., and Jonason, P. K., 'The dark and not so humble: School-type effects on the Dark Triad traits and intellectual humility', *Personality and Individual Differences*, 163, (2020), p. 110068.

Connor, J. D., Renshaw I., and Farrow D., 'Defining cricket batting expertise from the perspective of elite coaches', *PLoS ONE*, 15(6), (2020), https://doi.org/10.1371/journal .pone.0234802

Dennis, R., Farhart, R., Goumas, C., and Orchard, J., 'Bowling workload and the risk of injury in elite cricket fast bowlers', *Journal of Science and Medicine in Sport*, 6(3), (2003), pp. 359–367.

Dennis, R. J., Finch, C. F., and Farhart, P. J., 'Is bowling workload a risk factor for injury to Australian junior cricket fast bowlers?', *British Journal of Sports Medicine*, 39(11), (2005), pp. 843–846.

Forrest, M. R., Scott, B. R., Hebert, J. J., and Dempsey, A. R., 'Injury prevention strategies for adolescent cricket pace bowlers', *Sports Medicine*, 48(11), (2018), pp. 2449–2461.

Green, F., Henseke, G., and Vignoles, A., 'Private schooling and labour market outcomes', *British Educational Research Journal*, 43(1), (2017), pp. 7–28.

Green, F., Machin, S., Murphy, R., and Yu Zhu, 'The changing economic advantage from private schools', *Economica*, 79, no. 316, (2012), pp. 658–679.

Gucciardi, D. F., 'The relationship between developmental experiences and mental toughness in adolescent cricketers', *Journal of Sport and Exercise Psychology*, 33(3), (2011), pp. 370–393.

Johnstone, J. A., Mitchell, A. C., Hughes, G., Watson, T., Ford, P. A., and Garrett, A. T., 'The athletic profile of fast bowling in cricket: A review', *The Journal of Strength & Conditioning Research*, 28(5), (2014), pp. 1465–1473.

Jones, B. D., 'Game Changers: Discriminating Features Within the Microstructure of Practice and Developmental Histories of Super-Elite Cricketers: A Pattern Recognition Approach', Bangor University (2019).

Jones, B., Hardy, L., Lawrence, G., Kuncheva, L., Brandon, R., Bobat, M., and Thorpe, G., 'It Ain't What You Do – It's the Way That You Do It: Is Optimizing Challenge Key in the Development of Super-Elite Batsmen?', *Journal of Expertise*, 3(2), (2020), pp. 144–168.

Jones, B., Hardy, L., Lawrence, G., Kuncheva, L., Brandon, R., Such, P., and Bobat, M., 'The Identification of "Game Changers" in England Cricket's Developmental Pathway for 3 Elite Spin Bowling: A Machine Learning Approach', *Journal of Expertise*, 2(2), 2019, pp. 92–120.

Jooste, J., Toriola, A. L., van Wyk, J. G. U., and Steyn, B. J. M., 'The relationship between psychological skills and specialised role in cricket', *African Journal for Physical, Health Education, Recreation and Dance*, 20(1), (2014), pp. 106–117.

McNamara, D. J., Gabbett, T. J., Naughton, G., Farhart, P., and Chapman, P., 'Training and competition workloads and fatigue responses of elite junior cricket players', *International Journal of Sports Physiology and Performance*, 8(5), (2013), pp. 517–526.

Mandle, W. F., 'The professional cricketer in England in the nineteenth century', *Labour History*, 23, (1972), pp. 1–16.

Müller, S., Brenton, J., Dempsey, A. R., Harbaugh, Allen G., and Reid, C., 'Individual differences in highly skilled visual perceptual-motor striking skill', *Attention, Perception, & Psychophysics*, 77(5), (2015), pp. 1726–1736.

Phillips, E., Davids, K., Renshaw, K., and Portus, M., 'The development of fast bowling experts in Australian cricket', *Talent Development and Excellence*, 2, (2010), pp. 137–148.

Phillips, E., Davids, K., Renshaw, I., and Portus, M., 'Acquisition of expertise in cricket fast bowling: perceptions of expert players and coaches', *Journal of Science and Medicine in Sport*, 17(1), (2014), pp. 85–90.

Smith, R. E., and Christensen, D. S., 'Psychological skills as predictors of performance and survival in professional baseball', *Journal of Sport and Exercise Psychology*, 17(4), (1995), pp. 399–415.

Weissensteiner, J., Abernethy, B., and Farrow, D., 'Towards the development of a conceptual model of expertise in cricket batting: A grounded theory approach', *Journal of Applied Sport Psychology*, 21(3), (2009), pp. 276–292.

Warmenhoven, J., Weissensteiner, J. R., and MacMahon, C., '"It takes a village": The sources and types of support in development of male cricket players', *Journal of Science and Medicine in Sport*, 24(2), (2021), pp. 164–170.

Weissensteiner, J. R., Abernethy, B., Farrow, D., and Gross, J., 'Distinguishing psychological characteristics of expert cricket batsmen', *Journal of Science and Medicine in Sport*, 15(1), (2012), pp. 74–79.

3. AN URBAN SPORT IN A RURAL COUNTRY: THE CHALLENGE OF INDIAN CRICKET

Ahluwalia, I. J., Kanbur, R., and Mohanty, P. K. (Eds.), *Urbanisation in India: Challenges, Opportunities and the Way Forward* (SAGE Publications India, 2014).

Asher, S., Nagpal, K., and Novosad, P., 'The cost of remoteness: evidence from 600,000 Indian villages', IZA working paper, (2017), http://conference.iza. org/conference_files /GLMLICNetwork_2016/asher_s10281.pdf.

Bose, M., *A History of Indian Cricket* (Andre Deutsch, 2002).

Bose, M., *The Magic of Indian Cricket: Cricket and Society in India* (Routledge, 2006).

Cashman, R., *Patrons, players and the crowd: the phenomenon of Indian cricket* (Orient Longmann, 1980).

Chandrasekhar, S., and Sharma, A., 'Urbanization and spatial patterns of internal migration in India', *Spatial Demography*, 3(2), (2015), pp. 63–89.

Das, D., and Pathak, M., 'The growing rural-urban disparity in India: Some issues', *International Journal of Advancements in Research & Technology*, 1(5), (2012), pp. 1–7.

Guha, R., *A Corner of a Foreign Field: The Indian History of a British Sport* (Picador, 2002).

Guha, R., *The Commonwealth of Cricket: A Lifelong Love Affair with the Most Subtle and Sophisticated Game Known to Humankind* (William Collins, 2020).

Guruprasad, K.R., *Going Places: India's Small Town Cricket Heroes* (Penguin, 2011).

Johnson, K., *Television and social change in rural India: a study of two mountain villages in Western Maharashtra* (Sage Publications India, 1998).

Lall, S. V., Shalizi, Z., and Deichmann, U., 'Agglomeration economies and productivity in Indian industry', *Journal of Development Economics*, 73(2), (2004), pp. 643–673.

Majumdar, B., *Indian Cricket Through the Ages: A Reader* (OUP, 2005).

Majumdar, B., *Twenty-two yards to freedom: A social history of Indian cricket* (Penguin, 2004).

Mukhopadhyay, P., Zérah, M. H., and Denis, E., 'Subaltern urbanization: Indian insights for urban theory', *International Journal of Urban and Regional Research*, 44(4), (2020), pp. 582–598.

Overman, H. G., and Venables, A. J., 'Cities in the developing world (No. 695)', Centre for Economic Performance, London School of Economics and Political Science (2005).

Panagariya, A., *India: The Emerging Giant* (Oxford University Press, 2008).

Rice, J. (Ed.), *Wisden on India: An Anthology* (Bloomsbury, 2011).

Sachs, J. D., Bajpai, N., and Ramiah, A., 'Understanding regional economic growth in India', *Asian Economic Papers*, 1(3), (2002), pp. 32–62.

Sharma, S., 'Persistence and stability in city growth', *Journal of Urban Economics*, 53(2), (2003), pp. 300–320.

Singhal, A., Doshi, J. K., Rogers, E. M., and Rahman, S. A., 'The diffusion of television in India', Media Asia, 15(4), (1988), pp. 222–229.

Sundaresan, B., *The Dhoni Touch: Unravelling the Enigma that is Mahendra Singh Dhoni* (Ebury, 2018).

Suri, S. S., and Sheel, V., 'Origin of Cricket in India', *International Research Journal of Management Sociology & Humanities,* 6(10), (2015), pp. 3–8.

Van Duijne, R. J., and Nijman, J., 'India's emergent urban formations', *Annals of the American Association of Geographers*, 109(6), (2019), pp. 1978–1998.

4. AN ASHES EDUCATION – WHY CRICKET'S OLDEST RIVALRY IS THE BATTLE OF PRIVATE SCHOOLS

Armstrong, E., 'Australian cultural populism in sport: The relationship between sport (notably cricket) and cultural populism in Australia', *ANU Undergraduate Research Journal*, 10(1), (2020), pp. 68–76.

Bairner, A., 'Irish Australians, postcolonialism and the English game', *Sport in Society,* 12(4–5), (2009), pp. 482–495.

Gemmell, J., 'All white mate? Cricket and race in Oz', *Sport in Society*, 10(1), (2007), pp. 33–48.

Ryan, C., and Sibieta, L., 'Private Schooling in the UK and Australia', https://dera.ioe.ac.uk/33198/1/bn106.pdf

Ryan, C., and Watson, L., 'The drift to private schools in Australia: Understanding its features', https://openresearch-repository.anu.edu.au/bitstream/1885/42681/2/DP479.pdf

The Ethics Centre, 'Australian Cricket: A Matter of Balance', (2018), https://www.cricket-australia.com.au/-/media/B9F2F708C1A540A08847A4758D02CB99.ashx

Vella, F., 'Do Catholic schools make a difference? Evidence from Australia', *Journal of Human Resources*, (1999), pp. 208–224.

Zakus, D., Skinner, J., and Edwards, A., 'Social capital in Australian sport', *Sport in Society*, 12(7), (2009), pp. 986–998.

5. THE RISE OF NEW ZEALAND: BY LUCK OR DESIGN?

Astle, A. M., 'Sport development – plan, programme and practice: a case study of the planned intervention by New Zealand cricket into cricket in New Zealand', School of Management, College of Business, Massey University, Palmerston North, New Zealand (2014).

Bradbury, T., and O'Boyle, I., 'Batting above average: Governance at New Zealand cricket', *Corporate Ownership and Control*, 12(4), (2015), pp. 352–363.

Ferkins, L., Shilbury, D., and McDonald, G., 'The role of the board in building strategic capability: Towards an integrated model of sport governance research', *Sport Management Review*, 8(3), (2005), pp. 195–225.

Gibbs, D. W., 'More English than the English? Cricket fan culture in New Zealand', Doctoral dissertation, (2018), University of Waikato.

McMillan, J., 'Rugby meets economics', *New Zealand Economic Papers*, 31(1), (1997), pp. 93–114.

McMillan, J., 'Managing Economic Change: Lessons from New Zealand', *World Economy*, 21(6), (1998), pp. 827–843.

Obel, C., 'Club versus country in rugby union: tensions in an exceptional New Zealand system', *Soccer & Society*, 11(4), (2010), pp. 442–460.

Stenling, C., and Sam, M., 'Professionalization and its consequences: How active advocacy may undermine democracy', *European Sport Management Quarterly*, 20(5), (2020), pp. 577–597.

Wagg, S., *Cricket: A Political History of the Global Game, 1945–2017* (Routledge, 2017).

Wilde, S., *England: The Biography: The Story of English Cricket* (Simon & Schuster, 2018).

6. WOMEN'S CRICKET – A HISTORY OF INNOVATION

Cashman, R., Tregear, M., and Weaver, A., *Wicket Women: Cricket and Women in Australia* (Hear a Book, 1993).

Duncan, I., *Skirting the Boundary: A History of Women's Cricket* (The Robson Press, 2013).

Heyhoe Flint, R., and Rheinberg, N., *Fair Play: The Story of Women's Cricket* (Angus & Robertson, 1976).

Heyhoe Flint, R., *Heyhoe! The Autobiography of Rachael Heyhoe Flint* (Pelham Books, 1978).

Joy, N., *Maiden Over: A Short History of Women's Cricket and a Diary of the 1948–49 Test Tour to Australia* (Sporting Handbooks, 1950).

Kimber, J., *Test Cricket: The unauthorised biography* (Hardie Grant Books, 2015).

McCrone, K. E., *Playing the game: Sport and the physical emancipation of English women, 1870-1914* (University Press of Kentucky, 1988).

Malcolm, D., Gemmell, J., and Mehta, N. (Eds.), *The Changing Face of Cricket: From imperial to global game* (Routledge, 2013).

Nicholson, R., *Ladies and Lords: A History of Women's Cricket in Britain* (Peter Lang, 2019).

Williams, J., *A Contemporary History of Women's Sport, Part One: Sporting Women, 1850–1960* (Routledge, 2014).

Williams, J., *Cricket and Race* (Berg Publishers, 2001).

7. HOW JAYASURIYA AND GILCHRIST TRANSFORMED TEST BATTING – BUT T20 DIDN'T

Ismail, Q., 'Batting against the break: On cricket, nationalism, and the swashbuckling Sri Lankans', *Social Text*, (50), (1997), pp. 33–56.

Narayanan, C., *Sanath Jayasuriya: a biography* (Rupa, 2019).

Roberts, M., 'Wunderkidz in a blunderland: tensions and tales from Sri Lankan cricket', *Sport in Society*, 12(4–5), (2009), pp. 566–578.

Roberts, M., and James, A., *Crosscurrents: Sri Lanka and Australia at Cricket* (Walla Walla Press, 1998).

8. LEAGUE CRICKET – THE GAME'S GREAT MISSED OPPORTUNITY

Arlott, J., *Concerning Cricket: Studies of Play and Players* (Longmans, 1949).

Constantine, L., *Cricket in the Sun* (Stanley Paul, 1946).

Constantine, L., and Batchelor, D., *The Changing Face of Cricket* (Eyre & Spottiswoode, 1966).

Davis, A. E., *First in the field: the history of the world's first cricket league: the Birmingham and District Cricket League, formed 1888* (K.A.F. Brewin, 1988).

Genders, R., *League Cricket in England* (Werner Laurie, 1952).

Heywood, B., 'Ashes cricketers and the Lancashire League', *Sport in Society*, 15(8), (2012), pp. 1134–1180.

Hill, J., 'First-class' cricket and the leagues: some notes on the development of English cricket, 1900–40', *The International Journal of the History of Sport*, 4(1), (1987) pp. 68–81.

Kay, J., *Cricket in the Leagues* (Eyre & Spottiswoode, 1970).

Mangan, J. A., *The Games Ethic and Imperialism: Aspects of the Diffusion of an Ideal* (Routledge, 2013).

Pycroft, J., *The Cricket Field* (St. James's Press, 1922).

Root, F., *A Cricket Pro's Lot* (Edward Arnold, 1937).

Sandiford, K. A., 'English cricket crowds during the Victorian age', *Journal of Sport History*, 9(3), (1982), pp. 5–22.

Sandiford, K., and Vamplew, W., 'The peculiar economics of English cricket before 1914', *The International Journal of the History of Sport*, 3(3), (1986), pp. 311–326.

Schofield, J. A., 'The development of first-class cricket in England: An economic analysis', *The Journal of Industrial Economics*, (1982), pp. 337–360.

Stone, D., '"It's all friendly down there": the Club Cricket Conference, amateurism and the cultural meaning of cricket in the South of England,' *Sport in Society*, 15 (2), (2012), pp. 194–208.

Stone, D., 'Cricket, Competition and the Amateur Ethos: Surrey and the Home Counties 1870–1970', PhD diss., (2013), University of Huddersfield.

Stone, D., *Different Class: The Untold Story of English Cricket* (Repeater, 2022).

Williams, J., 'Cricket in industrial Lancashire between the wars – the impact of leagues', *British Society of Sports History Bulletin*, (9), (1989), pp. 67–80.

Williams, J., 'The economics of league cricket: Lancashire league clubs and their finances since world war one', *British Society of Sports History Bulletin*, Vol. 9 (1990).

Williams, J., *Cricket and England: A Cultural and Social History of the Inter-War Years* (Frank Cass, 1999).

9. A FAIR RESULT IN FOUL WEATHER

Asif, M., and McHale, I. G., 'A generalized non-linear forecasting model for limited-overs international cricket', *International Journal of Forecasting*, 35(2), (2019), pp. 634–640.

Bhattacharya, R., Gill, P. S., and Swartz, T. B., 'Duckworth–Lewis and Twenty20 cricket', *Journal of the Operational Research Society*, 62(11), (2011), p. 1951–1957.

Duckworth, F. C., and Lewis, A. J., 'A fair method for resetting the target in interrupted one-day cricket matches', *Journal of the Operational Research Society*, 49(3), (1998), pp. 220–227.

Duckworth, F., 'A fair result in foul weather', *Significance*, 1(2), (2004), pp. 94–96.

Duckworth, F., 'A role for statistics in international cricket', *Teaching Statistics*, 23(2), (2001), pp. 38–44.

Perera, H., Davis, J., and Swartz, T. B., 'Optimal lineups in Twenty20 cricket', *Journal of Statistical Computation and Simulation*, 86(14), (2016), pp. 2888–2900.

Preston, I., and Thomas, J., 'Batting strategy in limited-overs cricket', *Journal of the Royal Statistical Society: Series D (The Statistician)*, 49(1), (2000), pp. 95–106.

Preston, I., and Thomas, J., 'Rain rules for limited-overs cricket and probabilities of victory', *Journal of the Royal Statistical Society: Series D (The Statistician)*, 51(2), (2002), pp. 189–202.

Stern, S. E., 'The Duckworth-Lewis-Stern Method: extending the Duckworth-Lewis methodology to deal with modern scoring rates', *Journal of the Operational Research Society*, 67(12), (2016), pp. 1469–1480.

Swartz, T.B., Gill, P.S., Beaudoin, D., and DeSilva, B.M., 'Optimal batting orders in one-day cricket', *Computers & Operations Research*, 33(7), (2006), pp. 1939–1950.

10. CRICKET'S CONCUSSION CRISIS

Bretzin, A. C., Covassin, T., Fox, M. E., Petit, K. M., Savage, J. L., Walker, L. F., and Gould, D., 'Sex differences in the clinical incidence of concussions, missed school days, and time loss in high school student-athletes: part 1', *The American Journal of Sports Medicine*, 46(9), (2018), pp. 2263–2269.

Brukner, P., Gara, T. J., and Fortington, L. V., 'Traumatic cricket-related fatalities in Australia: a historical review of media reports', *Medical Journal of Australia*, 208(6), (2018), pp. 261–264.

Covassin, T., Moran, R., and Elbin, R. J., 'Sex differences in reported concussion injury rates and time loss from participation: an update of the National Collegiate Athletic Association Injury Surveillance Program from 2004–2005 through 2008–2009', *Journal of Athletic Training*, 51(3), (2016), pp. 189–194.

Davis, Gavin A., Makdissi, M., Bloomfield, P., Clifton, P., Cowie, C., Echemendia, R., and Eanna, C., 'Concussion guidelines in national and international professional and elite sports', *Neurosurgery*, 87, No.2, (2020), pp. 418–425.

Goh, S. C., Saw, A. E., Kountouris, A., Orchard, J. W., and Saw, R., 'Neurocognitive changes associated with concussion in elite cricket players are distinct from changes due to post-match with no head impact', *Journal of Science and Medicine in Sport*, 24(5), (2021), pp. 420–424.

Hill, T., Orchard, J., and Kountouris, A., 'Incidence of concussion and head impacts in Australian elite-level male and female cricketers after head impact protocol modifications', *Sports Health*, 11(2), (2019), pp. 180–185.

Morton, A., 'Traumatic cricket-related fatalities in Australia: a historical review of media reports', *The Medical Journal of Australia*, 209(3), (2018), p. 142.

Perera, N. K. P., Kemp, J. L., Joseph, C., and Finch, C. F., 'Epidemiology of hospital-treated cricket injuries sustained by women from 2002–2003 to 2013–2014 in Victoria, Australia', *Journal of Science and Medicine in Sport*, 22(11), (2019), pp. 1213–1218.

Saw, A. E., Howard, D. J., Kountouris, A., McIntosh, A. S., Orchard, J. W., Saw, R., and Hill, T., 'Situational factors associated with concussion in cricket identified from video analysis', *Journal of Concussion*, 4, (2020) pp. 1–8.

Wasserman, E. B., Abar, B., Shah, M. N., Wasserman, D., and Bazarian, J. J., 'Concussions are associated with decreased batting performance among Major League Baseball players', *The American Journal of Sports Medicine*, 43(5), (2015), pp. 1127–1133.

11. STEREOTYPES

Alverstone, L. C. J., and Alcock, C. W., *Surrey Cricket: Its History and Associations* (Longmans, 1902).

Brown, T., Khawaja, I., Powell, A., Greetham, P., Gough, L. A., and Kelly, A. L., 'The sociodemographic profile of the England and Wales Cricket Board (ECB) talent pathways and first-class counties: considering the British South Asian player', *Managing Sport and Leisure*, (2021), pp. 1–15.

Chalke, S., *Summer's Crown: The Story of Cricket's County Championship* (Fairfield Books, 2015).

Fiske, S. T., Cuddy, A. J., Glick, P., and Xu, J., 'A model of (often mixed) stereotype content: competence and warmth respectively follow from perceived status and competition', *Journal of Personality and Social Psychology*, 82(6), (2002), p. 878.

Fiske, S. T., 'Stereotype content: Warmth and competence endure', *Current Directions in Psychological Science*, 27(2), (2018), pp. 67–73.

Marqusee, M., *Anyone but England: Cricket, Race and Class* (Bloomsbury, 2016).

Ranjitsinhji, K. S., *The Jubilee Book of Cricket* (Blackwood, 1897).

Schneider, D. J., *The Psychology of Stereotyping* (Guilford Press, 2005).

Vamplew, W., *Pay Up and Play the Game: Professional Sport in Britain, 1875-1914* (Cambridge University Press, 2004).

Webber, R., *County Cricket Championship: A History of the Competition from 1873* (Phoenix Sports Books, 1957).

12. WHAT WILL THE FUTURE OF WOMEN'S CRICKET LOOK LIKE? AND THE CASE FOR REPARATIONS

Davies, P. J., 'Bowling maidens over: 1931 and the beginnings of women's cricket in a Yorkshire town', *Sport in History*, 28(2), (2008), pp. 280–298.

Deaner, R. O., and Smith, B. A., 'Sex differences in sports across 50 societies', *Cross-Cultural Research*, 47(3), (2013), pp. 268–309.

Dees, M. J., 'Taco: son of cricket', (2019), https://mjdees.wordpress.com/2019/04/19/95-taco-son-of-cricket/amp/

Hyde, J. S., 'The gender similarities hypothesis', *American Psychologist*, 60(6), (2005), p. 581.

Hyde, J. S., 'Gender similarities and differences', *Annual Review of Psychology*, 65, (2014), pp. 373–398.

McCrone, K. E., 'Play Up! Play Up! And Play the Game! Sport at the Late Victorian Girls' Public School', *Journal of British Studies*, 23(2), (1984), pp. 106–134.

Mean, L. J., and Kassing, J. W., "I would just like to be known as an athlete": Managing hegemony, femininity, and heterosexuality in female sport', *Western Journal of Communication*, 72(2), (2008), pp. 126–144.

Nicholson, R., 'Like a man trying to knit? Women's cricket in Britain, 1945–2000', doctoral dissertation, Queen Mary University of London (2015).

Nicholson, R., 'Confronting the "Whiteness" of Women's Cricket: Excavating Hidden Truths and Knowledge to Make Sense of Non-White Women's Experiences of Cricket', Bournemouth University (2017).

Nicholson, R., *Ladies and Lords: A History of Women's Cricket in Britain* (Peter Lang, 2019).

Nicholson, R., 'Maidens and Man-kads: gendering cricket scholarship in the 21st century', *Sport in Society*, (2021), pp. 1–16.

Ralls, K., 'Mammals in which females are larger than males', *The Quarterly Review of Biology*, 51(2), (1976), pp. 245–276.

Saini, A., *Inferior: How Science Got Women Wrong and the New Research That's Rewriting the Story* (Beacon Press, 2017).

Seiler, S., De Koning, J. J., and Foster, C., 'The fall and rise of the gender difference in elite anaerobic performance 1952–2006', *Medicine & Science in Sports & Exercise*, 39(3), (2007), pp. 534–540.

Velija, P., 'A maiden over: a socio-historical analysis of the Women's Ashes', *Sport in Society*, 15(8), (2012), pp. 1121–1133.

Velija, P., '"Nice girls don't play cricket": the theory of established and outsider relations and perceptions of sexuality and class amongst female cricketers', *Sport in Society*, 15(1), (2012), pp. 28–43.

Velija, P., Ratna, A., and Flintoff, A., 'Exclusionary power in sports organisations: The merger between the Women's Cricket Association and the England and Wales Cricket Board', *International Review for the Sociology of Sport*, 49(2), (2014), pp. 211–226.

Wild, S., Rüst, C. A., Rosemann, T., and Knechtle, B., 'Changes in sex difference in swimming speed in finalists at FINA World Championships and the Olympic Games from 1992 to 2013', *BMC Sports Science, Medicine and Rehabilitation*, 6(1), (2014), pp. 1–29.

13. WHY DOESN'T SOUTH AFRICA PRODUCE MORE BLACK BATTERS?

Davies, R., Du Randt, R., Venter, D., and Stretch, R., 'Cricket: Nature and incidence of fast-bowling injuries at an elite, junior level and associated risk factors', *South African Journal of Sports Medicine*, 20(4), (2008), pp. 115–118.

Desai, A., *Reverse Sweep: A story of South African cricket since apartheid* (Jacana Media, 2016).

Desai, A., and Vahed, G., 'Beyond the nation? Colour and class in South African cricket', *The Race to Transform: Sport in Post-Apartheid South Africa* (2010), pp. 176–221.

Noorbhai, H., 'Attending boys-only schools: is it an incidental or a strategic contributing factor to South African cricket development and success?', *African Journal for Physical Activity and Health Sciences* (AJPHES), 26(1), (2020), pp. 21–40.

Pote, L., and Christie, C. J., 'Strength and conditioning practices of university and high school level cricket coaches: a South African context', *The Journal of Strength & Conditioning Research*, 30(12), (2016), pp. 3464–3470.

Rheeder, S., 'Transformation Success in South African Franchise First-Class Cricket: A brief statistical analysis', Mimeo, https://www.12thman-analytics.com.

Vahed, G., 'What Do They Know of Cricket Who Only Cricket Know? Transformation in South African Cricket, 1990–2000', *International Review for the Sociology of Sport*, 36(3), (2001), pp. 319–336.

14. THE VALUE OF BATTING V BOWLING

Epstein, D.J., *The Sports Gene: Inside the Science of Extraordinary Athletic Performance* (Penguin, 2014).

Forsyth, C., *The Great Cricket Hijack* (Widescope, 1978).

Smith, A., *An Inquiry into the Nature and Causes of the Wealth of Nations* (W. Strahan and T. Cadell, 1776).

Smith, E. T., *Playing Hard Ball: County Cricket and Big League Baseball* (Hachette UK, 2014).

Swartz, T.B., Gill, P.S. and Muthukumarana, S., 'Modelling and simulation for one-day cricket', *Canadian Journal of Statistics*, 37(2), (2009), pp. 143–160.

15. DID THE COLD COST INDIA A TEST SERIES VICTORY IN ENGLAND?

Borghesi, R., 'The home team weather advantage and biases in the NFL betting market', *Journal of Economics and Business*, 59(4), (2007), pp. 340–354.

Cai, X., Lu, Y., and Wang, J., 'The impact of temperature on manufacturing worker productivity: Evidence from personnel data', *Journal of Comparative Economics*, 46(4), (2018), pp. 889–905.

Drane, P. J., and Sherwood, J. A., 'Characterization of the effect of temperature on baseball COR performance', *The Engineering of Sport*, 5(2), (2004), pp. 59–65.

Gibson, O. R., James, C. A., Mee, J. A., Willmott, A. G., Turner, G., Hayes, M., and Maxwell, N. S., 'Heat alleviation strategies for athletic performance: a review and practitioner guidelines', *Temperature*, 7(1), (2020), pp. 3–36.

Jones, D. M., Bailey, S. P., Roelands, B., Buono, M. J., and Meeusen, R., 'Cold acclimation and cognitive performance: A review', *Autonomic Neuroscience*, 208, (2017), pp. 36–42.

Koch, B. L. D., and Panorska, A. K., 'The impact of temperature on Major League Baseball', *Weather, Climate, and Society*, 5(4), (2013), pp. 359–366.

Mehta, R. D., Bentley, K., Proudlove, M., and Varty, P., 'Factors affecting cricket ball swing', *Nature*, 303(5920), (1983), pp. 787–788.

Mehta, R. D., 'An overview of cricket ball swing', *Sports Engineering*, 8(4), (2005), pp. 181–192.

Scobie, J. A., Shelley, W. P., Jackson, R. W., Hughes, S. P., and Lock, G. D., 'Practical perspective of cricket ball swing. Proceedings of the Institution of Mechanical Engineers, Part P', *Journal of Sports Engineering and Technology*, 234(1), (2020), pp. 59–71.

Tyler, C. J., Reeve, T., Hodges, G. J., and Cheung, S. S., 'The effects of heat adaptation on physiology, perception and exercise performance in the heat: a meta-analysis', *Sports Medicine*, 46(11), (2016), pp. 1699–1724.

16. IS THE IPL EFFICIENT?

Berkmann, M., *Deloitte Ratings: The Complete Guide to Test Cricket in the Eighties* (Partridge Press, 1990).

Haigh, G., *Silent Revolutions: Writing on Cricket History* (Aurum, 2007).

Lewis, M., *Moneyball: The Art of Winning an Unfair Game* (W.W. Norton & Co, 2004).

Lindsey, G. R., 'The progress of the score during a baseball game', *Journal of the American Statistical Association*, 56(295), (1961), pp. 703–728.

Lindsey, G. R., 'An investigation of strategies in baseball', *Operations Research*, 11(4), (1963), pp. 477–501.

Thorn, J., 'Chadwick's Choice: The Origin of the Batting Average' (2013), https://ourgame.mlblogs.com/chadwicks-choice-the-origin-of-the-batting-average-e8e9e9402d53

17. A DAY AT THE CRICKET

Bhattacharya, M., and Smyth, R., 'The game is not the same: The demand for Test match cricket in Australia', *Australian Economic Papers*, 42(1), (2003), pp. 77–90.

Blackham, J., and Chapman, B., 'The value of Don Bradman: additional revenue in Australian Ashes Tests', *Economic Papers: A journal of applied economics and policy*, 23(4), (2004), pp. 369–385.

Cashman, R. I., 'Australian Cricket Crowds: The Attendance Cycle: Daily Figures, 1877–1984', History Project Incorporated (1984).

Cashman, R. I., *'Ave a Go, Yer Mug! Australian Cricket Crowds from Larrikin to Ocker* (Collins, 1984).

Harte, C., *A History of Australian Cricket* (Andre Deutsch, 1993).

Hynds, M., and Smith, I., 'The demand for Test match cricket', *Applied Economics Letters*, 1(7), (1994), pp. 103–106.

Moyes, A. G., *Australian Cricket: A History* (Angus and Robertson, 1959).

Paton, D., and Cooke, A., 'Attendance at county cricket: An economic analysis', *Journal of Sports Economics*, 6(1), (2005), pp. 24–45.

Sacheti, A., Paton, D., and Gregory-Smith, I., 'An economic analysis of attendance demand for one day international cricket', *Economic Record*, 92(296), (2005), pp. 121–136.

Sacheti, A., Gregory-Smith, I., and Paton, D., 'Uncertainty of outcome or strengths of teams: an economic analysis of attendance demand for international cricket', *Applied Economics*, 46(17), (2014), pp. 2034–2046.

Schofield, J. A., 'The demand for cricket: the case of the John Player League', *Applied Economics*, 15(3), (1983), pp. 283–296.

18. HOW THE BARMY ARMY ARE KEEPING TEST CRICKET ALIVE – FROM THEIR SOFAS

Baade, R. A., and Matheson, V. A., 'Going for the gold: The economics of the Olympics', *Journal of Economic Perspectives*, 30(2), (2016), pp. 201–18.

Baum, T., and Butler, R. (Eds.), 'Tourism and Cricket: Travels to the Boundary', Channel View Publications, (Vol. 41), (2014).

Crompton, J. L., 'Economic impact studies: instruments for political shenanigans?', *Journal of Travel Research*, 45(1), (2006), pp. 67–82.

Fourie, J., and Santana-Gallego, M., 'The Impact of Mega-sport Events on Tourist Arrivals', *Tourism Management*, 32, (2011) pp. 1364–70.

Garicano, L., Palacios-Huerta, I., and Prendergast, C., 'Favoritism under social pressure', *Review of Economics and Statistics*, 87(2), (2005) pp. 208–216.

James, C. L. R., *Beyond a Boundary* (Duke University Press, 2013).

McCarrick, D., Bilalic, M., Neave, N., and Wolfson, S., 'Home Advantage during the COVID-19 Pandemic in European football', (2020).

Siegfried, J. J., and Zimbalist, A., 'The economics of sports facilities and their communities', *Journal of Economic Perspectives*, 14(3), (2000), pp. 95–114.

20. HOW AFGHANISTAN IS BRINGING CRICKET TO GERMANY

Breuer, C., Feiler, S., and Wicker, P., 'Sport clubs in Germany', *Sport clubs in Europe*, Springer Cham, (2015), pp. 187–208.

Breuer, C., and Feiler, S., 'Sports clubs in Germany: organisations and internal stakeholders', Sport Development Report for Germany, 18, (2017).

Michelini, E., Burrmann, U., Nobis, T., Tuchel, J., and Schlesinger, T., 'Sport offers for refugees in Germany. Promoting and hindering conditions in voluntary sport clubs', *Society Register*, 2(1), (2018), pp. 19–38.

INDEX